HARVARD STUDIES
IN COMPARATIVE LITERATURE
VOLUME VII

CHAUCER

AND

THE ROMAN POETS

CHAUCER

AND

THE ROMAN POETS

BY

EDGAR FINLEY SHANNON

NEW YORK

RUSSELL & RUSSELL · INC

1964

TO MY WIFE

ELEANOR DUNCAN SHANNON

WHOSE ABIDING INTEREST AND CONSTRUCTIVE CRITICISM
HAVE MADE THE BOOK POSSIBLE

We knowe in olde bokes men may finde
The maner makers wol hir thinges binde
Fro other makers, that with steppes before
Han shewed hem the place of swiche a store.

PREFACE

MY STUDY of the relation of Chaucer to Ovid was begun as a doctoral dissertation in Harvard University. The ultimate purpose I had in mind was to consider Chaucer's relation to all the Roman poets, the consummation of which is the present volume.

I am naturally much indebted to the work of previous scholars, who have recorded their findings of references and allusions to the Classics in various books and journals. To these I have endeavored to give proper credit in notes and elsewhere.

I wish to express my thanks to Professor E. K. Rand of Harvard University for a helpful conference at the very inception of my study; to Professor D. B. Easter of Washington and Lee University for suggestions in interpreting the spirit of some Old French passages; and to Professor J. O. Lofberg, formerly of Washington and Lee and now of Oberlin College, for aid in solving some problems in connection with Ovid's use of poetic forms. Especially do I desire to acknowledge my obligation to Professor F. N. Robinson of Harvard for constant encouragement and advice most generously given me; and to Professor G. L. Kittredge,

who suggested the subject of study to me, and
who has from his own fund of rich scholarship in
this particular field furnished me assistance in a
way that only those who have worked with him
can appreciate.

E. F. S.

CONTENTS

PART II

CHAUCER AND THE OTHER ROMAN POETS

CONTENTS

xi

INTRODUCTION

THE range of Chaucer's intellectual interests continually surprises the student of his works. Especially is the reader impressed with his use of stories and illustrations from the Classics. It seems altogether unlikely that he was acquainted with Greek literature at first hand. Such information concerning it as appears in his writings was no doubt conveyed to him through the Latin, though it may be possible that some knowledge of Greek civilization and culture seeped into the Middle Ages through later unknown channels. But an intimate knowledge of several of the Roman poets is very evident from Chaucer's works.

Chaucerian commentators and scholars have from time to time called attention to borrowings from most of these poets, but up to the present no attempt has been made to bring all these references together, to discuss them, and to add such new material as a comparative study could not fail to produce. Such an undertaking must of necessity lead beyond the investigation of analogies in details and incidents and involve a consideration of the influence of the Classics upon Chaucer's poetic development. For through contact with the early Renaissance in Italy he became a participant in the stimulation from the classical revival.

Chaucer's greatest obligation is to Ovid. From this ancient Roman far more than from any other poet he drew his inspiration as well as his great store of classical and mythological information.

All Ovid's works were known and often quoted by mediaeval writers.[1] Indeed, he was considered the great authority on love in the Middle Ages, and such parts of his poems as seemed too licentious were interpreted allegorically. His two works that appear to have had the greatest influence upon mediaeval literature are the *Metamorphoses* and the *Ars Amatoria*.[2]

In France especially the influence of Ovid manifested itself in the great abundance of mediaeval love-poetry.[3] Particularly were the French love-poets influenced by the *Ars Amatoria*, and to a less

[1] Manitius has made a most useful collection of references to Ovid by writers in the various countries of Europe in the Middle Ages. Though this list does not include Chaucer, it is instructive to know that Chaucer's predecessors in England were well acquainted with Ovid. See Manitius, *Philologus*, Supplement, VII, 723–758.

[2] See A. Graf, *Roma nella memoria e nelle immaginazione del medio evo*, 1882, II, 296, 305, 312, 313, 314; Bartsch, *Albrecht von Halberstadt und Ovid im Mittelalter*, *Bibliothek der deutschen National-Literatur*, vol. XXXVIII, Einleitung.

[3] For a full discussion of the influence of Ovid's *Metamorphoses* upon French poetry, see M. Sudre's dissertation, *Publii Ovidii Nasonis Metamorphoseon Libros quomodo nostrates medii aevi poetae imitati interpretatique sint*, Paris, 1893.

degree by the *Remedia Amoris*. But these mock-
didactic poems were wholly misunderstood by the
Middle Ages, which accepted them in all serious-
ness, being accustomed to consider the poets of
antiquity learned men who imparted useful information. In their lack of historical perspective
mediaeval readers failed to recognize the vast differences in thought and ideals that separated them
from the Augustan Age.[1] It was only natural that
such men should imitate seriously the *Ars Amatoria*
and the *Remedia Amoris*. Besides this, Ovid was
responsible for the idea prevalent in the Middle
Ages that love could be reduced to a system of
rules and practised as an art. Though the mediaeval
Court of Love was very different from Ovid's art
of love, yet the conceptions were alike in that they
assumed that love could be made to submit to
laws and that lessons could be given concerning it.[2]
The *Heroides* [3] does not seem to have been imitated
by the French poets as were the *Metamorphoses*,
Ars Amatoria, and *Remedia Amoris*, though, as has
been suggested by Schick,[4] the *genre* of the complaint may have been influenced in its origin by the
Heroides. The *Amores* by reason of its personal
revelations and its frank lasciviousness did not

[1] See Gaston Paris, *La Poésie du Moyen Age*, pp. 190–191.
[2] *Ibid.*, pp. 208–209.
[3] See *Histoire Litteraire*, Paris, XXIX, 488–489.
[4] J. Schick, *Temple of Glass*, E. E. T. S., p. cxxii.

lend itself readily to imitation,[1] yet it was frequently referred to. The *Fasti*, *Tristia*, and *ex Ponto Epistles* have little in subject-matter to commend them to imitators.

Though it was through the inspiration of French love-poetry that Chaucer began his career as a poet, he no doubt early became acquainted with Ovid as the recognized authority in matters pertaining to love and felt the importance of a first-hand knowledge of him for a poet who was to treat of love. At any rate his intellectual activity impelled him to a close study of the Latin poet's works. It is impossible to discover when Chaucer's reading of Ovid began. It may have been even before he began to write verse himself. By the time he wrote the *Book of the Duchess* we are sure he knew the *Metamorphoses*. Yet he used the Ovidian material there very much in the same manner as his predecessors and contemporaries. It may be that Chaucer's penetrating eye saw deeper than they did into the meaning of Ovid's mock-didactic poems. His spirit no doubt kindled in sympathy with the Latin poet's spirit of fun, which so completely escaped the Middle Ages generally.

So far as I am aware, the first person to call at-

---

[1] For an instance of indirect influence of the *Amores* in French poetry, see *Histoire Litteraire*, XXIX, 488.

tention to that special congeniality between Ovid
and Chaucer which was productive of such important results upon the English poet's work was
John Dryden. In the Preface to the *Fables* [1] he
discusses some of the similarities between the two
poets. As the criticism of the founder of modern
prose style upon the forerunner of modern English
must of itself have a special interest, and as it is
so pertinent to our subject, I make no apology for
quoting some extracts from it.

But to return: having done with Ovid for this time,
it came into my mind, that our English poet, Chaucer,
in many things resembled him, and that with no dis-
advantage on the side of the modern author, as I shall
endeavor to prove when I compare them; . . .
With Ovid ended the golden age of the Roman
tongue; from Chaucer the purity of the English tongue
began. The manners of the poets were not unlike. Both
of them were well-bred, well-natured, amorous, and
libertine, at least in their writings; it may be, also in
their lives. Their studies were the same, philosophy and
philology. Both of them were knowing in astronomy;
of which Ovid's books of the *Roman Feasts*, and Chaucer's *Treatise of the Astrolabe*, are sufficient witnesses.
But Chaucer was likewise an astrologer, as were Virgil,
Horace, Persius, and Manilius. Both writ with wonderful facility and clearness; . . . Both of them built on the
inventions of other men; yet since Chaucer had something of his own, as the *Wife of Bath's Tale*, *The Cock
and the Fox*, which I have translated, and some others,

[1] W. P. Ker, *Essays of John Dryden*, II, 248-257.

I may justly give our countryman the precedence in that part; since I can remember nothing of Ovid which was wholly his. Both of them understood the manners; under which name I comprehend the passions, and, in a larger sense, the descriptions of persons and their habits. For example I see Baucis and Philemon as perfectly before me, as if some ancient painter had drawn them; and all the Pilgrims in the *Canterbury Tales*, their humours, their features, and the very dress, as distinctly as if I had supped with them at the *Tabard* in Southwark. Yet even there, too, the figures of Chaucer are much more lively, and set in a better light; . . . The thoughts remain to be considered; and they are to be measured only by their propriety; that is, as they flow more or less naturally from the persons described on such and such occasions. The vulgar judges, which are nine parts in ten of all nations, who call conceits and jingles wit, who see Ovid full of them, and Chaucer altogether without them, will think me little less than mad for preferring the Englishman to the Roman. Yet, with their leave, I must presume to say, that the things they admire are only glittering trifles, and so far from being witty, that in a serious poem they are nauseous, because they are unnatural. . . . Chaucer makes Arcite violent in his love, and unjust in his pursuit of it; yet, when he came to die, he made him think more reasonably: he repents not of his love, for that had altered his character; but acknowledges the injustice of his proceedings, and resigns Emily to Palamon. What would Ovid have done on this occasion? He would certainly have made Arcite witty on his deathbed; . . . As for the turn of words, in which Ovid particularly excels all poets, they are sometimes a fault, and sometimes a beauty, as they are used properly or improperly; but in strong passions always to be shunned, because passions are serious, and will admit no playing. The French have a high value for them; and I confess, they are often what may be called delicate, when they are introduced with judgment; but Chaucer writ with more simplicity, and followed nature more closely than to use them.

With these judgments of Dryden we can in the main still agree.

The next comparison between Ovid and Chaucer, with some consideration of Virgil also, — this time with considerable scholarly accuracy and some literary appreciation, — is by Fiedler [1] in 1847. Lounsbury,[2] Skeat,[3] and J. Koch [4] all indicate many references and allusions to Ovid and the other Latin poets.

Professor G. L. Kittredge has rendered inestimable service to the study of Chaucer's relation to the Roman poets, particularly Ovid, by the citation of many passages that owe their origin to these sources; and especially has he, by his illuminating suggestions with regard to Chaucer's use of the Classics, pointed the way for comparative criticism.[5]

---

[1] *Archiv für das Studium der Neueren Sprachen und Literaturen*, II, 151–169.

[2] *Studies in Chaucer*, II, 250–252.

[3] *The Complete Works of Geoffrey Chaucer*, Oxford, 1899.

[4] *Chaucer's Belesenheit in den Römischen Klassickern, Englische Studien*, Band LVII, Heft 1, pp. 8–84.

[5] See particularly *Chaucer's Medea and the Date of the Legend of Good Women; Date of Chaucer's Troilus and Other Chaucer Matters; Chaucer's Lollius;* etc.

Though Virgil's poetry was universally popular during the Middle Ages,[1] Chaucer seems to have been acquainted only with the *Æneid*.[2] His use of Virgil is so closely interwoven with material from Ovid that it will be necessary to consider his relation to these two poets simultaneously.

That Statius was well known to Chaucer has long been recognized. He is cited by name, and his *Thebaid* is used in several poems. A study of the obligation that Chaucer owes to the *Thebaid* has been made by Professor B. A. Wise.[3]

Lucan, who with Suetonius and Valerius Maximus is cited as a source for the story of Julius Cæsar in the *Monk's Tale*, was recognized by Chaucer as one of the great poets of antiquity. He is named in *Troilus*, v, 1792, along with Homer, Virgil, Ovid, and Statius.

Though indications of some borrowings from the *Argonauticon* have been pointed out in the *Legend of Hypsipyle*, it has been thought impossible for Chaucer to have known Valerius Flaccus because

[1] A. Graf, *Roma nella memoria e nelle immaginazione del medio evo*, Torino, Ristampa, 1915, pp. 520–566; Comparetti, *Vergil in the Middle Ages*, trans. into English by E. F. M. Benecke, Macmillan, 1895; J. E. Sandys, *History of Classical Scholarship*, I, 633–635.

[2] Professor A. S. Cook (*Conn. Acad. of Arts and Sciences*, XXIII, 1–21) suggests Virgil's *Georgics* as the source for lines 1–11 of the Prologue to the *Canterbury Tales*, but his discussion is not convincing.

[3] *The Influence of Statius upon Chaucer*, Baltimore, 1911.

of the supposedly universal ignorance with regard to his work until Poggio's discovery at St. Gallen in 1416. But a study of the history of the manuscripts of the *Argonauticon* throws some new light on this question. It now seems possible that Valerius Flaccus may have been known in England during the Middle Ages though he was not known upon the Continent.

The poetry of Claudian was familiar to Chaucer. He signifies clearly that he knows the contents of the *De Raptu Proserpinae;* he translates a stanza from another poem of Claudian; and he alludes to him in the Prologue to the *Legend of Good Women* in a way that indicates a knowledge of still another poem, the *Laus Serenae.*

As to Horace, much as we may deplore the failure of Chaucer to come in contact with the work of this urbane poet, we must conclude from the evidence presented by Miss Siebert [1] that Horace was known to Chaucer only through an intermediate channel, such as John of Salisbury or some collection of Latin poetry.

Juvenal he cites by name as the author of the two quotations which he uses from him. Persius appears in a single quotation and without any indication of his authorship.

[1] *Modern Language Notes,* XXXI, 304-307.

Catullus, I believe, has never before been mentioned in connection with Chaucer; yet we shall find, along with some contributory evidence, one statement in the *Legend of Ariadne* which seems to prove that Chaucer was acquainted with at least one of Catullus' poems.

I

CHAUCER, OVID, AND VIRGIL

THE MINOR POEMS

The Book of the Duchess

THE earliest of Chaucer's poems which shows any borrowing from the Classics is the *Book of the Duchess*. The story of Ceys and Alcyone, lines 60–220, is drawn largely from the *Metamorphoses*, xi, 410–748. In an analysis of Chaucer's indebtedness to Ovid here, there are a few interesting points to add to what has been done by ten Brink.[1] The claim was made by Sandras[2] that Chaucer's story of Ceys and Alcyone was a servile imitation of Machaut's version of the same story in the *Dit de la Fontaine Amoureuse*. In discussing this question ten Brink makes the following points.

As Chaucer got from Machaut the idea of weaving in this story from Ovid, it is to be expected that he would follow in some measure the general form given to the story by Machaut. So also it is to be expected that the treatment which Machaut has given to the material borrowed from Ovid has remained not without influence

---

[1] Ten Brink, *Studien*, pp. 7–12.

[2] Sandras, *Etude sur Chaucer*, p. 95: "ce poeme qui, dans son ensemble et souvent dans ses details, n'offre qu'une imitation servile de Machaut est certainement une des plus faibles productions de Chaucer." For a full discussion of Machaut's influence in the *Duchess*, see Kittredge, "Guillaume de Machault and the Book of the Duchess," *P. M. L. A.*, XXX, 1.

upon the form it took under Chaucer's hands. Chaucer
has several times gone back to Ovid; and if in carrying
out the details he often approaches nearer to Machaut,
this is not always to be explained as an imitation of the
French poet, but sometimes is due in part to the similar
relation in which the modern poets stand to their ancient
model. In several cases, however, Chaucer departs from
both Ovid and Machaut; other points he takes from
the Latin, though he did not find them at all with the
French poet. Chaucer indicates, not exactly but still
quite clearly, that his source is the *Metamorphoses*. The
book in which he read during that night which he represents as sleepless contains without doubt writings of
different authors. The peculiarities, however, which he
has mentioned as belonging to these writings, correspond
better with Ovid's *Metamorphoses* than with any collection of allegorical poems of Machaut:

> And in this boke were writen fables
> That Clerkes hadde, in olde tyme,
> And other poets, put in ryme
> To rede, and for to be in minde
> Whyl men loved the lawe of kinde.
> This book ne spak but of such thinges
> Of Quenes lyves, and of kinges,
> And many othere thinges smale.
> Amonge al this I fond a tale
> That me thoughte a wonder thing.
> This was the tale: . . .

This would seem to indicate that the book contained
a collection of similar stories from which this one of
Ceys and Alcyone was taken out. Though Chaucer
evidently had the *Metamorphoses* before him, he used
it in a very independent manner and adapted his borrowings to his own needs. As for the details of the story
Chaucer gives a short summing up of the shipwreck

which is given at great length by Ovid and is not mentioned at all by Machaut. This shows that he could not be following Machaut alone. In the treatment of Alcyone's conduct after the departure of Ceys, Chaucer expands Ovid's account and modifies it in laying the chief weight upon the uncertainty in which the heroine continues. In this he is nearer to Machaut, but not in direct imitation of him. The idea that Alcyone herself requests Juno for a dream-vision is original with Chaucer. Machaut uses general expressions here, while Ovid makes the goddess of her own motion send news to Alcyone of Ceys's death in order that she may drive off her polluted hands from the altar — an ancient motive which neither Chaucer nor Machaut could rightly understand. In referring to the dwelling of the God of Sleep Chaucer combines the descriptions given by Ovid and Machaut. There are three points in which he differs from both his sources. Instead of Iris Chaucer lets an unnamed and man-messenger fulfill Juno's command. The God of Sleep under the name of Morpheus which really belongs to his son, goes in his own persons to Alcyone. At the end of the story Chaucer breaks off immediately after the mention of the quick death of Alcyone and says nothing about hers and her husband's metamorphosis.

Besides this analysis of the story by ten Brink, there is the suggestion of Furnivall that Machaut gives too little of Alcyone's sorrow for Chaucer "to rede and make him pite," which indicates that the story he refers to is Ovid's.[1]

---

[1] Furnivall, *Trial Forewords*, Chaucer Society, 1871, p. 46. See also Max Lange in his dissertation on *Chaucer's Boke of the Duchess*, Halle, 1883.

In spirit and general conception, as ten Brink suggests, Chaucer's version certainly does agree with Machaut's in being mediaeval and Christian. In fact, he departs even further from the ideas of Roman mythology than Machaut does. Alcyone's prayer as given by Chaucer resembles Machaut's account, though the French poet gives little of the prayer in direct form. Both the mediaeval poets omit the pagan idea of Ovid where he makes Ceys, when he appears to Alcyone, request that she put on mourning in order that he may not go unlamented to the ghostly realms of Tartarus.

In referring to the God of Sleep, Chaucer combines the descriptions given by Ovid and Machaut. Here a question concerning the reading of Chaucer's MS. of Ovid is involved. Lines 155–156 of the *Duchess* are from Machaut:

> Til he com to the derke valeye
> That stant betwene rockes tweye.

The description taken from Ovid is in lines 163–164,

> . . . a cave
> That was under a rokke y-grave.

This *cave under a rock* depends upon a variation in the texts of Ovid. The line from which this is taken reads:

Tecta petit jussi *sub rupe* latentia regis. (*Met.*, xi, 591.)

Most modern texts read *sub nube* instead of *sub rupe*. But as evidence that some of the MSS read *sub rupe*, note the following quotation from Heinsius:

> *sub nube latentia* De nube nugae sunt. Scribe sub rupe cum primo Gronovii, quarto Mediceo, Rottendorph. Graeviano et aliis duobus: fec. Pal. et duo alii, *sub nocte:* frustra.[1]

Clearly, Chaucer's MS. read *sub rupe*.[2]

There are a few more details which Chaucer takes from Ovid and which Machaut omits, that have not been noted by ten Brink. Chaucer's specific mention of the breaking of the mast in the account of the shipwreck, Professor Kittredge [3] has noted as a following of Ovid's line:

> Frangitur incursu nimbosi turbinis arbor. (*Met.*, xi, 551.)

The phrase, "And clefte hir ship," is probably a reference to Ovid's

> Jamque labant cunei, spoliataque tegmine cerae
> Rima patet, praebetque viam letalibus undis.
> (*Met.*, xi, 514–515.)

Chaucer and Ovid both give the circumstance of Alcyone's swooning. In Ovid it takes place at the

---

[1] *Nic Heinsii Commentarius in P. Ovidii Nasonis Opera Omnia*, ed. Joh. Masson, 1758, p. 665.

[2] This has been previously published in "Notes on Chaucer," *Mod. Phil.*, XI, No. 2, 227.

[3] *The Date of Chaucer's Troilus*, Chaucer Society, 1905, p. 23, note 2.

departure of Ceys,[1] in Chaucer at the conclusion
of her prayer to Juno to reveal to her in a dream
her husband's fate.

Line 152 of the *Duchess*,

> Go now faste, and hy thee blyve,

harks back to Ovid's *"Vise . . .* velociter" (*Met.*,
xi, 586). A detail from the Latin, which has already
been noted by Max Lange,[2] is the "deedly sleeping
soun" made by the stream (l. 162). Ovid has the
following:

> Saxo tamen exit ab imo
> Rivus aquae Lethes, per quem cum murmure labens
> Invitat somnos creputantibus unda lapillis.
> > (*Met.*, xi, 602–604.)

> This cave was also as derk
> As helle pit over-al aboute
> > (*Duch.*, ll. 170–171.)

is a Chaucerian adaptation of Ovid's

> Quo numquam radiis oriens mediųsve cadensve
> Phoebus adire potest nebulae caligine mixtae
> Exhalantur humo dubiaeque crepuscula lucis.
> > (*Met.*, xi, 594–596.)

That Chaucer is not slavish in his borrowing
even in his early work is evidenced by his omission
in this story of some points given by both Ovid and

---

[1] " Amplexusque dedit, tristique miserrima tandem
Ore 'vale' dixit, collapsaque corpore toto est."
> (*Met.*, xi, 459–460.)

[2] *Chaucer's Boke of the Duchess*, pp. 24–25.

Machaut, and by his insertion of some character-istic touches of his own. In fact, he is much more independent of both Ovid and Machaut than Machaut is of Ovid. His version of Juno's direc-tions to her messenger is original, especially the order to take up the actual body from the sea and creep into it. Lange [1] mentions the barrenness of the space about the dwelling of the God of Sleep as a feature original with Chaucer:

> Ther never yet grew corn ne gras
> Ne tree ne nothing that ought was.
> *(Duch.*, ll. 157–158.)

Machaut says nothing about the vegetation. Ovid states that numerous plants grew in front of the cave:

> Ante fores antri foecunda papavera florent
> Innumeraeque herbae, quarum de lacte soporem
> Nox legit et spargit per opacas humida terras.
> *(Met.*, xi, 605–607.)

Chaucer makes nothing of the messenger and of her being nearly overcome by sleep on approaching the god's dwelling — a circumstance emphasized by both Ovid and Machaut. In fact, Chaucer's con-trast to his originals here forms one of his most characteristic passages. His messenger comes with a dash and blows his horn right in Morpheus' ear and cries, "'Awaketh!' wonder hye."

[1] *Chaucer's Boke of the Duchess*, p. 25.

Chaucer brings the story to a close with Alcyone's death. In this he departs from Ovid and Machaut, both of whom conclude their accounts with the transformation of the husband and wife into birds. Thus in his first adaptation of a story from the *Metamorphoses*, Chaucer indicates that he will have none of the metamorphosis. Gower, as might be expected, when he told the story of Ceys and Alcyone in the *Confessio Amantis*[1] gave the transformation. But Chaucer excluded this irrelevant device of pagan mythology, not only from this story but from all[2] the others which he later borrowed from the *Metamorphoses*, thus displaying the sure perception of a sound literary taste.

It is apparent from the detailed comparison which has been made of the three versions of the Ceys and Alcyone story that Chaucer had read both Ovid's and Machaut's versions, perhaps many times, since he could not lay his hands on a new book at will, and so with both at his fingers' ends he proceeded to write his own story, using much of each and departing from both where it suited him.

Chaucer alludes in the *Duchess* to some persons of antiquity, as Hector, Priam, Achilles, Jason,

---

[1] Bk. iv, ll. 3088–3123.

[2] The *Manciple's Tale* is no real exception to the statement above, for the change of the feathers of the crow from white to black is hardly to be classed as a true metamorphosis, and makes little strain upon the reader's credulity.

Medea, and so forth, whose names he might have learned from the *Metamorphoses*. But many of them appear also in the *Roman de la Rose*,[1] by which Chaucer seems to have been much more influenced at this time. Professor Kittredge [2] has shown good reason to believe, however, that the "Storie de Troie" (l. 326) has reference to the *Roman de Troie* of Benoit de Ste. More and that Chaucer drew chiefly upon that source for these classical allusions.

In lines 567–568 the *Remedia Amoris* is referred to in a way which implies that Chaucer was familiar with its contents. From this we may infer that he knew this one of Ovid's works besides the *Metamorphoses* at the time of the composition of the *Duchess*.

In referring to Orpheus, "god of melodye" (line 569), it is probable that Chaucer had Ovid's account in mind, for the story of the death of Orpheus is told in the opening lines of the same book of the *Metamorphoses* (xi, 1–66) which contains the story of Ceys and Alcyone.

In the *Book of the Duchess* Chaucer was plainly imitating the French mediaeval poetry. The material from the Classics in the poem is confined to the mere allusions mentioned above and to the one

[1] Skeat, *Oxford Chaucer*, I, 471 ff.
[2] "Chaucer's Medea and the Date of the Legend of Good Women," *P.M.L.A.*, XXIV, 2, 344 ff.

episode of Ceys and Alcyone. This episode is managed in the typical mediaeval manner, and even the idea of using it may have come to him from his reading of Machaut. The real influence of the Classics upon Chaucer was not to come until his mind was inspired through contact with the Renaissance spirit as the result of his Italian journeys.

THE COMPLAINT OF MARS

The basis for the *Complaint of Mars* Chaucer probably found in *Metamorphoses*, iv, 170–189, where Ovid tells of the intrigue between Mars and Venus and how Phoebus betrayed them to Vulcan. Vulcan made a net with invisible meshes by which he entrapped Mars and his faithless spouse and exposed them to the ridicule of the gods. Omitting the part that Vulcan plays in Ovid's story, and taking only the bare circumstance of the intrigue as a mythological setting, Chaucer proceeds with a poem full of astronomical lore. Various interpretations of the *Mars* have been suggested. Professor Manly [1] thinks that "it can hardly be regarded as anything else than a mere exercise of ingenuity in describing a supposed event in terms of human action and emotion." Professor Mather [2] terms

---

[1] "On the Date and Interpretation of Chaucer's Complaint of Mars," *Harvard Studies and Notes*, V, 107 ff.

[2] F. J. Mather, ed. of *Prologue*, etc., p. xxxiii.

the poem only a *jeu d'esprit* in versified astrology.
Like the *Book of the Duchess* it shows Chaucer's use
of material from Ovid in the manner of the mediaeval French poets.

THE PARLIAMENT OF FOWLS

Very slight and incidental is the amount of classical borrowing in the *Parliament of Fowls*.

In the proem, Chaucer, while disclaiming any
personal knowledge of love, says,

> Yet happeth me ful ofte in bokes rede
> Of his miracles, and his cruel ire;
> Ther rede I wel he wol be lord and sire,
> I dar not seyn, his strokes been so sore.
>
> (*P. of F.*, ll. 10–13.)

These lines recall very strikingly the first poem in
the *Amores* of Ovid, where the poet represents himself as preparing to write about war when Cupid
appears to him and commands him to compose
love-poetry:

> Questus eram, pharetra cum protinus ille soluta
>   Legit in exitium spicula facta neum
> Lunavitque genu simuosum fortiter arcum
>   "Quod" que "canas, vates, accipe," dixit "opus."
> Me miserum! certas habuit puer ille sagittas:
>   Uror, et in vacuo pectore regnat Amor.
>
> (*Amores*, i, i, 21–26.)

Love appears again as "lord and sire" to Ovid in
Amores, ii, i, and iii, i. Also, in *Ars Amatoria*, Ovid
says of Amor,

Ille quidem ferus est etqui mihi saepe repugnat.
(Ars Am., i, 9.)

Compare also *Remedia Amoris,* lines 1–40.
Line 217,

Som for to slee, and som to wounde and kerve,

which Chaucer has added to what he found in the
Teseide, seems to have been suggested by Ovid's
words about Cupid in *Metamorphoses,* i, 468–469:

Eque sagittifera prompsit duo tela pharetra
Diversorum operum: fugat hoc, fecit illud amorem.

These lines occur in a passage depicting the power
of Cupid in making Apollo love Daphne and in
causing her to flee from him. It is an example of
one of the "miracles of Cupid," which Chaucer
probably had in mind in line 11 of the proem.

Lines 253–256, though in the main from the
Teseide, show that Chaucer also knew the story of
Priapus in the *Fasti,*[1] for he calls him a god and
uses the Latin form of his name.

Professor Lowes [2] has called attention to the use
made by Chaucer of both Boccaccio and Dante in
lines 288 ff. To the lists of lovers taken from these
poets Chaucer adds the names of Candace, Troilus,
Scylla, and Rhea Silvia. Three of these [3] seem to

[1] *Fasti,* I, 415–438.

[2] *Mod. Phil.,* XIV, 706–707.

[3] Skeat, *Oxford Chaucer,* I, 515, says *Candace* here is a confusion
for *Canace.*

have been suggested by Ovid, who tells the story
of each one of them as a lover: Canace, *Heroides*,
xi; Scylla, *Metamorphoses*, viii, 6–151; Rhea Silvia,
Fasti, iii, 9–45. Though Skeat refers, for Rhea
Silvia, to Livy, i, ix, and *Æneid*, i, 274, neither of
these passages is so likely to have been in Chaucer's
mind as Ovid's poetic account in the *Fasti*.

ANELIDA AND ARCITE

The question as to the source of Chaucer's unfinished poem *Anelida and Arcite* has been an un-
solved problem. Professor Skeat points out in his
introduction to this poem [1] that the first three
stanzas are from Boccaccio's *Teseide*, as are also
stanzas 8, 9, and 10; and that stanzas 4 to 7 are
partly from Statius. The origin of the rest of the
poem, which is far the greater part, is unknown.

The poem belongs among that class of lyrics
known technically as *complaints*, as its title indicates, *The Compleynt of feire Anelida and Fals
Arcite*. Chaucer begins with a proem of three
stanzas taken largely from Boccaccio. This proem
ends with a verse giving his authorities:

First folow I Stace and after him Corinne.

The story then opens with an adaptation of some
verses from Statius' *Thebaid*, xii, 519 ff. The

---

[1] *Oxford Chaucer*, I, 77.

eighth, ninth, and tenth stanzas again are from Boccaccio. After line 70, we have no further trace of a source, and for three reasons we may fairly consider the story itself to be an original attempt. First, Chaucer takes his setting, the court of Theseus, from the *Teseide* of Boccaccio; but that source does not furnish the story which he here tells. It is improbable that he would have taken this setting from the *Teseide* if he had had another source for his story. Second, the names Anelida and Arcite come from different cycles of stories, Anelida apparently originating in the Arthurian romances,[1] and Arcite coming from the Alexandrian cycle.

[1] Schick, in his edition of the *Temple of Glass*, E. E. T. S., p. cxx, says in a note upon the list of lovers given in the *Intelligenza:* "This list is interesting as giving, amongst others, the following pair of lovers (stanza 75, l. 2):

'La bella Analida et lo bono Ivano.'

This seems to point to one of the Romances treating of *Iwain* and the *Round Table* for the origin of the name *Anelida*, which would at once upset Bradshaw's and Professor Cowell's ingenious etymologies from 'Αναΐτις and Anahita: for I do not believe that both the poet of the *Intelligenza* and Chaucer mistook a *t* for an *l*. We have also in Froissart's *Dit du bleu Chevalier* the line (ten Brink, *Studien*, p. 213):

'Ywain le preu pour la belle Alydes.'

One and the same personage is evidently indicated by the two names Analida and Alydes for Iwain's paramour: I am not, however, sufficiently acquainted with the Arthur-romances to know of the occurrence of such a name. Laudine in Chrestien's *Chevalier au Lion* is not very like it."

On the name Anelida being a misreading of the name of the goddess Anáhita of the Zoroastrian religion in some Latin text, see Professor Cowell's article on " Chaucer's Queen Anelyda " in *Essays on Chaucer*, Chaucer Society, 1892, p. 615.

Third, the story was left unfinished. If Chaucer had been following a definite source, he would no doubt have finished the story.

This would seem a simple enough theory and so we might let the matter rest, but there are two troublesome questions which refuse to down. These are: first, why should Chaucer insist upon giving us an authority, Corinne, whom he apparently never followed; and second, why is this complaint so different from the ordinary complaints of the period?

Let us consider first the possibilities of such an authority as Corinne. There are two whom it has been conjectured Chaucer might have had in mind, Corinnus, a reputed Greek author, and Corinna,[1] a Theban poetess. Either of these names would assume, of course, the form that we find in Chaucer's verse.

Modern historians of Greek literature, such as Christ and Croiset, make no mention of Corinnus. But from Roscher [2] we find that Corinnus was sup-

[1] See Lounsbury, *Studies in Chaucer*, II, 402–405; Skeat, *Oxford Chaucer*, I, 531; *Globe Chaucer*, p. 336.

Miss Hammond, *Chaucer: A Bibliographical Manual*, p. 88, has, "I have queried if a MS. could have given Chaucer *Corinnus* instead of *Corippus:* see Sandys, *Hist. of Classical Scholarship*, 436; but there appears no evidence of Corippus' influence."

[2] See Roscher, *Ausführliches Lexikon der Griech. u. Röm. Mythologie*, under Korinnos. Fabricius in his *Bibliotheca Graeca*, I, 16, gives something about Corinnus based also only upon Suidas.

posed to be an epic poet, a native of Ilium who
lived before Homer, and during the Trojan War
wrote an *Iliad* from which Homer borrowed the
argument for his poem. He wrote in the Doric
characters which had been invented by Palamedes;
for he was a pupil of Palamedes. He also wrote the
story of the war of Dardanus against the Paphla-
gonians. Roscher cites Suidas as his authority.

The mere recital of the reputed facts about Corinnus seems to remove him from the range of possibility. Certainly Suidas is poor dependence in the
way of an authority. Nobody contends that Chaucer knew of any work of Corinnus; for had there
been an abundance of it extant, Chaucer would not
have been able to read it on account of his lack of a
knowledge of Greek. The question involved in
considering Corinnus is whether Chaucer might
have heard of him as a great writer and, in his
desire to cite an authority, have seized upon his
name. There seems, indeed, little probability of
this being the case; for Corinnus was certainly little
known to the Middle Ages, even as a reputed
writer, if his name is found only in such doubtful
authorities as Suidas and "Eudocia."

In the case of the Theban poetess Corinna we
have a little more definite information, at least as
to her work. Guilelmus Crönert, in an article in
the *Rheinisches Museum* entitled "Corinnae quae

supersunt,"[1] gives, first, under the heading "Testimonia," a list of writers of antiquity who mention Corinna in any way. The names include Suidas, Themistocles, Pausanias, some Scholia, and Statius.

Crönert's second heading includes what he designates as "Fragmenta apud Veteres servata." This list is made up chiefly of Scholia and grammarians such as Hephaestion and Herodian.

A third list of "Fragmenta incertae Sedis" contains Priscian, Heyschinus, and Heraclides Milesius. Of the three classes, there are all told, according to Crönert, forty-one references to Corinna, the poetess. He adds a few which he designates as "Dubia" and which we need not consider. He says in a concluding paragraph that Corinna was much read by the Alexandrian poets, authors of antiquities, grammarians, and metricians.

Here, then, was a poetess who was much celebrated in antiquity, but only her name had come down to later times with a few fragments of her work. We have again the same question as in the case of Corinnus. There is no supposition that Chaucer knew Corinna's work or even thought he was copying it; but whether he might not have heard of her as a celebrated ancient who would sound well as an authority is the question. In

---

[1] Guilelmus Crönert, *Rheinisches Museum für Philologie*, N. F., LXIII (1908), 161–189.

other words, can it be that he was using her name
as a literary device in much the same way as he
seems to have done with the name Lollius? This
is, as anyone will admit, a tempting theory, but
before we can assume it, we must see if it is likely
that Chaucer had ever heard of Corinna. It is, of
course, dangerous to assert that Chaucer did not
know or could not know such and such a thing. We
can proceed only from what we can gather from his
writings and from what works we know to have
been available in his time. So far as has been ascer-
tained, there is no reasonable ground for assuming
that he knew any of these writers who mention or
quote from Corinna except Statius. Certainly we
have abundant evidence of Chaucer's knowledge of
Statius, for he quotes from the *Thebaid* in this very
poem. Statius' works include two epic poems —
the *Thebaid*, already mentioned, and the *Achilleid*
— and a series of occasional poems entitled *Silvae*.
Now Statius in his *Silvae* (Liber v, Eclogue iii,
l. 158), has the following mention of Corinna:

> Tu pandere docti
> Carmina Battiadae, latebrasque Lycophronis atri
> Sophronaque implicitum, tenuisque arcana Corinnae.

This evidence would go far toward showing that
Chaucer might have known the name Corinna as a
famous authority at least, if it were not true that,
though Statius' *Thebaid* and *Achilleid* were well

known and quoted, his *Silvae* was practically lost
during the Middle Ages. There is only one instance
known in all the literature of the Middle Ages of a
quotation from Statius' *Silvae*. This is the occurrence of one line which seems to be from the *Silvae*
in a letter written during the age of Charlemagne
and therefore not later than the early part of the
ninth century. After this the *Silvae* was apparently unknown until the discovery of a manuscript
at St. Gallen in 1416, sixteen years after Chaucer's
death.[1]

Such a theory, therefore, as to the origin of
Chaucer's use of the name Corinna must rest upon
the assumption that it is a literary device and that
the name of the Theban poetess was known to
Chaucer. For the first we can adduce the parallel
of Lollius, but for the second there seems no reasonable basis.

There is one other Corinna of ancient literature
whose name has never been connected with this one
of Chaucer, but the facts in the case seem much
more to point to her name as the one to which
Chaucer meant to refer than to either of the others
we have considered.

This Corinna was the mistress of Ovid whom he
addressed in the *Amores*. Chaucer in the *Anelida*

---

[1] See Sandys, *A History of Classical Scholarship*, p. 618; Manitius,
Phil., LII, 538–545; O. Müller, *Rheinisches Museum*, XVIII, 189.

was writing a love-poem, and Ovid was the great authority in the Middle Ages upon love. The great popularity of his works is attested by all authorities.[1] It is needless to dwell upon how universally Ovid was celebrated in the Middle Ages as the poet of love. One of his works on love so popular at that time was the work which is now known as *Amores*. Most of the poems in this collection, especially in Book i, are addressed to his mistress, Corinna, and from Manitius we learn that it was only the first book which was much quoted by mediaeval writers.[2]

But a curious fate seems to have overtaken this book of Ovid's in the Middle Ages. Its real title, *Amorum*, which was given it by Ovid, seems to have fallen pretty generally into disuse. For it various others were substituted. Numerous manuscripts refer to the work as *sine titulo;* and from the early editors of Ovid, who put themselves to great pains to explain the true name and get it reëstablished, we find that it was also called *Elegiae* and *Corinna*.

In enumerating Ovid's writings, Vincent of

[1] A. Graf, *Roma nella memoria e nelle immaginazione del medio evo*, II, 296–315; Sandys, p. 615.

[2] Manitius says: "Anführungen aus Lib. II fehlen: überhaupt ist im Mittelalter kein Buch so wenig berücksichtigt worden wie Am. II (und III), ausser den Medic. faciei, aus welchem ich überhaupt kein Citat gefunden habe" (*Phil.*, Supplement, VII, 736).

Beauvais gives the *Amores* under the name of *sine titulo*.[1]

In an *Ovidii Vita ex Lilii Gregor. Gyraldi de Poetarum Historia Libro IV*, prefixed to an edition of Ovid's works by Cornelius Schrevelius, volume I, we find another reference to the designation *sine titulo*. Gyraldus, who died in 1552, has the following on this point: "Quae vero ingenissimi Poetae opera supersint, breviter colligam Elegiae Amorum vel de sine titulo: de quibus sunt Grammaticorum controversiae."

Of the extant manuscripts of the *Amores* and those of which the descriptions have come down to us in the catalogues of mediaeval libraries now lost, six designate the work as *sine titulo*.[2] Three MSS indicate the title as *Amorum*.[3]

---

[1] Bartsch, *Bibliothek der deutschen National-Literatur*, XXXVIII, Einleitung, 111.

[2] Becker gives the description of four such MSS: *Catalogi Bibliothecarum Antiqui*, p. 174, No. 74; p. 196, No. 82; p. 233, No. 115; p. 239, No. 117. And the catalogues of French manuscripts give two: *Catalogue des Manuscrits*, Departments, V, 121; *Bibliothèque de l'Arsenal*, II, 156.

[3] These are described in the following: *Catalogue des Manuscrits*, Departments, XXXVII,[1] 635; *Catalogus Codicum MSS Bibliothecae Bodleianae*, pars tertia, p. 115 (this MS. is prefixed by this distich:

"Hoc opus est Naso titulo quo signat amorum
Cantata est libris una Corinna tribus");

Catalogus Codicum Manuscriptorum Bibliothecae Regiae, VIIM-CCCXI. This last MS. has *animorum*, which is plainly a mistake for *amorum*. See R. Merkel, *Ovidius*, 1855, p. iv, for a description of this MS.

Though we have preserved no MS. describing
this book as *Corinna*, we have excellent testimony
to the fact that such a designation was common.
From Fabricius, we learn that Hermolaus Barbarus, a distinguished Venetian scholar, born in
1454, called it by this name. This is what Fabricius
has to say upon the *Amores:* [1]

Amorum libri III, memorati Ovidio, Art. III, 343:

"Deve tribus libris, titulus quos signat Amorum,
Elige, quod docili molliter ore legas."

Hinc patet falli Hermolaum Barbarum, qui illos libros
laudat sub titulo *Corinnae* Ovidii: vel autorem glos-
sarum veterum, quas servo MSS et Jeremiam de Mon-
tagnano, qui in Epitoma Sapientiac Venet. 1505. 4.
edita vocat *Ovidium sine titulo*.

Further testimony upon the use of the title
Corinna we find in the early printed editions of
Ovid's works. In an edition at Frankfort, 1601,[2]
there is a preface to the reader by the Venetian,
Dominicus Marius Niger, who lived about 1490.
Niger makes it clear that *Elegiae, sine titulo*, and
Corinna were all known as titles to the work:

Praefandum illud mihi tantum, studiose lector, ex
multis, quae Grammatici hac in parte quaerenda tradi-
dere, hisce in libris, quis videlicet eorum sit titulus;
atque eo quaerendum diligentius existimavi, quod doc-
torum hominum hac in re sententiae variant. Ele-

[1] J. A. Fabricius, *Bibliotheca Latina*, ed. J. A. Ernesti, I, 444.
[2] *Ovidius*, 3 tom., Francofurti, 1601, fol., I, 177.

giarum nomine multi treis hos libros appellant: sed parum recte, ut mea quidem fert opinio. Nam Elegiae quoque sunt, quas in Tristibus scripsit Naso; unde incertus et ambiguus his titulus redderetur. Alii Corinnam vocant: inter quos est noster Hermolaus Barbarus, qui quoties ex hoc opere carmina citat: Ovidius, inquit, in Corinna, etc. Verum non de Corinna solum hic loquitur auctor, neque Corinnam solam amavit, quod liquido patet ex elegia 4 et 19 libri 2 Amorum, atque ex aliis in quibus factetur ingenue Naso, se multarum puellarum captum fuisse. Non tamen inficias eo, Corinnam ei caeteris chariorem fuisse, de eademque frequentius scriptum esse: ut si a majori parte ducendus sit titulus, parum peccet qui Corinnae nomine hoc opus vocant. Gravius autem illi errare mihi videntur, qui licet manuscriptorum, depravatorum tamen exemplarium auctoritatem secuti, hos treis libellos De sine titulo nominant: ex quibus (quod maxime miror) sunt Laurentius Vallensis et Joannes Tortellius, qui non ineruditi habentur. Horum opinionem pluribus argumentis refellere non oportet: satis enim fuerit poetae sententiam et voluntatem de hujus operis titulo, ipsius verbis adduxisse. Naso igitur lib. 3 de Arte, hujus sui operis ita meminit: De tribus libris, titulos quos signat Amorum, Elige, quod docili molliter ore legas.

Nicolaus Heinsius (1620–1681), the great Ovid commentator, in a note on the *Amores* which Burmann copied, says: "Amorum libros dici oportere quicquid obstrepant MSS ipse Ovidius lib. III. Art. 343 docet: 'Deque tribus libris, titulus quos signat Amorum Elige.'"

Burmann after quoting this note adds his testimony as follows: "Amores inscribi debere hos

libros docet quoque Spartianus in Vita Aelii Veri
Cap. V. ubi narrat, Verum Ovidii libros Amorum
in lecto semper habuisse." [1]

Jahn,[2] a nineteenth-century editor, assigns a
reason for the substitution of the titles *Corinna*
and *sine titulo*. In addition he cites an instance
of the controversy of the grammarians over *sine
titulo* as a name:

Inscripsit autem *Amorum* nomine [v. Art. Am. iii,
343] qui titulus tamen librariis displicuit, qui in codicibus haec carmina plerumque aut *Corinnam* aut *libros
sine titulo* inscripserunt. Quam mirifico modo illi
homines in hac re versati sint, apparet ex scholiis codicis
Lipsiensis [senatorii], in quibus haec leguntur: *De tituli
carentia diversi diversa sentiunt. Quidam enim dicunt,
hunc librum intitulatum fuisse ab armis, solum auctoris
attendentes propositum. Proposuerat enim Ovidius de
Gigantomachia facere quinque libros, i. e., de bello Caesaris, quod fuit inter Augustum, Cleopatrum et Antonium,
habens Antonium et Cleopatrum pro Gigantibus et Augustum pro Jove. Sed cum tanto operi sufficere non posset, eo
relicto de amore [scripsit]. Sumerem titulum ab operis
exsecutione, praesertim quia ab illo proposito fuit a
Cupidine abstractus. Erant alii, qui dicebant, hunc librum intitulatum esse ab amore, sumentes titulum ab
operis exsecutione, ubi solum de amoribus tractat. Alii
vero dicunt, quod prae metu invidorum titulum apponere
non est ausus. Erant enim Romae quidam invidi, qui
titulos libris abradentes suos apponebant et, quia sic de
titulo dissentiebant, idem liber iste sine titulo quasi sub*

[1] See *Ovidii Opera*, ed. Burmann, 1727, I, 323.
[2] *Ovidii Opera Omnia*, ed. Jahn, 1828, I, 227.

incertitudine tituli manet. Alii dicunt, quod damnato Ovidio librisque suis ab Augusto propter librum de arte amandi quidam, hunc librum reticere volentes, titulum abstraxerint, qui talis erat: Incipit liber amorum qualem habemus in libro de arte amatoria.

Whatever may have been the reason that the real title, *Amorum*, was discarded or lost, the copyists seem generally to have followed two courses, sometimes giving the title of *sine titulo*, and sometimes giving the name of the mistress to whom the majority of the elegies were addressed, *Corinna*. Ovid's prediction about her name and his being indissolubly united had come true:

Nos quoque per totum pariter cantabimur orbem,
Iunctaque semper erunt nomina nostra tuis.
(*Am.*, i, iii, 25–26.)

When the Renaissance came, and men began again to read the classics for themselves in a critical way instead of *Scholia* upon them, they noticed that Ovid himself, in the *Ars Amatoria*, iii, 343, had given the name of *Amorum* to this book which had been masquerading widely as *sine titulo* or *Corinna*. Consequently the printed editions, which were, of course, published in the light of this knowledge, all give the correct title, *Amores* or *Amorum Liber*. But the early editors, who had access to the MSS with the titles *sine titulo* and *Corinna*, found it necessary to explain why they made the change. There are similar instances of substitution or loss of names during the Middle Ages and their re-discovery after the Renaissance. A striking illustration of the loss of a name is the case of the Roman poet Martial, who was called almost universally in the Middle Ages by the name Coquus.[1]

Chaucer is usually found to cite his authorities quite accurately. Why he does not do so in the case of Boccaccio we do not know. At any rate, he has no aversion to citing ancient authorities, and he refers to Ovid under the names of Ovide, Naso, and *Metamorphoseos*. From the foregoing evidence we must admit that it would also be very natural for him to refer to Ovid under the name of Corinna. Let us now see whether there is any reason for his referring to Ovid in this particular poem. This brings us to a consideration of our second question, why the *Compleynt of Anelida* is so different from the ordinary complaints of the period.

A study of the complaints of this period not only fails to disclose a single poem which might appear to be a source for the *Anelida*, but it also shows that the *Anelida* is essentially different from the general type to which the other complaints conform. The conventional complaint was so general and abstract that it conveys an impression of a literary exercise rather than the expression of sincere feeling. It is this stereotyped poem which we find so

---

[1] Sandys, *Hist. Class. Schol.*, p. 619.

abundant in the French love-poetry of the Middle Ages.[1] It had become the fashion, and the poets expressed their artificial complaining with little or nothing in the way of incident or situation as a basis. The *Compleynt of Anelida*, on the other hand, is based upon a distinctive situation, and is full of a spirit of reality and genuine feeling which places it quite outside this type. For the sake of illustrating the difference it may be well to quote some single examples of the French complaint to be compared with the *Anelida*. For such a comparison it would seem necessary to select poems which bear as close similarity in situation as possible to Chaucer's complaint. But just here is the difficulty. The situation in all of them is so little elaborated, the theme is so general and conventional, that there is little choice to make. The selections, however, have been made on the basis

[1] Rutebeuf, a *trouvère* of the thirteenth century, wrote complaints, but none of them deals with love. See *Œuvres Complètes de Rutebeuf*, ed. Jubinal, pp. 13 ff., 40 ff., 55 ff., 91 ff., 100 ff. For Machault's "complaintes," see *Guillaume de Machaut, Poésies Lyriques*, ed. Chichmaref, I, 241–269. Froissart wrote amorous ballads of the conventional type; see *Œuvres de Froissart, Poésies*, ed. Scheler, II, 366 ff. Granson, from whom we know Chaucer translated his *Compleynt of Venus*, wrote a *Complainte de Saint Valentin*. For a discussion of this poem and others of Granson's, see A. Piaget, *Romania*, XIX, 405–407. Deschamps wrote many "balades amoureuses." See *Œuvres Complètes de Eustache Deschamps*, ed. Saint-Hilaire, III, 209 ff. Christine de Pisan wrote "amorous complaints" of the established type. Her work was probably done too late to influence Chaucer. See *Œuvres Poétiques de Christine de Pisan*, ed. Roy, I, 281–295, and III, 203–208.

of similarity of situation, distinguishing details,
and sincerity of spirit, as far as it has been possible
to find these qualities.

The following is a little poem in Froissart's typical manner. The theme is the complaining of a
lover to his obdurate mistress.

> A vous sui tout, dame gente,
> Apareillies d'obeir,
> De coer, de foi et d'entente
> A faire votre plaisir;
> Loyalment vous ai servi
> En espoir d'avoir merci.
>
> Mais ce trop fort m'espoente
> Que ne me dagniés oïr;
> Je voi bien que longe atente
> Me menra jusqu'au morir
> Las! j'ai vescu jusqu'a ci
> En espoir d'avoir merci.
>
> La riens qui plus me contente
> En confortant mon desir
> Et l'assaut que j'ai de rente
> C'est un tres doulc souvenir
> Dont Amours m'a enrici
> En espoir d'avoir merci.[1]

As the following selection from Deschamps is
analogous in theme with the *Compleynt of Anelida*,
a comparison may more easily be made.

> *Plaintes d'une dame.*
> Se j'ay amé longuement
> De vray cuer et bonnement
> Mon doulz ami,

---

[1] *Œuvres de Froissart, Poésies*, ed. Scheler, II, 387.

Et il s'est retrait de mi
   Soudainement,
Sanz cause et sans mouvement,
   Amours regni.

Car je l'ay long temps servi,
Amé, doubté et chery
   Tresloyaument.
N'onques a autre qu'a ly
Mon las cuer ne s'assenty
   Aucunement.

Et je voi tout clerement
Que malicieusement
   M'a deguerpy
Et qu'il a amours choisi
   Nouvellement,
Sanz dire au departement:
   Adieu vous dy
Se j'ay amé longuement.

Et pour ce l'eure maudy
Qu'amours en moy s'embaty
   Premierement,
Et les yeux dont je le vy
Et moy quant mon cuer ravi
   Si folement:
En amours n'a que tourment,
A Dieu du tout le commant
   Des ce jour cy.

De moy n'ot onques mercy
   Certainement
Aincoiz m'a couvertement
   Le cuer ocy.
Se j'ay amé longuement,
   De vray cuer et bonnement.[1]

---

[1] *Œuvres Complètes de Eustache Deschamps*, ed. Saint-Hilaire, **IV**, 185.

Of Machaut's complaints, the example which suggests a situation most like that of the *Anelida*, is one where a lady avows her love and complains of the lover's absence:

Mes dous amis, à vous me vueil compleindre
Dou mal qui fait mon cuer palir et teindre,
Car de vous vient, si le devez savoir,
Ne sans vous seul confort ne puet avoir.
Or vueilliez dont entendre ma clamour
Et avec ce considerer l'amour
Dont je vous aim, car brief seroit ma fin
Se ne m'amiés de cuer loial et fin.
Amis, je n'ay nulle joieuse vie,
Eins suis toudis en grant merencolie,
Mais je ne fais jour et nuit que penser
A vous veoir; mais po vaut mon penser,
Quant il n'est tour, subtilité ne voie,
Ne maniere que j'y sache ne voie;
Si qu'einsi sont mi mortel anemy
Tuit mi penser, et toudis contre my.
Si n'ay confort, amis, fors que tant plour
Que je cuevre ma face de mon plour.
Et quant je suis saoulé de plourer,
Souvenirs vient mon las cuer acorer;
Car il n'est biens ne joie qu'il m'aporte,
Einsois toudis me grieve et desconforte,
Dont j'ay souvent estranglé maint souspir.
Pour ce que trop parfondement souspir.
Après desirs ne me laisse durer.
Si n'ay pas corps pour tel fais endurer,
Car foible sui, dont piessa fusse morte,
S'espoirs ne fust qui un po me conforte,
Et si ne say que c'est de cest espoir,
Car pas ne vient: si me deçoit espoir,
Et s'ay cause de penser le contraire
De ce qu'il dit; pour ce ne say que faire.
Or soit einsi come Dieu l'a ordonné;

Mais je vous ay si franchement donné
Moy et m'amour que c'est sans departir,
Et s'il convient m'ame don corps partir,
Ja ceste amour pour ce ne finera,
Tu apres ma mort m'ame vous amera.[1]

It is easy to see that these complaints vary little from the characteristics of the general type which have been pointed out. They are conventional and impersonal in style. They might apply to the case of almost any lover. It is the artificial complaining of courtly love that we find in all the love-poems of the period. Some of Chaucer's complaints are of this conventional type. The *Compleynt of Venus*, which is merely a translation from the French of Granson, deals with the usual abstractions, jealousy, constancy, and the like. The *Compleynt unto Pite* has the characteristic personifications, Love, Pity, and so forth. The *Compleynt to his Lady*, though it exhibits the stereotyped characteristics, especially in parts 1, 2, and 3, shows in part 4 more resemblances to Anelida's complaint in the *Anelida and Arcite*. But the *Anelida and Arcite* itself differs greatly from all of these complaints. In the first place, Chaucer has a story to tell, and the *Compleynt of Anelida* is woven into the story so as to make a component part of it.[2] For instance, the story part

[1] *Guillaume de Machaut, Poésies Lyriques*, ed. Chichmaref, I, 254.
[2] It may be well to indicate what is meant by *complaint* as it is used in this discussion. Skeat, in the *Oxford Chaucer*, I, 61, has defined

of the poem, told in the third person, narrates how
Anelida in her faithfulness to Arcite showed him all
the letters written to her by other lovers (ll. 113–
115). This same idea is brought into the *Compleynt*

complaint as follows: "The word *compleynt* answers to the O. F. *complaint*, sb. masc., as distinguished from O. F. *complainte*, sb. fem., and
was the technical name, as it were, for a love-poem of a mournful tone,
usually addressed to the unpitying loved one." This is a somewhat
technical limitation of the word, but this seems to be the kind of complaint that was fashionable among the French love-poets of the Middle
Ages, and the kind that Chaucer imitated in his early complaints.
Professor Neilson has shown in his discussion of the Court of Love
genre that it was common enough for someone to present himself before
Venus or her representative in the Court of Love with a complaint.
("The Origins and Sources of the Court of Love," *Harvard Studies and
Notes*, Boston, 1899, VI, 231–232.) In these instances the complaint
may be said to be an organic part of the story. But the word *complaint*
is in such cases used in its broadest sense to mean any kind of griev-
ance, and it really is a petition or "bill" presented to Venus for her
judgment and is not a love-poem addressed to the unpitying loved one.
In the same way we may call the *débat* a complaint. For instance,
there is the complaint of the White Canonesses against the Gray Nuns
in Jean de Conde's *Le Messe des Oisiaus et li Plais des Channonesses et
des Grises Nonains* (see Neilson, pp. 67–69). Here the Canonesses
come before Venus, who is to decide the question, to complain that
the Gray Nuns have taken their lovers. It will readily be seen, however, that these petitions are not *complaints* in the sense in which
Skeat defines the term and in which I am using it in discussing Chaucer's complaints. There are numerous instances later than Chaucer
where the complaint or lament is made an organic part of a story.
Professor Neilson has called my attention to three instances of such
complaints in Scottish poetry which show likewise the nine-line stanzas of the *Complaint of Anelida*. These are *Sir William Wallace*, ii,
170–359, "Scottish Text Society," 1889; "The Complaint of Cresseid"
in *The Testament of Cresseid*, ll. 407–469, Henryson, *Poems and Fables*,
ed. David Laing, Edinburgh, 1865; and the complaint in the *Quare of
Jalusy*, ll. 191 ff., *The Kingis Quair and the Quare of Jalusy*, Alexander
Lawson, London, 1910. But Chaucer in the *Compleynt of Mars* and in
the *Anelida and Arcite* appears to be the first poet to use the complaint
in this way.

in lines 264–265. In this respect Chaucer's *Compleynt of Mars* is similar to the *Anelida;* for it has a story in which appears a complaint containing reference to the story. But as we have seen, Chaucer was not writing there altogether in the manner of his French contemporaries; for he took his story from Ovid. Except for these direct references to the preceding story, the complaint in the *Mars* is of the artificial type. In the *Pite* there may be said to be a story in which a "bill" to Pity is introduced. But the whole poem is really a complaint written in the first person, and into this complaint of the death of Pity in his lady's heart the poet introduces a "bill" addressed to Pity herself. But the *Compleynt of Anelida* is more concrete and personal throughout. There is genuine feeling and passion in it. We are made to feel that Anelida is an individual, and our sympathies are aroused in her behalf.

Thus it will be seen that though this poem is generally thought to be an early one, and though Chaucer's early work was much influenced by French writers, there is not to be discovered any close relationship between Chaucer's *Anelida* and the work of his French contemporaries.

There is, however, one fertile field as yet unnoted from which Chaucer may have conceived his idea of this love-poem and complaint, and that is Ovid's *Heroides*.[1] From Chaucer's works written before the *Anelida*, it appears that Statius and Ovid were the Latin writers with whom he was up to that time familiar. We know that he drew upon his knowledge of Statius for this poem; and I believe a careful study of it will be convincing that, although the story of Anelida is Chaucer's own creation, he modelled it after the *Heroides* of Ovid and drew thence various details. The situation in all of the Epistles of the *Heroides* is practically the same: a lovely woman, who has fondly trusted her lover, suddenly and without apparent reason finds herself basely deserted. Under these circumstances Ovid makes each heroine address a letter

[1] J. Schick, in discussing Lydgate's *Complaint of the Black Knight*, has suggested that the origin of the complaint may have been influenced by Ovid's *Heroides*. He says: "Further, the 'Complaints' of the Lady and the Knight as they present them to the goddess, recall to us a certain species of poetry which was at one time much in vogue in England and France. These 'Complaints' are usually put into the mouth of a rejected or forsaken lover, bewailing his wretched state and calling upon his lady for pity. It is not impossible that their origin may have been influenced by Ovid's *Heroides*, which enjoyed so remarkable a popularity in the Middle Ages. We have such 'Complaints' from French poets — for instance, from Rutebeuf, Christina de Pisan and Machault: Chaucer wrote the 'Complaints' of Mars, of Venus, and of Anelida (of somewhat different *genre*, the *Complaint to Pity*, and turned jokingly, the *Compleint to his Purse*)." *Temple of Glass*, E. E. T. S., p. cxxii.

If in its origin the *genre* owed something to the *Heroides*, it is interesting to observe that Chaucer in the *Compleynt of Anelida* has broken away from his French masters who were by this time producing a type of complaint very different from Ovid's poems, and has gone back to the original source for his model.

to her lover, expressing her grief and resentment at his faithlessness and at the same time entreating him to return. Have we not exactly a parallel case in the *Anelida?* To be sure, Ovid's work in each case is based upon a legend which attributes to his heroine the fate which she is experiencing. The story itself was already presumably known to his reader; as, for instance, the story of Ariadne, who was deserted on the island of Naxos by Theseus and was supplanted by her sister Phaedra, whom Theseus carried to Athens with him.

These Epistles of the *Heroides*, we may presume, had fired Chaucer's imagination to attempt something of his own upon a similar theme. He found first of all that he needed what Ovid had already, a story that would furnish the occasion of the complaint to the unfaithful lover. Quite naturally he drew upon such storehouse of knowledge as he possessed at that time. Thus he took the setting of Theseus' court from the *Teseide*, linked together the euphonious names of Anelida and Arcite, and introduced a complaint addressed by the heroine to her lover and modelled after the *Heroides* of Ovid.

The spirit of the *Anelida*, to be sure, is more refined than that of the *Heroides*, but this is to be expected. Earthly as Chaucer sometimes is in his treatment of love, in drawing from Ovid he always elevates the theme.

Besides the general similarities mentioned, the details in the *Anelida* point to the *Heroides* as a source.[1]

In the Epistle of Ariadne to Theseus, *Her.*, x, 137–140, we find:

> Adspice demissos lugentis more capillos
> Et tunicas lacrimis sicut ab imbe gravis!
> Corpus, ut impulsae segetes aquilonibus, horret,
> Litteraque articulo pressa tremente labat.

These ideas may be found in the *Anelida:* the weeping of the heroine,

> Upon a day, ful sorowfully weping (l. 207);

---

[1] It may be noted that Penelope, to whom Chaucer compares Anelida (l. 82), is Ovid's heroine in the first Epistle of the *Heroides*, and that Lucretia, referred to in the same line, is celebrated by Ovid in *Fasti*, II, 721–852. But the linking together of the names of Penelope and Lucretia as models of goodness and constancy was a favorite idea of Chaucer's caught from a passage in the *Roman de la Rose*. Professor Skeat notes this as follows in the *Oxford Chaucer*, I, 490, note to line 1081 of the *Duchess:*

"*Penelope* is accented on the first *e* and on *o*, as in French. Chaucer copies this from the *Roman de la Rose*, line 8694, as appears from his coupling it with Lucrece, whilst at the same time he borrows a pair of rimes. The French has:

> 'Si n'est-il mès nule Lucrece,
> Ne *Penelope* nule *en Grece.*'

In the same passage, the story of Lucretia is told in full, on the authority of Livy, as here. The French has: 'ce dit Titus Livius,' line 8654. In the prologue to the *Legend of Good Women*, Chaucer alludes again to Penelope (line 252), Lucrece of Rome (line 257), and Polixene (line 258); and he gives the Legend of Lucrece in full. He again alludes to Lucrece and Penelope in the lines preceding the Man of Lawes Prologue (B. 63, 75); and in the Frankelein's Tale (F. 1405, 1443)." To these instances may be added this mention of the two names in *Anelida*, line 82.

the trembling of her body,

> That turned is in quaking al my daunce (l. 214);

and the writing of the letter with her own hand,

> She caste hir for to make a compleyning,
> And with hir owne honde she gan hit wryte.
>   (ll. 208–209.)

In *Her.*, xii, 175–178, Medea says:

> Forsitan et stultae dum te jactare maritae
>   Quaeris et iniustis auribus apta loqui,
> In faciem moresque meos nova crimina fingas,
>   Rideat et vitiis laeta sit illa meis.

Anelida's reference in lines 229–234 to Arcite's new attachment and to his laughing at her pain is akin to Medea's words. Anelida says:

> Now is he fals, alas! and causeles,
> And of my wo he is so routheles,
> That with a worde him list not ones deyne
> To bring ayein my sorowful herte in pees,
> For he is caught up in another lees.
> Right as him list, he laugheth at my peyne.

Both are thinking of the happiness of the lover and his new love; with Medea it is her rival who laughs at her in her grief, with Anelida it is her lover.

The idea that the heroine trusted too much to the flattering words of her lover, expressed in *Her.*, ii, 49,

> Credidimus blandis, quorum tibi copia, verbis,

Chaucer uses for a whole stanza (ll. 247–255):

> Alas! wher is become your gentilesse!
> Your wordes fulle of plesaunce and humblesse?
> Your observaunces in so low manere,
> And your awayting and your besinesse,
> Upon me, that he calden your maistresse,
> Your sovereyn lady in the worlde here?
> Alas! and is ther nother word ne chere
> Ye vouchesauf upon myn hevinesse?
> Alas! your love, I bye hit al to dere.

The suggestion that to be untrue in love will bring no glory to a man's name is expressed in two of the Epistles and in the *Anelida*. Ovid in *Her.*, ii, 63–66, has on this subject:

> Fallere credentem non est opera puellam
> Gloria: simplicitas digna favore fuit.
> Sum decepta tuis et amans et femina verbis:
> Di faciant, laudis summa sit ista tuae.

The same idea is found in *Her.*, iii, 144, where Briseis, after asserting that Achilles will cause her to die by his neglect, says:

> Nec tibi magnificum femina iussa mori.

A fairly close parallel to this is the following passage from the *Anelida*, lines 273–277:

> And thenke ye that furthered be your name
> To love a newe, and been untrewe? Nay!
> And putte you in sclaunder now and blame,
> And do to me adversitee and grame,
> That love you most, god, wel thou wost! alway?

Ovid and Chaucer give almost identically the ideas that separation from her lover means death to the heroine, and that his neglect has already banished the color from her face:

> Aut, si versus amor tuus est in taedia nostri,
>   Quam sine te cogis vivere, coge mori!
> Utque facis, coges: abiit corpusque colorque.
>   (*Her.*, iii, 139–141.)

> For either mot I have yow in my cheyne,
> Or with the dethe ye mot departe us tweyne;
> Ther ben non other mene weyes newe;
> For god so wisly on my soule rewe,
> As verily ye sleen me with the peyne;
> That may ye see unfeyned of myn hewe.
>   (*Anelida*, ll. 284–289.)

The circumstance of the heroine seeing her lover in her dreams is given by both authors:

> Tu mihi cura, Phaon! te somnia nostra reducunt,
>   Somnia formoso candidiora die
> Illic te invenio, quamvis regionibus absis;
>   Sed non longa satis gaudia somnus habet.
>   (*Her.*, xv, 123 ff.)

> And if I slepe a furlong wey or tweye,
> Than thinketh me, that your figure
> Before me stant, clad in asure,
> To profren eft a newe assure
> For to be trewe, and mercy me to preye.
> The longe night this wonder sight I drye,
> And on the day for this afray I dye.
>   (*Anelida*, ll. 328–334.)

Probably the most striking resemblance between
any single one of Ovid's Epistles and the *Anelida* is
found in the suggestions of both Dido and Anelida
that their laments are swan- songs. Both, in declaring that fate is against them and that they
must accept the inevitable, compare themselves to
the dying swan:

> Sic ubi fata vocant, udis abjectus in herbis
> Ad vada Maeandri concinit albus olor.
> Nec quia te nostra sperem prece posse moveri,
> Adloquor (adverso movimus ista deo).
> (Her., vii, 3–6.)

> Than ende I thus, sith I may do no more,
> I yeve hit up for now and ever-more;
> For I shal never eft putten in balaunce
> My sekernes, ne lerne of love the lore.
> But as the swan, I have herd seyd ful yore,
> Ayeins his deth shal singe in his penaunce,
> So singe I here my destiny or chaunce.
> (Anelida, ll. 342–348.)

Besides these similarities to the *Heroides*, there
is another indication that Chaucer was under the
influence of Ovid in this work. In the *Amores* Ovid
harps much upon the theme that we eagerly desire
what we cannot get:

> Quod licet, ingratumst: quod non licet, acrius urit.
> (Am., ii, xix, 3.)
> Nitimur in vetitum semper cupimusque negata.
> (Am., iii, iv, 17.)
> Quicquid servatur, cupimus magis, ipsaque furem
> Cura vocat: pauci, quod sinit alter, amant.
> (Am., iii, iv, 25–26.)

Chaucer refers to this same theme as follows:

> The kinde of mannes herte is to delyte
> In thing that straunge is, also god me save!
> For what he may not get that wolde he have.
> (*Anelida*, ll. 201–203.)

Not only does the similarity to the *Heroides* indicate that the *Anelida* was written under the influence of Ovid, but Chaucer's continued use of the *Heroides* in his subsequent work reinforces the belief that he was using it here.

Some of the foregoing points may seem slight in themselves, and it may be that Chaucer was not consciously borrowing in every case. At any rate, he had so absorbed Ovid's Epistles that he could write one in imitation of them and use perhaps unconsciously many of Ovid's details. Another example of such assimilation is to be found in Milton's *Lycidas*, which shows that its author was thoroughly saturated with the classical pastoral, though specific borrowings would be difficult to locate.

Thus we have found that the *Anelida* is like the *Heroides:* first, in general theme: man's unfaithfulness in love; second, in situation: a fair and faithful woman deserted by her false lover addresses a letter of complaint to him, bemoaning the confidence she has placed in him, but avowing her constancy and offering forgiveness if he will return to her; third, in details: for almost every idea expressed in the *Anelida* has a parallel in some one of the *Heroides*.

Now, as we have seen, it is quite probable that Chaucer's MS. copy of Ovid, which he calls his "owne booke" [1] designated the *Amores* as *Corinna*. It is probable that this book included all of Ovid's amatory verse; for Chaucer's works indicate familiarity with all of it. If the *Amores* came first with the *Heroides* following, as may very reasonably have been the case, we should have an explanation of why Chaucer refers to his use of the *Heroides* in the *Anelida* under the name of *Corinna*. However that may have been, the striking similarity of this poem to the Epistles of the heroines points to the *Heroides* as the model for the *Compleynt of Anelida*. And we may conclude that Chaucer intends to indicate his indebtedness to Ovid under the name *Corinna* when he says,

First folow I Stace and after him Corinne.[2]

[1] *House of Fame*, ii, 712.

[2] Since the publication of this discussion as an article in *P.M.L.A.*, XXVII, 4, Professor Frederick Tupper in *P.M.L.A.*, XXXVI, 2, 216, has called attention to the occurrence of the name "Corinna" in Propertius, ii, iii, 21. But this is by no means proof that Chaucer had ever seen it in any MS. of Propertius. On the contrary the probabilities are strongly against his having done so. Professor Tupper cites the Codices Neapolitanus, Vossianus, and the one in Petrarch's library. The Codex Neapolitanus (XIIC) was probably of German origin, and subsequently passed into Italy. It seems to have been at Florence in the fifteenth century and then passed to Naples,

The Former Age

In the *Former Age* Chaucer combines material from Boethius,[1] *Romance of the Rose*,[2] and Ovid. The three strands are so interwoven that it is difficult sometimes to feel sure that an idea is due more to one of these sources than to another.

Line 12 seems to be due to Ovid:

> No man yit knew the forwes of his land.

> Ipsa quoque immunis rastroque intacta nec ullis
> Saucia vomeribus per se dabat omnia tellus.
> > (*Met.*, i, 101–102.)

> Mox etiam fruges tellus inarata ferebat. (*Met.*, i, 109.)

The suggestion for lines 23–24 probably came from Ovid's description of conditions in the Golden Age:

where it remained until the seventeenth century, being then carried to Wolfenbüttel. The Vossianus (XIVC) is a fragment which extends only to Bk. ii, i, and consequently does not contain the passage which Mr. Tupper cites. And it may always have been a fragment. Petrarch seems to have had a Propertius MS. in his library. (For the facts with regard to these MSS, see H. E. Butler, *Sexti Properti Opera Omnia*, Introduction, pp. 9–11.) There is no evidence that Chaucer could have had access to any of these MSS, nor is there any indication of anything being known of Propertius' writings in England.

But if Chaucer had by some means seen the passage in Propertius where Corinna is mentioned, there is nothing in it to connect her name with Thebes. Still granting that Chaucer had heard of her as a Theban poetess, it is not inconceivable that he should have referred to her, to whom he owed nothing, because of the identity of her name with that of the mistress and one of the works of the poet to whom he did owe the inspiration for his poem.

[1] See Skeat, *Oxford Chaucer*, I, 539.
[2] Fansler, *Chaucer and the Roman de la Rose*, p. 223.

No trompes for the werres folk ne knewe,
No toures heye, and walles rounde or square.

Nondum praecipites cingebant oppida fossae,
Non tuba directi, non aeris cornua flexi,
Non galeae, non ensis erant: sine militis usu
Mollia securae peragebant otia gentes.

(*Met.*, i, 97–100.)

Likewise lines 27–32 may be due to Ovid's words about going into the bowels of the earth and digging up the riches, which at once became sources of evil among mankind:

But cursed was the tyme, I dar wel seye,
That men first dide hir swety bysinesse
To grobbe up metal, lurkinge in darknesse,
And in the riveres first gemmes soghte.
Allas! than spronge up al the cursednesse
Of covetyse, that first our sorwe broghte.

Nec tantum segetes alimentaque debita dives
Poscebatur humus, sed itum est in viscera terrae,
Quasque recondiderat Stygiisque admoverat umbris,
Effodiuntur opes, inritamenta malorum.

(*Met.*, i, 137–140.)

Though lines 41–48 seem to be more or less imitated from the *Roman de la Rose*, the use of caves as dwelling places is perhaps a suggestion from Ovid:

Tum primum subiere domos; domus antra fuerunt
Et densi frutices et vinctae cortice virgae.

(*Met.*, i, 121–122.)

Lines 57–59, which characterize Jupiter, are more likely from the *Roman de la Rose* [1] than from *Metamorphoses*, i.[2]

[1] Fansler, *Chaucer and the Roman de la Rose*, pp. 55–56.
[2] *Oxford Chaucer*, I, 542.

THE HOUSE OF FAME

THE classical influence is so considerable throughout the *House of Fame* that it may be well first of all to give a summary of the poem.

The proem gives some reflections upon dreams, their times and their causes, and a prayer that they may all turn out well. This leads the author to his own particular dream which he says took place on "the tenthe day of Decembre." Very appropriately he begins the account of his dream with an invocation to the God of Sleep, in which he prays

> that he wol me spede
> My sweven for to telle aright.

In the dream the poet finds himself in a temple of glass, which he recognizes as the temple of Venus from the portraiture he sees there of that goddess. Among many other wonderful things he finds graven upon the walls the story of Virgil's *Æneid*. These scenes he describes in comparatively short space with the rapid, telling strokes of his masterly pen, dwelling more particularly upon the love-story of Æneas and Dido, and laying the chief emphasis upon Dido's distress at her lover's desertion.

Leaving the temple then in search of someone to tell him where he is, Chaucer beholds about him a great lonely desert and a wonderful golden eagle descending toward him. With this situation to stimulate his reader's interest, he closes the first book.

The second book opens with a proem in the form of an invocation to Venus, the Muses, and Thought. Then, continuing the dream, Chaucer tells how the eagle swooped down upon him, caught him in his talons, and carried him swiftly heavenward. The poet is terrified, and in spite of the eagle's friendly assurances he begins to wonder if he is to be placed in the heavens as a constellation, and to compare himself with Enoch, Elijah, Romulus, and Ganymede. The eagle then makes known that he is the messenger of Jupiter sent to carry the poet to the house of Fame, where he can learn tidings of Love's folk as a recompense for his faithful service to the God of Love. The palace of Fame, he says, stands

> Right even in middes of the weye
> Betwixen hevene, erthe and see,

in just such a place that whatever is spoken by any tongue on earth secretly or openly must of necessity come there. In order to explain how this may be possible the eagle enters into a lengthy discussion of the laws of sound waves and the transmission of sounds up to Fame's house.

After this, in the course of their flight, the eagle calls the poet's attention to the distance they have come from the earth, to the constellations that are about them, and to their having passed above the elements, and bids him look down upon the clouds, and so forth. Finally, they hear a great rumbling sound like the beating of the sea upon the hollow rocks, and soon they arrive at the site of the house of Fame. The eagle says he will wait there, and Chaucer approaches the palace. This brings the second book to a close.

The third book opens with an invocation, this time to Apollo, after which the account of the dream is continued. Upon the pinnacle of a rock of ice Chaucer finds the dwelling of the Goddess of Fame. And on this rock of ice are written the names of people who had been famous on earth. The names on the side exposed to the sun are effaced to such an extent as to be illegible, but those protected by the shade of the castle of Fame are easily discernible. Outside this castle are seen all kinds of musicians, magicians, and so forth, who were famous on earth. Passing these by, the poet enters the gate and finds within the hall the goddess herself, a beautiful creature adorned with rich jewels, seated upon a dais and listening to "hevenish melodye of songes." On either side of this hall extending from the dais to the door are pillars of metal, upon which stand those writers who have had large fame in the world. The list includes Josephus and Statius; those great historians of Troy — Homer, Dares, Tytus (Dictys), Lollius, Guido de Columpnis, and English Gaufride; then Virgil, Ovid, Lucan, and Claudian. There were many more, but he deems these sufficient to mention.

While he is viewing the statues, a crowd enters the hall, worshipping the goddess Fame and praying her to give them worldly renown. She dispenses her judgments in a most capricious manner, wholly without regard to the merits of their requests, much in the fashion of the goddess Fortune. Æolus, God of the Winds, is the herald who by means of his two trumpets, Clere Laude and Sclaundre, proclaims to the world the decisions of Fame. After nine companies have passed before Fame and received their rewards, Chaucer is accosted by someone who inquires his name and the cause of his presence here. When the poet tells him that it is to learn tidings of Love's folk, the stranger volunteers to lead him to the place he seeks.

Departing from the castle they enter the valley where is the house to which all tidings come. The doors of this house are always open, and there is no porter to hinder the tidings from entering at will. There is no rest here, and there issues forth a great noise that might be heard a long distance. This house is made of twigs and is continually revolving, so that Chaucer cannot enter without the assistance of the eagle, who comes to do him this service.

Within he sees how a report runs from ear to ear, ever increasing as it goes until, full-grown, true or false, it issues from one of the windows. It then passes immediately to Fame, who gives it a name, and Æolus blows it abroad. This house is full of shipmen and all manner of wanderers from strange lands. As the poet goes about amusing himself and learning all he can, he hears a great noise in a corner of the hall where men are telling tidings of love. To this corner the people are crowding, and at last Chaucer sees a man of authority, but here he breaks off in the middle of a sentence and leaves the rest untold.

Professor Sypherd in his *Studies in Chaucer's Hous of Fame* [1] has shown, I think, quite conclusively that this poem is in form an example of the love-vision so extensively employed by the Old French poets. "It is," he says "with all its variations from the type, a love-vision of the *genre* to which belong the *Roman de la Rose*, the *Paradys*

[1] Chaucer Society, 1907.

d'Amours, and the *Duchesse*." [1]   Mr. Sypherd
thinks the motive which was present in Chaucer's
mind at the conception of the poem, namely, that
he was going to hear tidings of Love's folk, was
uppermost in his thoughts until the very end, although he modified it considerably in the course
of his work (p. 15). Chaucer's wide divergence
from his French models Mr. Sypherd explains as
due merely to his originality: "His feeling for the
real, his interest in actual men and women, and
his early developed intellectual tastes, have combined to endow his love-visions with qualities
which place these poems, in point of excellence,
at the apogee of the *genre* of love-vision literature"(p. 43).

As I have said, Mr. Sypherd has shown that the
House of Fame is a love-vision in form, but he goes
further than this and attributes also the essential
elements of the subject-matter to the influence of
the love-vision: "The essential point of contact
between the *Hous of Fame* and the Old French
love-visions is, as I have indicated above, that it
is a dream in which the experience of a love-poet
is described by means of mythological elements.
The underlying idea of the poem and the essential
elements of the form and subject-matter are clearly
due to the influence of the love-vision" (p. 18).

[1] Sypherd, p. 13.

Whether or not it is possible to agree with Mr. Sypherd on all points will appear later. At least we can accept at the outset this much of his conclusion, that the *House of Fame*, however much it may differ from the type, is a love-vision in form. This fact, it seems to me, is of great importance in any further study of the poem.

We are now ready to consider Chaucer's indebtedness in the *House of Fame* to Ovid and Virgil.

In his invocation near the beginning of the first book Chaucer describes the dwelling of the God of Sleep as follows:

> Unto the god of slepe anoon
> That dwelleth in a cave of stoon
> Upon a streem that comth fro Lethe,
> That is a flood of helle unswete;
> Besyde a folk men clepe Cimerie,
> Ther slepeth ay this god unmerie
> With his slepy thousand sones
> That alway for to sleep hir wone is.
>
> (*H. F.*, ll. 69-76.)

This is a short summary of the description of the habitation of the God of Sleep given by Ovid in the story of Ceyx and Halcyone (*Met.*, xi, 591-615, 633-634). Chaucer had previously introduced that story into the *Book of the Duchess*. It is interesting to notice how, after having given a full account of the god's dwelling in twenty-three lines in the earlier work, he here condenses it into eight lines. The description in the *Duchess*, it is true, agrees in some points with the version of Machaut in the *Dit de la Fontaine Amoureuse* [1] rather than with Ovid's, but these slight substitutions do not serve to expand the material but merely to vary it. In the passage in the *House of Fame* Chaucer has selected the prominent features of Ovid's recital and added nothing of his own except the explanatory line 72, identifying for his readers the river Lethe. A longer account here would, of course, have extended his invocation to too great length.

On the walls of the temple of Venus, Chaucer says he saw written upon a table of brass some verses, which are in reality a translation of the opening lines of the *Æneid*. Then, beginning with the destruction of Troy, he describes the scenes which he saw upon the walls. His portrayal of these scenes forms an outline of the *Æneid*, though, of course, he could not use Virgil's dramatic device of making Æneas later tell the story up to the point where the poem opens. Instead he gives the events in connected narrative from the fall of Troy.

When he comes to the story of Æneas' desertion of Dido, he goes into it at much length and devotes more space to it and to the digressions to which his interest in the subject leads him than he does to all the rest of the *Æneid*. His dwelling on this episode is no doubt due to his long acquaintance with it in Ovid's Epistle of Dido to Æneas

[1] See pp. 3 ff., above.

(*Heroides*, vii). Here he is on familiar ground. It is the old subject of the deserted heroine with which his mind was so saturated from Ovid's Epistles and which he himself had celebrated in the *Anelida*.[1] It is too much to expect that he should pass this by with a few words. It may be said that Chaucer gave prominence to this episode because of its appropriateness in a love-poem. Undoubtedly this is true, and it is also true that his familiarity with it in Ovid's Epistle made him appreciate its appropriateness and utilize it effectively. But he really places the emphasis upon the story as an illustration of man's unfaithfulness in love rather than as a mere love-story, for after mentioning (ll. 267–268) that Æneas

> to hir a traitor was;
> Wherfor she slow hirself, allas!

he indulges in some reflections on the folly of women in trusting to the goodly appearance and fair words of men. The first two lines in these observations recall some words of Helen to Paris in the *Heroides*:

> Lo, how a woman doth amis,
> To love him that unknowen is.
> (*H. F.*, ll. 269–270.)

> Certus in hospitibus non est amor; errat, ut ipsi,
> Cumque nihil speres firmius esse, fuit.
> (*Her.*, xvi, 191–192.)

[1] See pp. 15 ff., above.

Chaucer's entire passage upon the infidelity of men
(ll. 269–285) bears a marked similarity to one in
Catullus' version of the episode of Theseus and
Ariadne.[1]

As Chaucer goes on with his story, the influence
of the *Heroides* is manifest in his sympathetic
treatment of Dido and the very slight attention
which he bestows upon Æneas, the hero of the
narrative which he started to tell. Virgil's recital
of Æneas' struggle against love in order to give
obedience to the commands of the gods I think
Chaucer deliberately suppresses at this point:

> Ille Jovis monitis immota tenebat
> Lumina, et obnixus curam sub corde premebat.
> > (*Æn.*, iv, 331–332.)

> At pius Aeneas, quamquam lenire dolentem
> Solando cupit et dictis avertere curas,
> Multa gemens magnoque animum labefactus amore,
> Jussa tamen divum exsequitur, classemque revisit.
> > (*Æn.*, iv, 393–396.)

> Haud secus assiduis hinc atque hinc vocibus heros
> Tunditur, et magno persentit pectore curas;
> Mens immota manet.
> > (*Æn.*, iv, 447–449.)

Most of Chaucer's account is devoted to the complaint of Dido. This complaint is spoken, as it is
in the *Æneid;* not written, as in the *Heroides;* and
most of the circumstances also are from Virgil:

[1] See pp. 364–366.

"Alas!" quod she, "my swete herte,
Have pitee on my sorwes smerte,
And slee me not! go noght away!
O woful Dido, wel away!"
Quod she to hir-selve tho,
"O Eneas! what wil ye do?
O, that your love, ne your bonde,
That ye ben sworn with your right honde,
Ne my cruel deeth," quod she,
"May holde yow still heer with me!"

(*H. F.*, ll. 315-324.)

Per ego has lacrimas dextramque tuam te —
Quando aliud mihi jam miserae nihil ipsa reliqui —
Per connubia nostra, per inceptos Hymenaeos,
Si bene quid de te merui, fuit aut tibi quidquam
Dulce meum, miserere domus labentis et istam,
Oro, si quis adhuc precibus locus, exue mentem.

(*Æn.*, iv, 314-319.)

O widde Fame! for ther nis
Nothing so swift, lo, as she is!

(*H. F.*, ll. 349-350.)

Extemplo Libyae magnas it Fama per urbes,
Fama malum, qua non aliud velocius ullum.

(*Æn.*, iv, 173-174.)

And called on hir suster Anne,
And gan hir to compleyne thanne;
And seyde, that she cause was
That she first lovede Eneas.
And thus counseilled hir therto.

(*H. F.*, ll. 367-371.)

Tu lacrimis evicta meis, tu prima furentem
His, germana, malis oneras atque obicis hosti.
Non licuit thalami expertem sine crimine vitam
Degere, more ferae, tales nec tangere curas!

(*Æn.*, iv, 548-551.)

But Chaucer's conception of the character and spirit of Dido had evidently already been formed from the *Heroides*. A reading of his entire account in connection with Ovid's reveals the same attitude toward the heroine. Her complaint in Chaucer's version is much more like that of Ovid's Epistle. She bemoans her disgrace as in Ovid; the prevailing note is one of woe and distress, not of wrath as in the *Æneid*. The spirit of such passages as the following from Ovid runs all through Chaucer's complaint:

> Sic ubi fata vocant, udis abiectus in herbis
>   Ad vada Maeandri concinit albus olor;
> Nec quia te nostra sperem prece posse moveri,
>   Adloquor (adverso movimus ista deo),
> Sed merita et famam corpusque animumque pudicum
>   Cum male perdiderim, perdere verba leve est.
>   (*Her.*, vii, 1–6.)
>
> Non tamen Aenean, quamvis male cogitat, odi,
>   Sed queror infidum questaque peius amo.
>   (*Her.*, vii, 29–30.)
>
> Non ego sim tanti, (quidni cuncteris, inique?)
>   Ut pereas, dum me per freta longa fugis.
>   (*Her.*, vii, 45–46.)
>
> Perdita ne perdam, timeo, noceamve nocenti,
>   Neu bibat aequoreas naufragus hostis aquas.
> Vive, precor! sic te melius quam funere perdam:
>   Tu potius leti causa ferere mei.
>   (*Her.*, vii, 61–64.)
>
> Exige, laese pudor, poenas! violate Sychaei. . . .
>   Ad quas, me miseram, plena pudoris eo.
> Est mihi marmorea sacratus in aede Sychaeus
>   (Oppositae frondes velleraque alba tegunt):

Hinc ego me sensi noto quater ore citari;
Ipse sono tenui dixit "Elissa, veni!"
Nulla morast, venio, venio tibi dedita coniunx;
Sum tamen admissi tarda pudore mei.
Da veniam culpae! decepit idoneus acutor:
Invidiam noxae detrahit ille meae.

(Her., vii, 97–106.)

Especially to be compared with the above selections, as emphasizing Dido's still-faithful love coupled with shame, are the following portions of Chaucer's complaint:

O, haveth of my deeth pitee!
Y-wis, my dere herte, ye
Knowen ful wel that never yit,
As fer-forth as I hadde wit,
Agilte I yow in thoght ne need.
O, have ye men swich goodliheed
In speche, and never a deel of trouthe?
Allas, that ever hadde routhe
Any woman on any man!
Now see I wel, and telle can,
We wrecched wommen conne non art;
For certeyn, for the more part,
Thus be we served everichone.

(H. F., ll. 325–337.)

O, welaway that I was born:
For through you is my name lorn,
And alle myn actes red and songe
Over al this lond, on every tonge.

. . . .
. . . .

O, sooth is, every thing is wist,
Though hit be kevered with the mist.
Eek, thogh I mighte duren ever,
That I have doon, rekever I never,

That I ne shal be seyd, allas,
Y-shamed be through Eneas,
And that I shal thus juged be —
    Lo right as she hath doon, now she
    Wol do eftsones hardily.
                (*H. F.*, ll. 345–359).

There is in neither Ovid nor Chaucer anything of the raving fury and spirit of revenge which characterize all of Dido's utterances in Virgil's account.[1]

In concluding his story of Dido and Æneas, Chaucer indicates his sources by suggesting that anyone who cares to know more about it should

        Red Virgile in Eneidos
        Or the Epistle of Ovyde.

But as further examples of "swich untrouthe" he cannot refrain from calling attention to some of the other stories celebrated in the *Heroides*.[2] The fol-

---

[1] That this fury was the dominant idea with Virgil may be seen from the following passages: *Æn.*, iv, 298–303, 362–387, 590–629.

[2] On Chaucer's use of the *Heroides* here Professor Kittredge has the following (" Chaucer's Medea and the Date of the Legend of Good Women," *Publications of the Modern Language Association of America*, XXIV, 2, 350–351): "In the *House of Fame* Chaucer's acquaintance with the *Heroides* is abundantly evident. The well known passage (vv. 378 ff.) in which he expressly refers to the 'Epistle of Ovyde' from Dido to Aeneas (*Heroides*, vii), appending further examples of masculine perfidy (Demophoon to Phyllis; Achilles to Briseis; Paris to Oenone; Jason to Hypsipyle; 'eft Iason to Medea'; Hercules to Deianira; Theseus to Ariadne) is conclusive. For, however much this passage may have been influenced by the *Roman de la Rose*, it contains several things that Chaucer did not learn from that poem and that he did learn from the *Heroides*. These are, besides the fact that Ovid wrote an epistle of Dido to Aeneas, the following: the knowledge that Demophoon was 'duk of Athenes' and that Phyllis was daugh-

lowing cases he merely enumerates: Briseis and Achilles, found in *Her.*, iii; Oenone and Paris, *Her.*, v; Hypsipyle and Jason, *Her.*, vi; Medea and Jason, *Her.*, xii; and Deianira and Hercules, *Her.*, ix. The episodes of Phyllis and Demophoon, *Her.*, ii, and Ariadne and Theseus, *Her.*, x, he briefly recounts, no doubt because they furnish closer parallels to the Dido and Æneas story. In each of these stories the hero comes a stranger in peril to the home of the heroine, who befriends him. In gratitude for her services he becomes her lover, but later rewards her faithfulness by desertion.

The story of Phyllis and Demophoon presents a situation closely similar to that of Dido and Æneas. Demophoon, overtaken by storms at sea as he is returning from the Trojan War, makes his way after much wandering into the harbors of Thrace, where he is received with great hospitality by the virgin ruler of that country, Phyllis. Like that of Dido, this was another instance where hospitality went too far, and Phyllis became the mistress of Demophoon. Like Dido again, she is willing to bestow on the stranger the governing of her realm. In both stories interest in a kingdom of his

ter to the Thracian king; Demophoon's forswearing himself (which is strongly emphasized by Ovid); the infidelity of Achilles to Briseis, of Jason to Hypsipyle, of Hercules to Deianira, and of Theseus to Ariadne. It is clear that, when he wrote the *House of Fame*, Chaucer had read the second, third, sixth, seventh, ninth, and tenth epistles of the *Heroides*."

own leads the hero to desert his royal entertainer, *hospita* — a word which Ovid makes each of his heroines apply to herself when she discovers that she can never claim the name of wife. Demophoon leaves Thrace in order to recover the kingdom of Athens, but promises Phyllis that he will return in a month. Four months have already expired without his return, when she writes her Epistle and expresses her determination to end her grief by a violent death. She bemoans, like Dido, her disgrace in the eyes of her people. The two Epistles close in very much the same way with the thought that the betrayer's name will appear on the heroine's tomb as the cause of her death:

> Hoc tamen in tumuli marmore carmen erit:
> "Praebuit Aeneas et causam mortis et ensem;
> Ipsa sua Dido concidit usa manu."
>
> *(Her., vii, 194–196.)*

> Inscribere meo causa invidiosa sepulcro;
> Aut hoc aut simili carmine notus eris:
> "Phyllida Demophoon leto dedit hospes amantem:
> Ille necis causam praebuit, ipsa manum."
>
> *(Her., ii, 145–148.)*

Though Chaucer chose to give more prominence to the Phyllis and Demophoon story than to the others in the list except Ariadne and Theseus, he does not undertake to relate it at any length, but sums it up in a few lines. Professor Kittredge has pointed out three features which Chaucer took from Ovid: that Demophoon was duke of Athens, that Phyllis was the daughter of the Thracian king, and that Demophoon foreswore himself.[1]

Why Chaucer should have stated of Phyllis that

> She heng hir-self right by the hals (*H. F.*, l. 394.)

is not clear from Ovid's account, for in it she only mentions hanging among other methods of suicide to which she might resort:

> Est sinus, adductos modice falcatus in arcus;
> Ultima praerupta cornua mole rigent.
> Hinc mihi suppositas inmittere corpus in undas
> Mens fuit; et, quoniam fallere pergis, erit.
> Ad tua me fluctus projectam litora portent,
> Occurramque oculis intumulata tuis!
> Duritia ferrum ut superes adamantaque teque,
> "Non tibi sic," dices, "Phylli, sequendus eram!"
> Saepe venenorum sitis est mihi; saepe cruenta
> Trajectam gladio morte perire juvat.
> Colla quoque, infidis quia se nectenda lacertis
> Praebuerunt, laqueis inplicuisse iuvat.
>
> (*Her.*, ii, 131–142.)

It seems probable, as Professor Kittredge has already suggested,[2] that the *Roman de la Rose* was

---

[1] See p. 61, note, above. Cf. *Her.*, ii, 6, 13, 67–68, 78; 81–83, 106–112; 23–26, 29–44, 53.

[2] *The Date of Chaucer's Troilus* (Chaucer Society, 1905), p. 23, note 4. The statement that Phyllis hanged herself occurs also in the *Book of the Duchess*, l. 729, and in the *Legend of Good Women*, l. 2485, and it is to these passages that Professor Kittredge's note relates as follows: "As to Phyllis, use of the *Roman de la Rose* is practically certain. Professor C. G. Child, in his interesting essay on Chaucer's *Legend of Good Women* and Boccaccio's *De Genealogia Deorum* (Modern Language Notes, XI, 478–479, cf. X, 380), remarking that Ovid nowhere

Chaucer's authority for the statement that Phyllis hanged herself, for that death is attributed to her in the short passage devoted to the story in the *Roman:*

> Philis ausinc tant atendi
> Demophon qu'ele se pendi
> Por le terme qu'il trespassa
> Dont serement et foi cassa.[1]

Skeat has called attention to the phrase, "Por le terme qu'il trespassa," corresponding to Chaucer's "His terme passe." [2] Though there is a close verbal resemblance between the two phrases, Ovid's

> Ultra promissum tempus abesse queror (*Her.,* ii, 2.)

alone might be responsible for Chaucer's phrase, as has been suggested by Mr. Fansler.[3] Nevertheless, with these two resemblances between Chaucer's version and the French there can be little doubt that he recalled the passage from the *Roman* in addition to the Epistle of Ovid.

says in so many words that Phyllis hanged herself, quotes the *De Genealogia* (XI, 25, ed. 1511, fol. 84 verso) as the source of Chaucer's knowledge on this point in the Legend (v. 2485). It may be added that Boccaccio's *De Casibus* supplies the same information: 'Phillis amoris Demophoontis impaciens se suspendit' (i. 18, ed. 1544, p. 29). But Chaucer got a plain statement of Phyllis's suicide from the *Roman de la Rose,* II, 82 ('Qu'ele se pendi'; 'heng hirself,' *B. Duch.,* V, 729), years before he could have known Boccaccio's handbooks. However, the use of the *Roman de la Rose* is no proof that Chaucer did not know the *Heroides.*"

   [1] *Roman de la Rose,* ed. Méon, Paris, 1814, ll. 13414–13417.
   [2] *Oxford Chaucer,* III, 252.
   [3] *Chaucer and the Roman de la Rose,* pp. 45–46.

The story of Ariadne and Theseus does not afford so close a parallel to the Dido and Æneas story as that of Phyllis and Demophoon, but the idea that the hero's debt of gratitude to the heroine adds to the guilt of his betrayal is stronger in the case of Theseus than in that of any of the other heroes Chaucer mentions. By Medea's aid, to be sure, Jason is enabled to overcome the dragon, but in this she assists him merely in accomplishing an adventure, not in escaping from an unavoidable peril. According to the agreement of human tribute to be paid by the Athenians to Minos, King of Crete, Theseus is condemned by lot to be devoured by the Minotaur in his labyrinthine abode. Ariadne, the daughter of Minos, has compassion on the stranger and reveals to him a way by which he can kill the monster and find his way out of the Labyrinth, from which no victim has ever yet returned. In his gratitude Theseus swears that she shall be his wife and that he will be faithful to her as long as they both shall live. They make their escape to the island of Naxos, and there he deserts her. Taking with him her sister Phaedra, he steals away by night and sails for Athens. Ovid's Epistle expresses Ariadne's grief and despair when she finds herself alone on the desert island. This episode, presenting as it does the extreme of cruel and ungrateful treachery, affords a fitting climax to Chaucer's

treatment of man's unfaithfulness. And it is interesting to note how, even in the short space which
he allows himself, he brings out the force of the
story.

There is a brief account of Ariadne in *Metamorphoses*, viii, 169–182, but it was chiefly *Heroides*, x,
and Boccaccio's *De Genealogia Deorum* which furnished the material for Chaucer here. In addition
to the Æneas–Dido and Demophoon–Phyllis stories, which have just been discussed, the other five
instances of false lovers that he has enumerated in
this connection are to be found in the *Heroides*.
In both Ovid and Chaucer the emphasis is upon
the falseness of Theseus, who deserted Ariadne
after she had saved his life. This is the burden
of Ovid's Epistle, and Chaucer strikes this note in
the beginning of his story:

> How fals eek was he, Theseus;
> That as the story telleth us,
> How he betrayed Adriane.
> 　　　　　　(*H. F.*, ll. 405–407.)

Nothing in Ovid or Boccaccio corresponds to
Chaucer's line in the *House of Fame* (l. 409),

> For had he laughed, had he loured.

Professor Lowes,[1] who has suggested Machaut's
Le Jugement dou Roy de Navarre as the source of

---

[1] *P. M. L. A.*, XXXIII, 324.

the story of Ariadne, offers as a parallel to this line one from the *Jugement*:

Mais riens n'i vausist fer ne fust.

But there is no trace of similarity here. The antithesis which Chaucer uses may have been common enough in everyday speech, and, unless it should be found expressed in almost his identical words, I think we may assume that the line is his own.

There is a close verbal similarity between line 441,

If Adriane ne had y-be,

and Machaut's

Se belle Adriane ne fust.

This parallelism may be purely accidental, for certainly both Chaucer and Machaut could independently reach the conclusion from Ovid's account that there would have been no rescue for Theseus without Ariadne's help.

Lines 412–413 of the *House of Fame*,

And, for she had of him pitee,
She made him fro the dethe escape,

are derived from *Heroides*, x, 71–72:

Cum tibi, ne victor tecto morerere recurvo,
Quae regerent passus, pro duce fila dedi.

She gave him the clue for his return in order that he might not die even after he was victor over the monster. It was her aid that saved him from death, as Ariadne fully recognized. The same idea is repeated in *Heroides*, x, 103, where Ariadne, after she finds herself so cruelly abandoned by Theseus, says she wishes she had never given him the thread by which he could find his way out of the Labyrinth:

> Nec tibi, quae reditus monstrarent, fila dedissem.

Again in *Metamorphoses*, viii, 172–173, Ovid says that Theseus' escape from the Labyrinth was due to the assistance given him by the maiden:

> Utque ope virginea nullis iterata priorum
> Janua difficilis filo est inventa relecto.

And Theseus' promise to wed Ariadne was on the condition,

> That, so she saved him his lyf,
> He wolde have take hir to his wyf.
> (*H. F.*, ll. 423–424.)

Machaut [1] has nothing of the life of Theseus being saved by Ariadne. He states that she showed him how to kill the monster in order that he might save himself "from bondage":

> Pour lui delivrer *dou servage*.

The climax to Chaucer's story is in Ariadne's being deserted on an island in the sea while she was on the way home with Theseus.

[1] *P. M. L. A.*, XXXIII, 324.

He lefte hir sleping in an yle,
Deserte alone, right in the see,
And stal away, and leet hir be;
And took hir suster Phedra tho
With him, and gan to shippe go.

(H. F., ll. 416–420.)

This setting Chaucer found in the vivid picture of
Ariadne which Ovid gives when she found herself
abandoned. She wakes only to realize that there is
nothing but shore around her; the place is an island. This makes her conscious of her helpless
state, for escape is hopeless. She rushes to the top
of a mountain and gazes over the billowy deep,
only to behold the sails of Theseus' ship receding
from view. She calls with all the might of her voice
for him to turn back his ship, which did not have
its full number on board. Failing in this, she tries
signalling with her veil upon a pole until the ship is
carried beyond her vision. Then she breaks down
in despair. No wonder this realistic description of
Ariadne left alone on a desert island made a deep
impression upon Chaucer's mind, so that he used it
in both the *House of Fame* and the *Legend of Good
Women*.

Ovid reiterates that the place on which Ariadne
was deserted was an island:

     . . . vacat insula cultu.   *(Her.,* x, 59.) [1]

---

[1] See also *Her.,* x, 61, 86.

And it was the vanishing vessel with Theseus and her sister on board that brought home to her so overwhelmingly that she had been abandoned:

"Quo fugis?" exclamo "scelerate revertere Theseu,
Flecte ratem, numerum non habet illa suum."

Ariadne's final appeal to Theseus in *Heroides*, x, is to turn his ship and come back with the changed wind:

Flecte ratem, Theseu, versoque relabere vento. (l. 151.)

Machaut says nothing about an island, calling it instead a strange country, *en estrange contrée.* Nor does he mention the ship in which Theseus sailed away.

Two points which Chaucer and Machaut have in common are that Ariadne was left "sleeping" and "alone," *dormant, seulette.* But Ovid has dwelt far more upon these; he makes her say that sleep has evilly betrayed her, and Theseus by crime plotted against her in her sleep:

In quo me somnusque meus male prodidit et tu
Per facinus somnis insidiate meis.
(*Her.*, x, 5–6.) [1]

And her state of aloneness on this sea-girt isle Ovid has reiterated:

Aut ego diffusis erravi sola capillis. (*Her.*, x, 47.) [2]

---

[1] See also *Her.*, x, 9–10.
[2] See also *Ibid.*, ll. 59, 129.

In *Metamorphoses* (viii, 175–176) Ovid speaks of Ariadne as *deserted* until Bacchus gave assistance to her:

> comitemque suam crudelis in illo
> Litore destituit; desertae et multa querenti
> Amplexus et opem Liber tulit.

The part of Phaedra is the only element in the story which did not come from Ovid. Though she is mentioned by Machaut, she also appears in *De Genealogia Deorum*, from which Chaucer borrowed considerably in telling this story in the *Legend of Good Women*: [1]

. . . et Ariadna relicta Phedram sibi conjugio copulavit. (*De Gen.*, x, 49.)

Haec [Phaedra] cum Ariadna sorore superato minotauro cum Theseo abiit et Ariadna ut supra dictum est relicta ejus facta est conjunx. (*De Gen.*, xi, 30.)

Professor Child [2] has pointed out that Chaucer's information about Phaedra could have come also from Boccaccio's *Amorosa Visione*.

In the *House of Fame* Theseus swears to Ariadne to make her his wife in connection with her efforts to save his life:

> And yet he had y-sworen to here
> On al that ever he mighte swere
> That, so she saved him his lyf
> He wolde have take hir to his wyf.
> (*H. F.*, ll. 421–424.)

---

[1] See pp. 250 ff.   [2] *M. L. N.*, X, 381.

Likewise in the *Heroides* Ariadne recalls to Theseus' mind that when she gave him the thread for his guide out of the Labyrinth he swore he would make her his wife:

> Cum tibi, ne victor tecto morerere recurvo,
> Quae regerent passus, pro duce fila dedi,
> Cum mihi dicebas "per ego ipsa pericula juro,
> Te fore, dum nostrum vivet uterque, meam."
> *(Her.*, x, 71–74.)

The situation is very different in *Le Jugement*. Since the text of Machaut has been disarranged by Professor Lowes in an effort to show verbal parallelisms between the French poet and Chaucer, it becomes necessary to quote a brief passage from the *Jugement* in its continuity:

> Se belle Adriane ne fust   2742
> Qui oublia Minos, son pere,
> Et Androgeus, son chier frere,
> Sa terre et ses charnels amis,
> Pour Theseüs, ou elle a mis
> Son cuer, si qu'elle li moustra
> Comment occis le fier moustre a,
> Pour lui delivrer dou servage;
> Et li donna son pucelage   2750
> Par si qu'a femme la penroit   2751
> Et qu'en son païs l'en menroit
> Avec Phedra, sa chiere suer,
> Qu'elle ne lairoit a nul fuer.
> Theseüs qui se parjura   2755
> Ses dieus et sa loy li jura
> Que jamais ne li fausseroit
> Et qu'envers li loiaus seroit.[1]   2758

---

[1] *Le Jugement dou Roy de Navarre*, ll. 2742–2758.

As will be seen from the context, Machaut, beginning with line 2742, makes Ariadne the active agent. She it is who has shown Theseus how to kill the monster. It is she who gave up her virginity to him, provided that he would take her as his wife and lead her to his own country. The suggestion that she be taken as his wife came from her. After that Theseus swore by the gods and his faith that he would *never be false to her and that he would always be loyal to her.* Professor Lowes's arrangement of the text so that lines 2750–2751 come after 2755–2758 destroys the significance of the passage. With Machaut, Theseus' oath is in connection with Ariadne's giving him her virginity. With Ovid and Chaucer it is in connection with the hope of her saving his life.

We cannot say definitely what book Chaucer had in mind when he wrote, at the end of this story,

> He wolde have take hir to his wyf,
> For she desired nothing elles,
> In certein, as the book us telles.
> (*H. F.*, ll. 424–426.)

But these words point more significantly to the *Heroides* than to any other. We have seen that for the Dido–Æneas story he was chiefly indebted to the *Heroides*, that he cited other instances of man's unfaithfulness from the same source, and that in summarizing the Demophoon–Phyllis story he took most of his facts from the *Heroides*. Later, when he wrote the story of Ariadne more fully in the *Legend of Good Women*, he again used the *Heroides* and *Metamorphoses* supplemented by some facts from *De Genealogia Deorum*.

After concluding these stories from Ovid of faithful women and their untrue lovers, Chaucer returns to his summary of the *Æneid*. But in order to go back to Æneas as Virgil's hero, he finds it necessary after all to excuse his conduct toward Dido. And so at last he admits Virgil's explanation that Æneas was acting at the command of Mercury and that this excused him "fulliche of al his greet trespas."

Then in a short space Chaucer describes the remaining scenes of the *Æneid* which he saw painted upon the walls of the temple.

In regard to the origin of Chaucer's story of Dido and Æneas Mr. Sypherd says (p. 19):

The story of Dido and Aeneas came probably from his favorite author, Virgil, but was enlarged by Chaucer himself in a manner consonant with the nature of a love-poem.

Again (p. 83), in comparing Boccaccio's version of the Dido and Æneas story in the *Amorosa Visione* with Chaucer's in the *House of Fame*, Mr. Sypherd writes:

Chaucer and Boccaccio treat independently the Virgilian story, each writer preserving features of this love-episode neglected by the other, Boccaccio probably adhering more closely to his source. The diversity in the treatment of Dido's lament illustrates the different points of view. Chaucer emphasizes the fickleness of Æneas and the disgrace brought on Dido; Boccaccio the longing of Dido for the pleasures of the nuptial bed.

From all this one might suppose that Mr. Sypherd had failed to heed the latter part of Chaucer's injunction to

> Red Virgile in Eneidos
> Or the Epistle of Ovyde.

The enlarging of the story "in a manner consonant with the nature of a love-poem" was really done by Ovid; and "the diversity in the treatment of Dido's lament" indicates the different authors followed. I have already shown clearly enough, I think, that, though Chaucer stamped the story with his own poetic individuality, it was the emphasis upon precisely the features which Mr. Sypherd mentions, the fickleness of Æneas and the disgrace of Dido, that he got from Ovid.

Scattered at short intervals through the second book of the *House of Fame* are brief outlines of stories from Ovid which have already been noted by Professor Skeat.[1] The presence of these stories in the poem shows that Chaucer's mind was at this time well stocked with classical lore as a result of his long acquaintance with Ovid.

[1] *Oxford Chaucer*, III, 256 ff.

A reference to Ovid is found in lines 589–592, where Chaucer, as the eagle is carrying him through the air, "gan to wonder in his minde" what was to be his fate and said to himself:

> I neither am Enok, ne Elye,
> Ne Romulus, ne Ganymede
> That was y-bore up, as men rede,
> To hevene with dan Jupiter
> And maad the goddes boteler.

Usually the mention of classical proper names as coming from any particular source is scarcely worth while, as they may often have come from any one of a number of authors, but in this instance, as Professor Skeat has hinted, the evidence clearly points to Ovid as one of the sources of Chaucer's information. For the circumstance of Romulus' being carried up to heaven by Mars, Ovid is the most obvious source, for he tells the story in *Met.*, xiv, 805–844, and again in *Fasti*, ii, 475–512. The case of Ganymede is mentioned by three authors whom Chaucer used in this poem, Ovid, Virgil and Dante; but the subject is merely mentioned by Virgil (*Æneid*, i, 28), and Dante (*Purgatorio*, ix, 22–24). Virgil gives a somewhat longer account in *Æneid*, v, 252–257. Only Ovid (*Met.*, x, 155–161) gives the information which Chaucer has in line 592 that Ganymede was made cupbearer to the gods:

> . . . qui nunc quoque pocula miscet,
> Invitaque Iovi nectar Iunone ministrat.
>
> (*Met.*, x, 160.)

In lines 711–724, there is some material from Ovid's description of the palace of Fame (*Met.*, xii, 39–63), which forms the basis for Chaucer's whole treatment of the house of Fame. This passage contains the famous reference to the *Metamorphoses* (how many of Ovid's other works the book may have contained we do not know) as Chaucer's own book in the line:

And so thyn owne book hit telleth.

These lines and the others in Book ii concerning the house of Fame will be taken up later in connection with the account of it in Book iii.

The next Ovidian material is found in lines 919–924, which refer to the story of the flight of Daedalus and Icarus given by Ovid in *Met.*, viii, 183–235. Though this story is referred to in the *Roman de la Rose* [1] and in Dante's *Inferno*,[2] neither of these gives so much of the story as Chaucer does. So it is evident that he got his fuller information from the *Metamorphoses*.

Again in lines 941–956 is a brief recital of Phaethon's fatal adventure with the chariot of his father, Phoebus, taken from Ovid's graphic story, *Met.*, ii, 32–328. Warton mentions that probably this story of Ovid's suggested to Chaucer the idea of making the eagle call attention to the constellations — "eyrish bestes" — in the course of their

[1] Ed. Méon, ll. 5241–5242 and 21633. [2] Bk. xvii, ll. 109–111.

flight.[1] Phaethon in his journey saw the Triones,
Serpens, and Scorpius, and was terrified by these
vast beasts:

> Sparsa quoque in vario passim miracula caelo
> Vastarumque videt trepidus simulacra ferarum.
> *(Met.,* ii, 193–194.)

Chaucer (lines 925–932) makes the eagle, before
pointing out the constellations, warn him not to be
afraid. Then he shows him the Milky Way and
tells him how it was once burnt with heat when
Phaethon drove the chariot of the Sun through the
heavens. He then goes on to tell the story of Phaethon, and how when he saw the Scorpion he lost his
wit from fear and let the reins of his horses go, and
so forth.

For lines 1004–1007 Skeat gives the following
references to Ovid:

> As the Raven or either the Bere. *(Fasti,* ii, 243–266.)
> Or Ariones harpe fyn. *(Fasti,* i, 316; ii, 76.)
> Castor, Pollux, or Delphyn. *(Fasti,* i, 457, or ii, 117.)
> Or Atlantes doughters sevene. *(Fasti,* v, 83.)

It seems best to consider next the various passages in both the second and third books concerning the house of tidings, although the account of
this house in the third book occurs later than the
description of the palace where Fame dispenses her
judgments upon worldly honor.

---

[1] Warton, *History of English Poetry,* (London, 1775), I, 391; see also
Fiedler, *Archiv für das Studium der Neueren Sprachen,* II, 168.

Chaucer's description of the house of Fame to which all tidings come is based upon *Metamorphoses*, xii, 39–63:

> Orbe locus medio est inter terrasque fretumque
> Caelestesque plagas, triplicis confinia mundi:
> Unde quod est usquam, quamvis regionibus absit,
> Inspicitur, penetratque cavas vox omnis ad aures.
> Fama tenet, summaque domum sibi legit in arce,
> Innumerosque aditus ac mille foramina tectis
> Addidit, et nullis inclusit limina portis.
> Nocte dieque patet: tota est ex aere sonanti;
> Tota fremit, vocesque refert, iteratque quod audit.
> Nulla quies intus, nullaque silentia parte.
> Nec tamen est clamor, sed parvae murmura vocis:
> Qualia de pelagi, siquis procul audiat, undis
> Esse solent; qualemve sonum, cum Iuppiter atras
> Increpuit nubes, extrema tonitrua reddunt.
> Atria turba tenet: veniunt leve vulgus euntque;
> Mixtaque cum veris passim commenta vagantur
> Milia rumorum, confusaque verba volutant.
> E quibus hi vacuas implent sermonibus aures,
> Hi narrata ferunt alio, mensuraque ficti
> Crescit, et auditis aliquid novus adicit auctor.
> Illic Credulitas, illic temerarius Error
> Vanaque Laetitia est consternatique Timores,
> Seditioque repens dubioque auctore Susurri.
> Ipsa, quid in caelo rerum pelagoque geratur
> Et tellure, videt, totumque inquirit in orbem.

This account of Ovid's is a piece of almost pure description. Chaucer, true to his purpose as a narrative poet, weaves into his story from time to time the details given by Ovid until finally he has used them all. Not only has he done this, but he has developed each suggestion until from Ovid's short and rather general description he has evolved a very ample and concrete account of this house.

The passages in the second book in which the eagle is made to describe the house of Fame are suggested altogether by this description of Ovid's. Thus in the *Metamorphoses* the dwelling of Fame is the place to which comes all speech of whatsoever nature it may be. In lines 672–699 Chaucer applies this idea specifically to love-tidings and enumerates the various stages and characteristics of love.

The eagle anticipates the poet's incredulity at the idea of all speech being heard in the house of Fame and undertakes to expound the reasonableness of it. This brings him to tell of the location of the house in lines 711–724. In these lines Chaucer translates almost directly from Ovid, but even here he makes his details more specific. Ovid's general statement that the voice is reëchoed becomes with Chaucer

> Or what so comth fro any tonge,
> Be hit rouned, red, or songe,
> Or spoke in seurtee or drede,
> Certein, hit moste hider nede.

In a discussion of the laws of sound-waves, Chaucer reiterates the idea of every speech or word coming to Fame's house in lines 782–786, 817–821, 849–852, 881–882. The location of the house is also repeated in lines 843–847.

In describing the sound which issues from Fame's house (ll. 1025–1042), Chaucer follows Ovid closely. When they approach the house, the eagle asks the poet if he hears the noise. In the dialogue which ensues Chaucer manages to put part of the description into the eagle's mouth and part into his own replies. With characteristic concreteness he has rendered Ovid's "siquis procul audiat":

> And lat a man stonde, out of doute,
> A myle thens, and here hit route.

One interesting feature of Chaucer's adaptation is his representing the speeches as taking the bodily form of the men who uttered them on earth (ll. 1068–1083). In Ovid's account the rumors are personified and run to and fro, filling each other's ears with all manner of tales. From Ovid's personification Chaucer seems to have evolved the idea that the speech assumes the likeness of the speaker.

It should be noted that in the second book the eagle gives only the location of the house and an account of what might be heard there. Nothing is said about the house itself until the poet gives the record of his own observation in the third book, and it is here that the story takes a surprising turn. The palace which is first described is not Ovid's house of a thousand openings. In fact, the conception of this palace seems to be entirely independent of any suggestion from Ovid. Though Chaucer has introduced here a new development of his idea, he later comes back to his original design and gives a description of the house of tidings in lines 1918–1985.

This house of tidings Chaucer compares to the house of Daedalus, which is described in *Metamorphoses*, viii, 159. This comparison was perhaps suggested by the innumerable entrances which Ovid gives to both habitations. In the description of the house of Daedalus he uses the phrases "variarum viarum" and "innumeras vias," and in the description of the palace of Fame "innumerosque aditus." These phrases seem to represent the only points of similarity between the two structures, for in the case of the Labyrinth the *intricacy* of the passages is the chief feature, while in the abode of Fame the many avenues emphasize its *openness* and *easiness* of access. Line 1921, "That Laborintus cleped is," is a reference to *Æneid*, v, 588, for Ovid does not give the structure the name of Labyrinthus.

The features of the house of tidings given in lines 1924–1926, where it is represented as a revolving house, and in lines 1935–1944, where it is said to be built of twigs, are not suggested by Ovid and are no doubt mediaeval additions.[1]

---

[1] For a discussion of these features, see Sypherd, pp. 138–155.

The following passage shows how Chaucer has used all the details about the house which Ovid has furnished him:

> And eek this hous hath of entrees
> As fele as leves been on trees
> In somer whan they grene been;
> And on the roof men may yit seen
> A thousand holes, and wel mo,
> To leten wel the soun out go.
>   And by day, in every tyde,
> Ben al the dores open wyde
> And by night, echoon, unshette;
> Ne porter ther is non to lette
> No maner tydings in to pace;
> Ne never rest is in that place,
> That hit nis fild ful of tydinges
> Other loude, or of whispringes.
>
> (H. F., ll. 1945–1958.)

It is interesting to note that in making two of the points of this description more graphic, Chaucer has used ideas which occur in Ovid's description of the cave of the God of Sleep (*Met.*, xi, 592–615). Ovid uses the figure of the innumerable leaves on the trees in telling of the many phantoms of dreams which hover around the God of Sleep:

> Hunc circa passim varias imitantia formas
> Somnia vana iacent totidem, quot messis aristas,
> Silva gerit frondes, eiectas litus harenas.
>
> (Met., xi, 613–615.)

Chaucer employs this figure to indicate that the entrances to the house of tidings are innumerable:

> As fele as leves ben on trees
> In somer whan they grene be.

In describing the cave of Somnus, Ovid mentions that there is no porter there, and so forth:

> Ianua, ne verso stridores cardine reddat,
> Nulla domo tota; custos in limine nullus.
> (*Met.*, xi, 608–609.)

Chaucer, in amplifying the idea that the doors of the house are always open, says:

> Ne porter there is non to lette
> No maner tydinges in to pace.

These points no doubt represent almost an involuntary rather than deliberate use of the passages from the description of the cave of Somnus. They are significant of Chaucer's familiarity with that description, which he had used before in the *Duchess* [1] and in the invocation to the first book of the *House of Fame*.[2] This familiarity we may well believe amounted to a word-for-word memory of at least many of the lines, which naturally arose in his mind, when they were appropriate to the idea he had to express.

The enormous size of the house and the frailty of its structure (ll. 1977–1985) are features not given by Ovid.

In enumerating the tidings that he heard in this house Chaucer does not restrict himself to love-

[1] See pp. 6–7, above.   [2] See pp. 54–55, above.

tidings as he does in the second book. He here
mentions the greatest variety of subjects (ll.
1959–1976).

When the poet is set down by the eagle in the
house of tidings (l. 2034), he finds a great congre-
gation of folk roaming about. This is merely a
translation of Ovid's line:

> Atria turba tenet; veniunt leve vulgus euntque.
>
> (*Met.*, xii, 53.)

But Chaucer adds that there were so many that he
could hardly find a "foot-brede of space." Ovid
says (ll. 56–58) that these crowds are filling each
other's ears with rumors and that each fresh narra-
tor adds something new to what he has heard. This
furnished the basis for Chaucer's excellent description (ll. 2043–2080) with its bits of gossipy
conversation [1] and its account of how one person
ran to another with his news and added something
to it, and the second to the third, and so on. Chaucer also makes the comparison of the spread of a
rumor to the growth of a conflagration from a
spark.[2] Certainly no one would deny the superiority of Chaucer's concrete and spirited treatment to
Ovid's bare statement. It is this power of Chaucer
to take an idea from Ovid and quicken it into life

---

[1] Other bits of gossipy conversation Chaucer has given us in the
Squire's Tale, ll. 181–262, and *Knight's Tale*, ll. 1655–1664.

[2] Cf. passage in *Troilus*, iv, 183–184, where the shouting of a
crowd is compared to the fury of burning of straw.

for his reader that renders so interesting the comparison of the two poets.

Ovid's statement that the rumors were mixtures of the false and true (ll. 54–55) was enough to suggest to Chaucer the idea of describing how the mingling took place. Keeping up Ovid's personification of the rumors, Chaucer gives a lively account of a struggle between "a lesing and a sad soth-sawe" as to which of them should escape first through a window. Each finding his efforts to advance checked by the other, they form a compact of sworn brotherhood in true mediaeval style and go forth together. Hence it comes that the report is made up of both false and true.

Chaucer has now brought into his poem all the details given by Ovid in his description of Fame's dwelling. As has been pointed out, he has woven these in from time to time and enlarged them to suit himself, adding many a graphic touch suggested by his own imagination.

In the third book also there are several minor instances of indebtedness to Ovid, most, if not all, of which have been noted by Skeat. In lines 1203–1206 are mentioned three famous harpers of antiquity, Orpheus, Orion, and Eacides Chiron. The story of Orpheus is, of course, one of the best-known myths of the Classics. In *Metamorphoses*, x, 1–85, Ovid tells of the grief of Orpheus for the death of

his wife, Eurydice, and of his charming by his sweet
music all the realm of Pluto, so that he secures her
release on condition that he shall not gaze upon her
until they have gone beyond the confines of Hades.
Orpheus, however, neglects this injunction, and
Eurydice has to return to the phantom world. The
death of Orpheus, who had such power in his music
as to charm stones, trees, and wild beasts, is related in *Metamorphoses*, xi, 1–66.

Orion, Ovid's Arion, was likewise famous as a
harper according to the story in *Fasti*, ii, 79–118.

Chaucer's reference to Chiron as a musician
seems a little remarkable, for Chiron is chiefly
famous for having been the tutor of Achilles. But
Ovid in *Fasti*, v, 385–386, refers to Chiron as follows:

> Ille manus olim missuras Hectora leto
> Creditur in lyricis detinuisse modis.

In lines 1229–1232 is a reference to the legend of
the satyr Marsyas, whom Apollo defeated in a contest of musical skill and afterwards flayed alive.
Ovid has the story in *Met.*, vi, 382–400. It is rather
strange that Chaucer, who knew the *Metamorphoses* so intimately, should have mistaken Marsyas
for a woman. We might explain this as due to his
mistaking the Latin name Marsya for a feminine
form, in the passage, "Marsya nomen habet" (*Met.*,
vi, 400), but there is abundant indication in the

Latin preceding this phrase that the satyr was
masculine. Skeat [1] has suggested in his note on
this passage that Chaucer may have got the idea
that Marsyas was feminine from Dante's form of
the name, Marsia.[2] It may be that, with only an
indistinct recollection of Ovid's story from his own
reading, he trusted to Dante and judged from the
appearance of the form Marsia that it was feminine. Sufficient it was for his purpose here that he
or she was famed for musical skill.

After enumerating various kinds of magicians in
lines 1259–1270, Chaucer mentions some famous
practisers of magic. Among them he cites Medea,
Circe, and Calipsa. Medea's restoration of Æson,
her father-in-law, at the request of Jason is told in
detail in *Met.*, vii, 162–296. Circe's wonderful
magical skill Ovid relates in connection with several
heroes. In *Met.*, xiv, 1–74, Glaucus will not desert
Scylla for Circe, and this becomes the occasion of
her showing her power of enchantment. Again in
Met., xiv, 244–319, the companions of Ulysses are
transformed into swine at the court of Circe. In
Met., xiv, 320–440, Picus is enchanted by her.
Medea and Circe are mentioned together in *Ars
Amatoria* in a discussion of the uselessness of magic
arts as an aid to love:

---

[1] *Oxford Chaucer*, III, 269.

[2] See also Kittredge, "Chaucer's Medea and the Date of the
Legend of Good Women," *P. M. L. A.*, XXIV, 352, note 11.

> Non facient, ut vivat amor, Medeides herbae
> Mixtaque cum magicis naenia Marsa sonis:
> Phasias Aesoniden, Circe tenuisset Ulixem,
> Si modo servari carmine posset amor.
>
> (*Art. Am.*, ii, 101–104.)

These two enchantresses are referred to in the same passage again in *Remedia Amoris* where a similar argument is presented that magic arts are of no avail to cure love:

> Quid te Phasiacae juverunt gramina terrae,
> Cum cuperes patria, Colchi, manere domo?
> Quid tibi profuerunt, Circe, Perseides herbae,
> Cum sua Neritias abstulit aura rates.
>
> (*Rem. Am.*, ll. 261–264.)

Calipsa is no doubt the Calypso famous in antiquity for having detained Ulysses so long in her embraces. Ovid has a reference to her in the *ex Ponto Epistles*, iv, x, 9–14, *Amores*, ii, xvii, 15–16, and *Ars Amatoria*, ii, 125–126. In none of these references is any mention made of Calypso as an enchantress, but she is represented as keeping the hero against his will, which to Chaucer's imagination might have suggested magic. As pointed out by Mr. Fansler in discussing Professor Root's attributing the *House of Fame*, lines 1271–1274, to the *Romance of the Rose*, Medea, Circe, and Calypso are all mentioned in close proximity in *Ars Amatoria*, ii, and may be due quite as much to Ovid as to the *Roman*.[1]

[1] See Fansler, *Chaucer and the Roman de la Rose*, p. 43.

In lines 1399–1404, there is a reference to the Nine Muses of classical fame, but in view of the many possible sources from which Calliope and her sisters might be known to Chaucer, one hardly dares to designate any source in particular.

In lines 1413–1414, we find Hercules mentioned and the cause of his death given. The story might, of course, have come to Chaucer from the *Roman de la Rose*[1] or from Boccaccio's *De Mulieribus Claris*[2] as well as from Ovid, *Met.*, ix, 101–272, and *Heroides*, ix. But we know he was much indebted to Ovid for the story of Hercules in the *Monk's Tale*, and we suppose that story to have been written much earlier than the *House of Fame*. Like some of Chaucer's other allusions, it is impossible to assign a particular source for this one when there are several possible sources having a common origin in Ovid.

We are fortunate in having Chaucer's own characterization of Ovid (lines 1486–1492). He is described as Venus' clerk who has spread far and wide the fame of the God of Love. Chaucer was apparently at this time acquainted with all of Ovid's love-poetry as well as with the *Metamorphoses*.

In lines 1571–1605, dealing with Æolus, God of the Winds, we have classical material perhaps from

[1] Ed. Méon, ll. 9230 ff.   [2] Cap. 22.

both Ovid and Virgil. The description in lines
1583–1590, of the god in his cave holding the winds
in check, is from *Æneid*, i, 52–57. Chaucer no
doubt had had a long acquaintance with Æolus
from *Met.*, i, 262–264:

> Protinus Aeoliis Aquilonem claudit in antris
> Et quaecumque fugant inductas flamina nubes,
> Emittitque Notum,

and also from *Met.*, xiv, 223–226:

> Aeolon ille refert Tusco regnare profundo,
> Aeolon Hippotaden, cohibentem carcere ventos:
> Quos bovis inclusos tergo, memorabile munus,
> Dulichium sumpsisse ducem.

The incident of Fame's sending her messenger in
haste to the cave of Æolus recalls vividly the com-
mission of Juno to the God of Sleep in the *Book of
the Duchess*. This latter episode is told by Ovid
(*Met.*, xi, 585–632).

The conception of Æolus as a trumpeter de-
serves special consideration. None of the passages
from the Classics already referred to represents
him with a trumpet. Lounsbury [1] thinks this idea

---

[1] Lounsbury, *Studies in Chaucer*, II, 381–382. Lounsbury says
Albricus Philosophus is described as a Londoner of the early part of
the thirteenth century. "No dictionary of English biography contains his name or gives the slightest account of his life. The work by
which he is known — if he can strictly be said to be known at all —
is a treatise entitled *De Deorum Imaginibus*. It consists of a series of
sketches of heathen gods and goddesses and of a few other mythological personages." This treatise, which is very short, is contained in Van

may have come to Chaucer from Albricus Philosophus, who has in a treatise called *De Deorum Imaginibus* the following passage:

In manu autem utraque tenebat cornua: quae ori admovens, ea subflare, et ab unoquoque cornum sex ventox emittere videbatur.

But I think we need to look no further than *Æneid*, vi, 162–174, for the idea of Æolus as a trumpeter:

Atque illi Misenum in litore sicco,
Ut venere, vident indigna morte peremptum,
Misenum Aeoliden, quo non praestantior alter
Aere ciere viros, Martemque accendere cantu.
Hectoris hic magni fuerat comes; Hectora circum
Et lituo pugnas insignis obibat et hasta.
Postquam illum vita victor spoliavit Achilles;
Dardanio Aeneae sese fortissimus heros
Addiderat socium, non inferiora secutus.
Sed tum, forte cava dum personat aequora concha,
Demens, et cantu vocat in certamina divos,
Aemulus exceptum Triton — si credere dignum est —
Inter saxa virum spumosa immerserat unda.

Modern commentators have generally taken this Æolus who was the father of Misenus to be a mortal and probably the man whose death is related in *Æneid*, xii, 542. But the father of Misenus was for a long time supposed by commentators to

Steveren's *Auctores Mythographi Latini*. Albricus, to whom Lounsbury traces also slight obligations in the *Knight's Tale*, is mentioned in the *De Causa Dei* of Bradwardine, whose name appears in the *Nun's Priest's Tale*.

be Æolus, God of the Winds. Dryden[1] translated *Æneid*, vi, 164, as follows:

> Misenus lay extended on the shore
> Son of the God of the Winds: none so renown'd.

In a revision of Dryden's translation[2] in 1803 the editor allowed this passage to remain unchanged. Davidson in his translation of Virgil,[3] also of 1803, understood this name to refer to the God of the Winds and gives his explanation of why Misenus was called his son. In a note on *Æneid*, vi, 164, he says:

> Misenum Aeoliden, Misenus, the son of Aeolus. This is only a figurative genealogy, as we call warriors sons of Mars, so Misenus, who excelled in blowing the trumpet, which is a wind instrument, is called a son of the god of the wind.

Not until the day of modern accurate scholarship do we come upon a different explanation of who this Æolus was. In the Heyne–Wagner edition[4] of 1832 occurs this comment on *Æoliden:*

> Æolidum appellat Misenum, Æoli filium, tanquam ejusdem Æeoli Trojani, quem in pugna cum Latinis occubuisse narrat. (XII, 542 sq.)

---

[1] *The Works of Virgil Translated into English Verse*, London, 1721, vol. II, Bk. vi, ll. 242–243.

[2] *The Works of Virgil Translated into English Verse*, ed. Carey, London, 1803, II, 220.

[3] *The Works of Virgil Translated into English Prose*, N.Y., 1803, vol. II.

[4] *P. Virgilii Maronis Opera*, ed. Heyne–Wagner, Leipsic and London, 1832, Excursus 7 to Bk. vi, ll. 162 ff.

Anthon [1] in his edition of Virgil sums up the matter thus:

Aeoliden, "Son of Æolus." Many commentators suppose that as Misenus played upon a wind instrument, the poet, by a figurative genealogy, makes him the son of the wind god. Not so, however. Virgil calls him Æolides, as indicating merely his descent from a natural father, named Aeolus, probably the same with the one who is said to have fallen in battle with the Latins (*Æn.* xii, 542 seqq. — Heyne, Excursus VII ad Aen. vi).

Roscher likewise considers the Æolus here mentioned a mortal.[2]

In the light of this history of the commentary upon the name, it seems not an unwarranted assumption to suppose that Chaucer's knowledge was no more accurate than that of the commentators, and that he shared the common idea that the Æolus here referred to was the God of the Winds. As Misenus was called "son of Æolus" because he was such a great trumpeter, the inference would naturally be that Æolus himself was a great trumpeter. The winds as a means of spreading tidings would be an easy conception to Chaucer. We say

[1] *The Æneid of Virgil,* ed. Anthon, N. Y., 1853.

[2] "Vgl. auch Aen. 6, 164 and 9, 774, wo Söhne eines Troianers Aiolos (Misenus und Clytius) genannt werden." *Ausführliches Lexikon der Griech. u. Röm. Mythologie,* XI, 195. However, *Harper's Dictionary of Classical Literature and Antiquities,* 1897, gives again the old explanation that the Æolus referred to here is the God of the Winds.

to-day of telling a secret to a gossipy person, "As well tell it to the winds." So Æolus, God of the Winds, with his mighty trumpet would make a suitable herald of renown. Altogether then, it seems quite probable that Chaucer may have had no other source than Virgil for his conception of Æolus with his trumpet acting as the herald of the goddess Fame.

But there is another source which may have furnished Chaucer an interpretation of this passage of Virgil's. Boccaccio in the *De Genealogia Deorum* commenting upon Virgil's *Misenum Æoliden* not only takes this Æolus to be the God of the Winds but also offers an explanation of why a trumpeter should be called his son:

Misenus Aeoli fuit filius ut ait Virgilius. Misenum Aeoliden quo non praestantior alter Aere ciere viros, martem que accendere cantu. . . . Nunc quoniam simpliciter a Virgilio dicta vera non sunt, quod sit absconditum advertendum. Fingit ergo Misenum Aeoli filium eo que fuit bubicen: nam tubae sonus nil aliud est quam spiritus per fistulam ab ore emissus: sicuti et ventus et aer impulsus, et per terrae fistulas e cavernis emissus: et quia ventorum Aeolus deus dicatur, quasi eorum auctor sit: a similitudine operis Misenus ejus dicitur filius.[1]

This commentary from a contemporary of Chaucer's indicates that the Æolus, the father of Mise-

---

[1] *De Genealogia Deorum*, 1511, lib. xiii, cap. xxiii.

nus, was generally understood in the Middle Ages to be the God of the Winds.

The idea that the cave of Æolus where he "held the windes in distresse" was to be found in Thrace (ll. 1571, 1584–1587) seems to have come from Valerius Flaccus, *Argonauticon*, i, 596–613. For a discussion of this point and the whole question of Chaucer's acquaintance with the *Argonauticon*, see the chapter on Valerius Flaccus (pp. 340 ff.).

Triton, who is represented by Chaucer as the companion of Æolus, was in classical mythology a famous trumpeter. He appears in the *Æneid* three times, at least, as a sea god. In Book i, line 144, he is merely assisting in pushing off the ships that have been driven upon the sand by the storm. In Book ii, line 173, the passage already quoted in the discussion of Æolus, Triton is represented as causing the death of Misenus, because Misenus had boasted of rivalling the gods with the blasts upon his trumpet. Again in *Æneid*, x, 209–210, Triton is referred to as a trumpeter:

> Hunc vehit immanis Triton et caerula concha
> Exterrens freta.

In *Met.*, i, 330–342, there is a more detailed account of Triton and his trumpet:

> Nec maris ira manet, positoque tricuspide telo
> Mulcet aquas rector pelagi, supraque profundum
> Exstantem atque umeros innato murice tectum
> Caeruleum Tritona vocat, conchaeque sonanti

Inspirare iubet, fluctusque et flumina signo
Iam revocare dato: cava bucina sumitur illi
Tortilis, in latum quae turbine crescit ab imo,
Bucina, quae medio concepit ubi aëra, ponto,
Litora voce replet sub utroque iacentia Phoebo.
Tunc quoque, ut ora dei madida rorantia barba
Contigit, et cecinit iussos inflata receptus,
Omnibus audita est telluris et aequoris undis,
Et quibus est undis audita, coërcuit omnes.

A mere knowledge of Triton as a trumpeter would, of course, have been sufficient to suggest him to Chaucer as a suitable person to accompany Æolus on this journey to the palace of Fame, but it is especially significant that his name and function appear in the same passage from which it may be supposed that Chaucer derived his idea of using Æolus as a herald of tidings.

All the direct or detailed borrowings which the *House of Fame* owes to Ovid have now been noted. There is still to be considered the classical influence upon some of the organic features of the poem.

Without any desire to underestimate the value of Mr. Sypherd's thorough investigation of the mediaeval French influence upon the *House of Fame* and his conclusion that it is a love-vision in form, I must nevertheless differ from him in his assertion that the essential elements of the subject-matter are due to the mediaeval love-visions. Mr. Sypherd has, I think, minimized the influence of the Classics upon some of these essential elements. An instance of this, which I have already discussed, is his theory that the story of Dido and Æneas, though from the Classics, was modified by the influence of the love-visions. As has been shown, Chaucer's modification of Virgil's story was due to Ovid's Epistle in the *Heroides*, to which Chaucer himself refers the reader, and not to the mediaeval love-poetry.

Another element which Mr. Sypherd attributes to the love-vision is the temple of Venus. He says (pp. 18–19):

The Temple of Venus, with the story of Troy graven on its walls, is a most appropriate element of the love-vision. A disregard of this fact has led to unjust estimates of its importance in the poem. The long description of the scenes painted on the walls is by no means, as someone has said, a digression. The temple itself and the story of Dido and Æneas are in perfect accord with the spirit of the love-vision. The length of the story is no evidence of a digression, when we consider the interest that this feature of the poem would have for the court-circle for whose delectation the poem was evidently written. It is only when we look at the poem from the position of the modern reader at his library table, or when we wrongly assume that Chaucer's chief purpose in the work was to portray allegorically his reflections on fame, that we are at all justified in calling the story of Dido and Æneas a digression. The suggestion of the temple of Love came from the love-vision; the story of Dido and Æneas came probably from his favorite author Virgil, but was enlarged by Chaucer himself in a manner consonant with the nature of a love-poem.

The appropriateness in a love-vision of a temple of Venus with the story of Æneas and Dido graven upon its walls, is apparent, but Mr. Sypherd's statement that the suggestion of the temple of Love came from the love-visions is not so obvious. Let us see what Mr. Sypherd himself has to say on this point in another place: [1]

In his second vision he is in the temple of Venus, upon the walls of which is graven the story of Æneas. The chief significance of this temple for Chaucer is that it is a building devoted to the worship of Love. It offers a happy medium through which he may tell the story of Æneas and Dido. Here he is little concerned, as it seems, with the description of the temple. From his brief account of the images and the portraiture and from his own statement later (l. 473) we know that this building is of the nature of a shrine or chapel, devoted to the worship of Venus. It has no connection with the actual residence of the goddess.

Such temples or shrines do not, I believe, exist in the old French love-visions to which Chaucer owes so many of the conceptions of the dream-poems. The medieval love-poet as a rule felt no necessity for the introduction of a shrine at which his divinity might be worshipped. Venus, as goddess of Love, was not a divinity whose home was far away, and who could only be prayed to at an altar erected by her devotees. The realm of love was here on earth, and Venus, in the poet's imagination, could be prayed to in person. Humanity — at least that part of humanity represented by the great world of lovers — was in close touch with divinity. Hence

[1] Page 80.

when Venus is to be worshipped, she appears in her
palace seated on her throne or in the garden conse-
crated to Love.

The idea of a temple or shrine for the worship of
the goddess rather than the palace in which the
goddess could be seen in person, Mr. Sypherd says,
is a "departure from the traditions of the love-
visions" which is easily explained. His explanation
of this departure is, first, that it is to furnish "a
suitable setting for the story of Æneas and Dido."
But this does not explain why it should be the
shrine instead of the palace of the goddess. The
story might just as well have appeared upon the
walls of a palace, in the same way that the stories
were depicted upon the walls of the palace of Venus
in the *Parliament of Fowls*.[1] Though Chaucer designates this building in the *Parliament* as a *temple*,
yet the goddess is there in person disporting herself
among her subjects.[2] So it is in no sense a shrine as
is the temple in the *House of Fame*, which in line
473 Chaucer calls a *chirche*.

The second reason which Mr. Sypherd gives for
Chaucer's use of a shrine instead of a palace is "that
he had yet to portray a goddess in her dwelling —
the goddess Fama in her house to which all sounds
ascend." From this we are to understand that
Chaucer avoided describing the abode of Venus

[1] *Parliament of Fowls*, ll. 284 ff.   [2] *Ibid.*, ll. 260 ff.

here because he did not wish to portray two goddesses in the same poem. Yet in the *Parliament of
Fowls* he describes Venus in her dwelling, and coming out of it, he immediately sees the goddess Nature, whom he describes as seated upon a hill of
flowers holding her court with the branches of the
trees forming her halls and her bowers.[1]

"Finally," Mr. Sypherd says, "the setting of his
poem, which was determined by the situation of the
palace of Fame, would almost force Chaucer to describe the chapel of the goddess of Love, rather
than the palace, which according to the requirements of the love-vision should be on earth in a
garden full of flowers and singing birds." I do not
understand exactly what Mr. Sypherd means by
this, unless it is that the material from the Classics
which Chaucer uses in this poem and which places
the palace of Fame above the clouds is incongruous
with the mediaevalism of the palace of Venus described according to the requirements of the love-
vision. For it is really this incongruity between the
classical mythology and the mediaeval love-
allegory which would make the typical palace of
the love-vision seem out of place.

From this consideration of Mr. Sypherd's own
discussion of the question it is clear, I think, not
only that the suggestion for the temple of Venus did

[1] *Parliament of Fowls*, ll. 295 ff.

not come from the love-vision, but that it is not a
mediaeval conception. Skeat [1] suggests a comparison between this temple and the temple of Venus
in the *Knight's Tale* (ll. 1060 ff.), which he says is
imitated from that in Boccaccio's *Teseide*. Certainly this temple of Venus in the *Knight's Tale* is
the same in function as the temple we have in the
House of Fame — that is, it is a shrine erected in
honor of the goddess and is not her abode. But this
conception does not come from the *Teseide*. The
temple in the *Teseide* is the dwelling of Venus on
Mount Cithaeron and the goddess appears there in
person. The scenes which were actually taking
place in Boccaccio's temple Chaucer represents as
painted on the walls of the temple in the *Knight's
Tale:*

> For soothly, al the mount of Cithaeroun
> Ther Venus hath her principal dwelling
> Was shewed on the wal in portreying.
>   (*K. T.*, ll. 1078–1080.)

Chaucer's description of these scenes follows Boccaccio's account at least to some extent. It may be
worth while to note here that the temple of Venus
in the *Parliament of Fowls* to which I have already
referred is closely copied from Boccaccio's temple.

The description of the portrait of Venus in the
House of Fame is very similar to that of her statue in
the *Knight's Tale* (ll. 1097–1108), but, as Lounsbury

---

[1] *Oxford Chaucer*, III, 249, note on l. 130.

has pointed out,[1] both of these were probably suggested by a passage in Albricus Philosophus' *De Deorum Imaginibus*. The scenes from the *Teseide* used in the *Knight's Tale* do not appear in the temple in the *House of Fame*. In fact, the temple in the *House of Fame* has nothing in common with the one in the *Teseide*.

Where then did Chaucer get the suggestion for this temple, which is so manifest a departure from love-vision traditions? Mr. Sypherd says that Chaucer's main interest in introducing the temple was to obtain "a suitable setting for the story of Æneas and Dido," which is certainly true. Now, as there is in the very story which Chaucer wished to introduce a temple dedicated to the worship of a goddess and decorated with paintings on the wall, does it not seem probable that he got from it the immediate suggestion for his temple? This classical temple, which is described in *Æneid*, i, 446–493, has the same function as Chaucer's — it is erected in honor of Juno and for her worship. Virgil says the temple of Juno was enriched with gifts and the powerful manifestation of the goddess (*numine divae*). This manifestation of power in the classical temples came in various ways. Sometimes it was the trembling of the statue of the goddess which was often, though not always, erected in the

[1] *Studies in Chaucer*, II, 381–382; see also Sypherd, p. 81.

temple. Chaucer's use of this idea in connection
with the temple of Venus in the *Knight's Tale*
clearly marks it as of classical origin:

> But atte laste the statue of Venus shook,
> And made a signe, wher-by that he took
> That his prayere accepted was that day.
>
> (*K. T.*, ll. 1407–1409.)

Boccaccio, being a poet of the Renaissance, would
also be expected to follow classical designs, and in
fact he makes use of this manifestation in the cases
of the statues of the other two divinities in the
Teseide, Diana and Mars.

As has already been brought out, the temple in
the *House of Fame* is the same in function as the
temple in the *Knight's Tale*, and it also is classical
in conception.

But the similarity between Virgil's temple and
the temple of Venus in the *House of Fame* does not
stop with their functions. Though neither the
Latin nor the English author pays much attention
to the description of the building, both being more
interested in the paintings on the walls, the two
structures are similar in their splendor and their
richness of decoration. The skill of the artists and
the elaborate works excite the wonder of Æneas
first, as the

> curious portreytures,
> And queynte maner of figures
> Of olde werke
>
> (*H. F.*, ll. 125–127.)

are marvelled at by Chaucer. The chief point of similarity, however, lies in the carvings on the walls and the way in which they are managed by the two authors. Virgil represents a series of pictures from the Trojan War given in their historical order (*ex ordine*), and in just the same way Chaucer describes successive scenes from the *Æneid*.

In view of these similarities between the temples and of Chaucer's larger use of the *Æneid* in the same connection, and also in view of the fact that the conception of Chaucer's temple is essentially classical, it seems altogether reasonable to believe that the suggestion for it came from Virgil's temple of Juno. As Chaucer is writing a love-poem, he of course dedicates his temple to Venus.

The most important element of the poem in which, it seems to me, Mr. Sypherd has not done justice to the classical influence, is that of the eagle which is messenger and guide to Chaucer on his journey.

In attempting to show that the Ganymede story from the Classics as the source of this conception is of little importance, Mr. Sypherd separates the functions of the eagle into three divisions: "1. the messenger of a divinity; 2, the guide to a hero on his journey; 3, the helpful animal" (p. 86). The third function, as Mr. Sypherd says, probably did not occur to Chaucer until late in the composition and had little or nothing to do with determining the eagle as a guide. Hence we need not consider it here. Mr. Sypherd admits that his division of the part played by the eagle into three distinct functions is somewhat arbitrary and leads to danger, but he proceeds nevertheless to try to find parallels to each function separately. This process leads him into the manifest error of his conclusions. First he cites (pp. 86–87) a number of examples from the Classics to indicate the source of the conception of the eagle as a messenger of Jove. But in none of these except the Ganymede story does the eagle carry a hero on an aërial journey.

As the messenger and the guide are the same in Chaucer's story, Mr. Sypherd naturally finds it difficult to distinguish between the two. He says (p. 87):

Chaucer's conception of the eagle as the messenger of Jupiter is undoubtedly based on the Latin classics. To what extent this conception was united in his mind with the idea of the eagle as guide, who is at the same time a carrying animal, it is not easy to determine. If such an episode as the Ganymede story, for instance, was at the very bottom of Chaucer's representation, it formed surely but the slightest foundation for the treatment of the episode by Chaucer. The contributory influences, if I may still regard as probable the Ganymede story as its basis, were such, it will in a moment be evident, as to obscure very largely this primary material.

From this Mr. Sypherd passes on to a discussion
of his second division, the function of the eagle as a
guide. In regard to this he says (p. 88):

The conception of the eagle as a guide on a journey
gradually assumes shape — not, I believe, starting from
any single legend such as that of Ganymede, but de-
pending upon the necessary conditions of the plan of his
poem, and evolved from the great storehouse of legen-
dary material concerning guides to a hero on a journey,
animals as guides, animals as hero-carriers, the eagle as
a messenger, the eagle who takes a hero up in the air,
famous journeys taken through the air by heroes, etc.
There is no starting-point from which may be traced the
whole course of this aerial journey with the eagle.

Further Mr. Sypherd says (pp. 89–90):

We are now concerned with the *rôle* of the eagle as a
guide. The legend of Ganymede as told by Ovid was
surely in Chaucer's mind. I am inclined to think, however, that the importance of the story for the eagle as a
guide and carrying animal has been over-estimated. Is
it entirely certain that the legend as told in the *Metamorphoses*, as Professor Lounsbury says, suggests to
Chaucer the central incident for which the bird is introduced? The eagle whose shape Jupiter assumed merely
performs the office of carrying Ganymede to heaven.
Chaucer's eagle performs the functions of a guide. The
likelihood of a pretty direct influence from the Ganymede story seems plausible in view of the dependence of
the *Hous of Fame* on material from the classics. Yet the
idea of the poem is purely mediaeval — the reward of a
poet for his service to Love; the framework is mediaeval;
and the material, though partly from the Classics, is
thoroughly imbued with the essence of mediaeval life.

The influence from the Classics on this poem is by no means to be disregarded; but the fact must be borne in mind that many a conception which seems to spring from the true ancient sources had been so thoroughly modified and enlarged by subsequent writers that the wider stream was more attractive to a mediaeval poet. Forgotten the original conception could not be; but not for that reason was it necessarily fundamental. The appeal which such an early conception would make to Chaucer's literary intelligence would be secondary to that which would be exerted by later portrayals often nearer to the poet's own tastes and more like the completed representation in his own poem. The eagle legend from Ovid should, I believe, be looked upon as one of the sources of Chaucer's large conception, but not necessarily as a point of departure.

But in the parallels which Mr. Sypherd cites in succeeding pages of eagles carrying heroes, the eagle is *not the bird of Jove*. Of the two that Mr. Sypherd offers, Chaucer certainly knew the story of Alexander's flight, for he refers to it in line 915. Yet it is not a close enough parallel to have furnished the suggestion for Chaucer's episode, since the eagle is not Jove's. The other story which Mr. Sypherd mentions, the Babylonian legend of Etana's flight with the eagle, Chaucer probably did not know. From eagles in general as guides, Mr. Sypherd wanders away to the extent of suggesting guides that were not eagles at all. Finally, in his suggestions for possible influence he drops the last distinctive feature, that of guide to a hero *on an aërial journey,* and cites the guides in the love-visions, damsels in the service of Love, who guide the hero to his mistress or to the house of Love. Thus the danger which Mr. Sypherd feared from his arbitrary division has overtaken him. The Ganymede story from the Classics furnishes the only parallel to the twofold function of the eagle as a messenger of Jove and the conductor of a hero on an aërial journey.

This story of Ganymede is found in both the Latin authors from whom Chaucer is borrowing so extensively in this poem, Ovid and Virgil. Ovid represents Jupiter as assuming the form of the eagle in order to carry away his beloved Ganymede, (*Met.*, x, 155–161):

Rex superum Phrygii quondam Ganymedis amore
Arsit; et inventum est aliquid, quod Iuppiter esse,
Quam quod erat, mallet. nulla tamen alite verti
Dignatur, nisi quae posset sua fulmina ferre.
Nec mora, percusso mendacibus aëre pennis
Abripit Iliaden; qui nunc quoque pocula miscet
Invitaque Iovi nectar Iunone ministrat.

In Virgil's account (*Æn.*, v, 252–257), it is the eagle of Jove, instead of Jove himself, which bears Ganymede up to heaven:

Intextusque puer frondosa regius Ida
Veloces jaculo cervos cursuque fatigat,
Acer, anhelanti similis, quem praepes ab Ida
Sublimem pedibus rapuit Jovis armiger uncis;
Longaevi palmas nequiquam ad sidera tendunt
Custodes, saevitque canum latratus in auras.

Virgil has another reference to the story in *Æneid*, i, 28: "et rapti Ganymedis honores."

In addition to the similarity between this story and Chaucer's there is other strong evidence in the *House of Fame* for the Ganymede story as the basis of Chaucer's conception. He uses the Ganymede story as a means of introducing the eagle's explanation that he is the bird of Jove sent to carry the poet up to the house of Fame. Of the four instances of men carried up to heaven which Chaucer mentions there, Ganymede is the only one he distinguishes by any outline of his story. Besides this, he is the only one of the four connected with Jove. Chaucer says that while his fancy is dwelling upon these stories and he is wondering if Jove means to place him in the heavens as a constellation, the eagle tells him he is mistaken, for Jove has no such intention with regard to him. Then he tells the poet that he is Jove's messenger often sent upon missions, and that Jupiter has sent him upon this one to reward Chaucer for his faithfulness to Love. If the Ganymede story did not furnish the suggestion for Chaucer's conception, why was it Jupiter who sent the eagle? Without this source the reward might more reasonably have come from Love himself or from Venus. Chaucer's imaginative mind was entirely capable of utilizing the time on the journey in conversation between the eagle and the poet without suggestions from any other source.[1] Nevertheless, in view of the manifest influence of the *Divina Commedia* upon Chaucer at this time, though any structural parallel between it and the *House of Fame* be denied, the rôle of Virgil in Dante's work may have had its effect upon Chaucer's portrayal of the eagle in the capacity of "guide, philosopher and friend."[2] Furthermore, such other stories as Chaucer knew of aërial journeys no doubt influenced him more or less. He has mentioned several in this poem — Enoch, Elijah, Romulus, Alexander of Macedon, Scipio, and Daedalus.

But none of these stories has anything like so much in common with Chaucer's as has the Ganymede story. If, as Mr. Sypherd suggests (p. 90), "there were later portrayals often nearer the poet's own tastes and more like the completed representation in his own poem" which would have made a primary appeal to Chaucer's literary intelligence, Chaucer has failed to mention them. Does it not seem a little strange that Chaucer should refer to seven stories of aërial flights and still deprive his readers of the ones which appealed most to him?

[1] I have already pointed out (p. 78) that the story of Phaethon probably influenced Chaucer in the part of this conversation dealing with the constellations.

[2] For a description of the eagle, see *Purgatorio*, ix. See also Jusserand, *Literary History of the English People*, I, 295.

Not only did Chaucer refrain from citing these closer parallels, but Mr. Sypherd himself has failed to disclose them.

Now we have seen that the Ganymede story furnishes the only known parallel to Chaucer's eagle as both the messenger of Jove and the conductor of a hero on an aërial journey; that in both stories it is Jupiter who is rewarding a mortal — Ganymede for his beauty, Chaucer for his service to Love; that Chaucer mentions the Ganymede story in introducing his eagle as the messenger of Jove; that, though Chaucer refers to other cases of men carried to heaven, he gives most prominence to the story of Ganymede. Furthermore, among these cases cited in connection with Ganymede and in the three other instance of aërial flights mentioned later, none has any connection with Jove, and in only one, the story of Alexander, does an eagle appear as guide. In view of these facts it seems only reasonable to conclude that the Ganymede story was the basis for Chaucer's conception of the eagle, or in other words, it was just what Mr. Sypherd says it was not, "the point of departure." [1]

After the foregoing discussion of various points in the *House of Fame*, many of which have to do

[1] Professor Manly in a paper entitled "What is Chaucer's 'House of Fame?'" published in *Kittredge Anniversary Papers*, pp. 73–81, sweeps away all the previous attempts to interpret the poem allegorically, and Brusendorf writing later (*The Chaucer Tradition*) fails, I

with matters of detail, it seems well now to weigh the results and see what we may arrive at as a deliberate judgment of the poem.

As the *House of Fame* is fortunately not the only love-vision in which Chaucer used classical material, we have some basis for a comparison of his methods in a poem where the essential elements in subject-matter are mediaeval and in this one in which many of the essential elements are derived from other sources. In the *Book of the Duchess*, the episode of Ceys and Alcyone is evidently used on

think, to establish such an interpretation. Professor Manly cites *Met.*, xii, 39 ff., as the source for Chaucer's house of Fame (or Report), and adds:

"In order to reach this house, located, as it is, between heaven and earth and sea, he has need of a winged carrier powerful enough to transport him. Such a supernatural creature can be provided only by some god or goddess, and the poet's service of the goddess of love motives the plan of her rewarding him by having him transported to the house where all good stories gather. Venus, of course, has no messenger capable of such a feat, but in the *Æneid*, i, 254 ff. (a passage remembered by Chaucer, *H. F.*, i, 212–220), Jupiter shows himself somewhat affectionately ready to aid his dear daughter; and so here Chaucer represents him as lending her his own messenger, the eagle, who had already shown his powers by the long flight with Ganymede. This is the framework of the story; the rest is decorative or subsidiary. The temple with its storied walls, the treeless plain, the splendor of the eagle, and his power of human speech, his conversations about the heavenly bodies and his explanation of the manner in which sounds reach the house of Fame, — all are determined by the fundamental idea" (p. 76).

As my discussion of the *House of Fame* was written though not published before Professor Manly's article was published, I am gratified to have his confirmation of my own independent study.

account of its appropriateness to the theme of the poem. But it bears no vital relation to the poem as a whole, and in it Chaucer is much more closely dependent upon his source than he is in the *House of Fame*. The story is merely one that he had been reading before he fell asleep. In the *House of Fame* the material from the Classics is an inseparable part of the whole. It may help to an appreciation of the importance of this material to enumerate the features of the poem that are furnished by the Classics. It will be noticed that these features form essential elements of the poem. They are as follows: (1) the temple of Venus and the scenes from the *Æneid* painted on the walls; (2) the messenger sent from Jove; (3) the location of the house of Fame; (4) the basis for the idea of the Goddess of Fame, though much expanded, and her herald Æolus; (5) the fundamental idea and most of the details of the house of tidings.

Even before this period of his literary activity, Chaucer had shown how he loved to tell over again tales from the Latin poets. Under the fresh impetus of the Italian Renaissance his mind was no doubt teeming with new stories recently acquired. Skeat [1] thinks that Chaucer became acquainted with Virgil only a short time before he wrote the

[1] *Oxford Chaucer*, vol. III, p. ix, note 2.

House of Fame. In discussing Chaucer's intellectual
activity at this time Professor Kittredge says:[1]

> He had been filling his head with information from
> various sources as well as cultivating his taste by read-
> ing Italian. And, in particular, he had been studying the
> Latin classics. Ovid he had long known, of course, but
> he had reverted to him just before he wrote the *House of
> Fame*, and he had recently read the *Æneid*, perhaps for
> the first time. I need not pursue the subject. The im-
> plications are obvious. It is neither accident nor whim
> that we have to thank for the Eagle's description of
> Chaucer's studious habits. The composition of the
> *House of Fame* was directly preceded by a time of read-
> ing and study, during which Chaucer, busy at the
> custom-house in the daytime, spent evening after even-
> ing over French, Latin, and Italian books. What he
> wrote in the meantime was not essentially different
> from the product of his French Period, though he was
> always growing. It included, besides many occasional
> lyrics, the *Tragedies* and the *St. Cecilia*, — perhaps also
> the translation of Boëthius, which fits this studious
> time and must have been a powerful educating influence.
> And then, still in the Transition Period, came the *House
> of Fame*, full of spirit and *verve* and conscious power, but
> not to be compared with what was to follow, in the
> Italian Period, when Chaucer had "found himself,"
> recognizing Boccaccio as his proper guide.

As Professor Kittredge shows, this was a transi-
tional period in Chaucer's intellectual development. Though he still had much of the spirit of the
mediaeval French poetry, he was full of new classi-

[1] *The Date of Chaucer's Troilus and Other Chaucer Matters* (Chaucer
Society, 1905), p. 54.

cal knowledge and inspiration to use it, as the result
of his visit to Italy. If he was casting about at this
time for a convenient form in which to launch some
of this new material, it would be natural for him to
seize upon the love-vision which he had already
used successfully in the *Duchess*. Mr. Sypherd,
however, has magnified the form and insisted that
Chaucer's chief interest in the *House of Fame* was
in the reward of a poet for his service to Love. A
careful reading of the poem will show, I think, that
the love-vision was merely a form to carry the
ideas. Chaucer sometimes found it hard to hold
himself to his plan. In the story of Dido and
Æneas he says (ll. 313–314) that he dreamed all
this and will not refer to any other author. But
later he seems to have become so absorbed in his
story as to forget that he was supposed to see it
painted on the walls of the temple in his dream and
mentions that the "book seyth" (l. 429). Moreover, if he was not more interested in his other
material than in his tidings of Love's folk, it seems
strange that he should have given us so much else
and should have left untold the tidings of lovers.
Chaucer, I believe, was carried so far away from
his love-vision idea by his classical material that
when he attempted to return to it, he found the
spirit of the poem so changed that he gave it up. It
was, I think, an attempt to put new wine into old

bottles. Failure to adapt the classical material to the pure love-vision type accounts for the unfinished condition of the poem.

When Chaucer essayed a love-vision in the *Parliament of Fowls*, he kept to mediaeval ideas and hence preserved the true love-vision spirit. In the *Legend of Good Women* he used classical material again, but not as an organic part of the love-vision. He wrote the Prologue with its May-day full of birds and flowers in true mediaeval fashion and told his stories from the Classics separately in the legends.

Though there is in the *House of Fame* much of mediaeval French influence, as Mr. Sypherd has shown, and much of the classical element, which I have endeavored to present in this discussion, there is still plenty of evidence of Chaucer's own developing powers. He is able now to take a mere hint and develop it for himself. Though the origin of his Goddess of Fame he owes to the Classics, from that conception he has evolved a Goddess of Fame hitherto unknown. The house of tidings, though fundamentally from Ovid, shows the play of Chaucer's imagination upon his material in many ways. It is necessary to mention also as evidence of his unfolding genius the presence in this poem of that delicious humor which was so characteristic of all his later work. Furthermore, his greatly increased virtuosity in the *House of Fame* becomes manifest when compared with his earlier poem in the same metre, the *Book of the Duchess*.[1] But most significant of his power is the very fact that the poem does combine mediaeval and classical elements. From Italy, as we have seen, Chaucer returned filled with the new spirit in regard to the Classics and an inspiration to use them in a creative way. The result was the *House of Fame*, which was the first attempt in English literature to engraft upon the formality of the Middle Ages the imaginative freedom of the Classics. Hence the poem may be said to mark a literary epoch.

[1] See my article on "Chaucer's Use of the Octosyllabic Verse in the *Book of the Duchess* and the *House of Fame*," *J. E. G. P.*, XII, 277–294.

TROILUS AND CRISEYDE

THOUGH the *Troilus and Criseyde* was derived from Boccaccio's *Filostrato*, a Florentine
romance, the story became in Chaucer's hands
practically a new creation, which has been called a
great psychological novel.[1] All the elements of
Chaucer's genius unite happily in it. His skill in
dramatic narrative [2] combines with keen insight
into human nature [3] to present action and characters with remarkable verisimilitude. Under the
poetic fiction that it is a story of ancient times
largely translated from one Lollius,[4] a historian of
the Trojan War, Chaucer weaves into it much
material from the Classics. In a love-poem such
as this, it was inevitable that Ovid's love-poetry
should be constantly in Chaucer's mind, while at
the same time he was making drafts upon his knowledge of the *Metamorphoses* to produce an atmosphere of antiquity. In Ovid also he found a proto-
type for the character of Criseyde, who is a much

[1] Kittredge, *The Date of Chaucer's Troilus and Other Chaucer
Matters*, p. 56.

[2] See T. R. Price, "Troilus and Criseyde, A Study of Chaucer's
Methods of Narrative Construction," *P. M. L. A.*, XI, 307-322.

[3] See W. G. Dodd, *Courtly Love in Chaucer and Gower*, pp. 141-
189; Kittredge, *Chaucer and his Poetry*, pp. 121-142; R. K. Root,
Chaucer's Troilus and Criseyde, pp. xi-l.

[4] Kittredge, *Harvard Studies in Classical Philology*, XXVIII, 47-
91.

more subtle and elusive personality in this poem than she had appeared in any previous treatment of the story.

Book I

In line 6 of the first of the eight stanzas that constitute the introduction to the poem Chaucer very properly invokes the aid of one of the Furies, Tisiphone (Thesiphone), for this tale is to be one of Love's tragedies. As this scrap of classical mythology was so well known, it is perhaps useless to try to identify its source, though Virgil in *Æneid*, vi, 555 and 571, and x, 76, refers to Thesiphone by name.[1]

A probable reminiscence of Virgil, as pointed out by Bell, occurs at the beginning of the story proper (i, 58 and 60), where the "thousand shippes" and "ten yeer" were suggested by "mille carinae" and "anni decem" (*Æn.*, ii, 198).[2] Compare also *Heroides*, xiii, 97,

> Inter mille rates tua sit millenima puppis.

"Apollo Delphicus" (i, 70) recalls Ovid's

> Pulchrior in tota, quam Larissaea Coronis,
> Non fuit Haemonia; placuit tibi, *Delphice*, certe.
> (*Met.*, ii, 542–543.)[3]

---

[1] Professor Wise (*Influence of Statius upon Chaucer*, p. 4) suggests that Chaucer's invocation of Tisiphone may have been due to *Thebaid*, i, 58. Professor Lowes (*Mod. Phil.*, XIV, 718) thinks the influence of Dante is to be seen in this passage.

[2] See Skeat, *Oxford Chaucer*, II, 462.   [3] *Ibid.*

Boccaccio has only Apollo. Chaucer's greater concreteness — a characteristic which we shall find
manifest throughout the poem — may be ascribed
in this instance to his knowledge of Ovid, for he
could not know Ovid without associating Apollo
with Delphi.

In i, 206–208, is presented the personification of
love as a god with his bow and arrows. This conception is an inheritance from classical times and a
good example may be found in the first elegy of
the *Amores*.[1] Professor Hamilton[2] has suggested
Guido's account of the *innamoramento* of Achilles
and Polyxena as the source for Chaucer's use of
Cupid here, but Professor Karl Young[3] thinks this
is no more probable a source than the *Filostrato*. In
view of Chaucer's thorough acquaintance with
Ovid at this time, it would seem unnecessary to derive the conception of the God of Love in these lines
from any other source than *Amores*, i, i.

In i, 652–658, Pandarus compares the sad state of
his own love affair with that of Oenone, who loved
Paris, Troilus' brother. Nothing could be more

[1] See W. G. Dodd, *Courtly Love in Chaucer and Gower*, p. 16. See
further in the same work, pp. 190 ff., where are clearly indicated the
differences among the classical, the mediaeval, and the ecclesiastical
conceptions of the power of love.

[2] *Chaucer's Indebtedness to Guido delle Colonna*, p. 71.

[3] *The Origin and Development of the Story of Troilus and Criseyde*,
p. 113.

apropos than the introduction here of Oenone's letter to Paris in the *Heroides*.[1] The utmost effect of reality is secured by Pandarus' question to Troilus,

> Ye say the lettre that she wroot, I gesse?

It is by such masterly strokes as this that Chaucer renders most vivid the local color of antiquity, which Professor Kittredge has shown is so important a feature of this poem.[2] Pandarus indicates to Troilus a part of the contents of Oenone's letter, giving the general sense of *Heroides*, v, 147–154, without making a literal translation of the lines.[3]

In i, 699–700, Pandarus tells Troilus that it is not the way to be successful in love,

> To walwe and wepe as Niobe the quene,
> Whos teres yet in marbel been y-sene.

The fate of Niobe, whose statue Pandarus refers to as if it were standing in Troy, is told at length by Ovid, who closes his account with the words which Chaucer has borrowed:

> Flet tamen, et validi circumdata turbine venti
> In patriam rapta est: ibi fixa cacumine montis
> Liquitur, et lacrimas etiam nunc marmora manant.
> (*Met.*, vi, 310–312.)[4]

---

[1] *Oxford Chaucer*, II, 465.

[2] *Harvard Studies in Classical Philology*, XXVIII, 50–54.

[3] For the suggestion that the *Teseide* may have influenced Chaucer here, see *Ibid.*, p. 113.

[4] *Oxford Chaucer*, II, 465.

In i, 712–714, Pandarus says that no further misfortune may come upon him because there is room for no more:

> So ful of sorwe am I, soth for to seyne,
> That certeynly no more hardy grace
> May sit on me, forwhy there is no space.

Ovid has expressed the same idea with regard to his own misfortunes in exile:[1]

> Sic ego continuo fortunae vulneror ictu,
> Vixque habet in nobis jam nova plaga locum.
> > (*ex Ponto*, ii, vii, 41–42.)

> Quid juvat extinctos ferrum demittere in artus?
> Non habet in nobis jam nova plaga locum.
> > (*ex Ponto*, iv, xvi, 51–52.)

In i, 786–788, Pandarus tells Troilus that he knows he is suffering woe

> As sharp as dooth he Ticius in helle,
> Whos stomak foules tyren ever-mo
> That highte Volturis, as bokes telle.

Whether Chaucer had in mind Boethius, Book iii, *Æneid*, vi, 595 ff., or *Met.*, iv, 457, one cannot say, but the passage may be noted as a classical allusion.[2]

Book i, lines 857–858, in which Pandarus attempts to persuade Troilus to disclose to him the

---

[1] I am indebted to Professor Kittredge for these references.
[2] See Kittredge, *Harvard Studies*, XXVIII, 52.

nature of his malady, recall a similar idea in the
Remedia Amoris: [1]

> For whoso list have helping of his leche,
> To him bihoveth first unwrye his wounde.

> Adgredior melius tum, cum sua vulnera tangi
> Jam sinet.   (*Rem. Am.*, ll. 125–126.)

Some touches which aid in heightening the effect
of antique verity in this first book are the two
oaths that are put into the mouth of Pandarus.

> To Cerberus in helle ay be I bounde (i, 859.)

is not found in the *Filostrato;* and

> for Joves name in hevene (i, 878.)

is substituted for Boccaccio's mediaeval Christian
oath, "I pray thee by God." In i, 1014, Troilus
invokes the aid of Venus.

The idea in i, 946–949, that the rose often grows
next to the nettle, is taken from Ovid:

> For thilke ground that bereth the wedes wikke,
> Bereth eek thise holsom herbes, as ful ofte
> Next the foule netle, rough and thikke,
> The rose waxeth swote and smothe and softe.

> Terra salutares herbas eademque nocentes
> Nutrit, et urticae proxima saepe rosast.
>   (*Rem. Am.*, ll. 45–46.) [2]

---

[1] See Kittredge, "Chaucer's Medea and the Date of the Legend
of Good Women," *P. M. L. A.*, XXIV, 349, note 2.

[2] See *Ibid.*

Book II

In line 8 the poet appeals to Clio, the muse of history, to aid him in his rhymes in this book. He needs, he says, to use no other art, as he is translating from the Latin:

> But out of Latin in my tonge it write. (ii, 14.)

The epithet "white" (*whyte bole*, ii, 55) Chaucer applies to the sign of Taurus, because he recalls the story of how Jupiter assumed the shape of a white bull when he carried off Europa on his back; see *Met.*, ii, 836–875.[1] The use of this epithet shows not only how Chaucer's classical knowledge had become a part of his literary equipment, but also how he could give a fresh poetic turn to a very commonplace scientific thing. Small wonder is it that the idea lingered in Chaucer's mind, for Ovid's words in describing the bull are very appealing to the imagination:

> Quippe color nivis est, quam nec vestigia duri
> Calcavere pedis nec solvit aquaticus auster.
> (*Met.*, ii, 852–853.)

In ii, 64–70, Chaucer, representing the swallow as waking Pandarus with her chirping in the morning, calls her by her classical name Progne:

> The swalwe Proigne, with a sorwful lay,
> Whan morwe com, gan make hir weymentinge,

---

[1] *Oxford Chaucer*, II, 468.

Why she forshapen was; and ever lay
Pandare a-bedde, half in a slomeringe,
Til she so neigh him made hir chiteringe
How Tereus gan forth hir suster take,
That with the noyse of hir he gan a-wake.

The unhappy fate of Progne, who was transformed into a swallow, is related by Ovid in *Met.*, vi, 424–674.[1] Chaucer tells the story of her wrongs at the hands of Tereus in the *Legend of Philomela.*

The pervasive spirit of antiquity in the poem is furthered by the author's prayer to the Roman god of beginnings that Pandarus may be successful in his appeal to Criseyde:

Now Janus, god of entree, thou him gyde. (i, 77.)

See *Fasti*, i, 125; [2] *Rem. Am.*, l. 561.

The passage (ii, 100–108) which tells how Pandarus found Criseyde with two other ladies reading "the sege of Thebes" indicates that both Pandarus and his niece knew the early history of Thebes and the contents of the twelve books of the *Thebaid* of Statius.[3] Chaucer was to revert to the story of the *Thebaid* again in v, 1485–1510, where he makes Cassandra give a brief outline of the whole epic to Troilus in order to explain his dream about the boar. The anachronism of introducing this poem of Statius into an account of the Trojan War need

---

[1] *Oxford Chaucer*, II, 468.   [2] *Ibid.*
[3] See Wise, pp. 9 and 10.

trouble us as little as it did Chaucer. It served the purpose of giving a charming realism to the episode.

Classical oaths which Chaucer has put into the mouths of his characters in Book ii are as follows:

By the goddesse Minerve. (l. 232.)
And Juppiter that maketh the thunder ringe. (l. 233.)
And by the blisful Venus that I serve. (l. 234.)
O lady myn, Pallas. (l. 425.)
By Neptunus. (l. 443.)
By Mars the god. (l. 593.)
And thou Minerva, the whyte. (l. 1062.)
Venus here to borwe. (l. 1524.)
Joves lat him never thryve. (l. 1607.)

Book ii, line 391,

As love for love is skilful guerdoninge,

was no doubt a common enough proverb, but it may have been suggested to Chaucer by Ovid's "ut ameris, amabilis esto" (*Ars Am.*, ii, 107).[1] In fact, the ideas that Pandarus presents to Criseyde here upon the wasteful effects of age (ii, 393–405) all seem to be rather reminiscent of Ovid's advice to the lover that beauty is only a fragile thing and decreases with the years. Then will come white hairs and wrinkles which will draw furrows over the body. See *Ars Am.*, ii, 113–118.[2]

The sentiments expressed by Criseyde in ii, 786–

[1] *Oxford Chaucer*, II, 469.
[2] *Ibid.*

788, about man's inconstancy to woman, are not in the *Filostrato:*

> eek men be so untrewe,
> That, right anoon as cessed is hir lest,
> So cesseth love, and forth to love a newe.

These words are very similar to the idea expressed by Ariadne in Catullus (*Ode*, lxiv, 143–148).[1] There is also a suggestion of the same idea in the Epistle of Helen to Paris (*Her.*, xvi, 39–40).

Though Boccaccio makes Pandarus suggest to Troilus that he write a letter to Criseyde telling her of his love-longing (ii, 1005), the concrete advice about what to include in the letter Chaucer adds on his own account:

> Touching thy lettre, thou art wys enough,
> I woot thow wilt it digneliche endyte;
> As make it with thise argumentes tough;
> Ne scrivenish or craftily thou it wryte;
> Beblotte it with thy teres eek a lyte.
>   (ii, 1023–1027.)

These details Chaucer remembered, no doubt, from the advice to the lover in *Ars Amatoria*, and from some of Ovid's phrases in the letters of the *Heroides*, as the following:[2]

> Sed lateant vires, nec sis in fronte disertus,
>   Effugiant voces verba molesta tuae!
> Quis, nisi mentis inops, tenerae declamat amicae?
>   Saepe valens odii littera causa fuit.
>   (*Ars Am.*, i, 463–466.)

---

[1] See discussion of Chaucer and Catullus, p. 365.
[2] *Oxford Chaucer*, II, 471–472.

Quascumque adspicies, lacrimae fecere lituras.

(Her., iii, 3.)

The detail of a Greek spy having come to Troy
(ii, 1111–1113) serves to keep up the illusion that
this was a story of Troy in ancient days.[1] Professor
Kittredge cites ii, 1394 ff., relating to the friendship of Deiphobus for Troilus, as indicative of local
color. Certainly we have here a lively picture of
private life among the Trojan nobility. It may be
noted that Deiphobus appears by name in the
Epistle of Paris to Helen (Her., xv, 360) and in the
Epistle of Oenone to Paris (Her., v, 94).

Book III

At the beginning of the third book Chaucer invokes Calliope (l. 45), whose aid he needs to tell
the gladness of Troilus to the praise of Venus
(l. 49).

In iii, 150, Pandarus makes use of a classical
oath,

Now nece myn, by natal Joves fest,

and Troilus, in iii, 383–384, swears,

And this, in alle the temples of this toun,
Upon the goddes alle, I wol thee swere.

When Troilus wishes to provide an excuse for
being absent, if he should be sought at any time

[1] See Kittredge, *Harvard Studies in Classical Philology*, XXVIII,
52.

while he is with Criseyde, he directs Pandarus to say that he is doing sacrifice in the temple of Apollo:

> And moste at swich a temple alone wake,
> Answered of Apollo for to be;
> And first, to seen the holy laurer quake,
> Er that Apollo spak out of the tree,
> To telle him next whan Grekes sholden flee.
>
> (iii, 540–544.)

The story of how Daphne was transformed into the laurel tree to escape from Apollo is told in *Met.*, i, 490–567.[1] As Apollo was eluded by Daphne herself, he adopted the laurel as his tree:

> "at quoniam conjunx mea non potes esse,
> Arbor eris certe," dixit, "mea."
>
> (*Met.*, i, 557–558.)

At the end of Apollo's speech, the laurel nods its approval,

> factis modo laurea ramis
> Adnuit, utque caput visa est agitasse cacumen.
>
> (*Met.*, i, 566–567.)

From these passages it is easy to see how Chaucer has here identified Apollo with the laurel and represents him as speaking out of the tree.

When Troilus has reached the culmination of his hopes and is waiting for Pandarus to bring him to Criseyde, he recalls (iii, 720–735) the love-affairs of the various gods and adjures them by these loves

---

[1] *Oxford Chaucer*, II, 477.

to aid him in his enterprise. Appropriately he calls upon Venus first, asking her to intercede with Jupiter, and begs her to do this

> For love of him thou lovedest in the shawe,
> I mene Adoon, that with the boar was slawe.
>
> (iii, 720–721.)

This has reference to the story of Venus and Adonis given by Ovid in *Met.*, x, 715–723.[1] Troilus next appeals to Jupiter for the love he bore Europa, (*Met.*, ii, 846–875);[2] then to Mars for his love of Venus, accounts of which are found in *Met.*, iv, 171–189, and *Ars Am.*, ii, 561–592; and to Apollo for his love of Daphne (*Met.*, i, 490–559).[3] Likewise the lover entreats Mercury for the love he had for Herse (*Met.*, ii, 708–832)[4] to assist him at this time, and beseeches even the chaste Diana that this attempt may not be hateful to her (*Ars Am.*, i, 261–262). He closes his invocation to the gods for help (ll. 732–735) with a final appeal to the Fates ("fatal sustren").

---

[1] For Professor Kittredge's suggestion that the allusion here may possibly be due to the *Teseide*, see *Harvard Studies*, XXVIII, 115.

[2] Mr. Wise (p. 11) attributes this allusion to *Thebaid*, vii, 191, where Bacchus, in pleading for his native city, uses Jupiter's love for Europa as the basis for his appeal. But surely this reference to the *Thebaid* cannot be accepted in the face of Ovid's full account of the intrigue in the *Metamorphoses*, particularly in its connection here with a series of love-episodes recalled from Ovid. The spirit of the patriotic appeal of Bacchus in *Thebaid* has nothing in common with the amatory feelings of Troilus at this crisis.

[3] *Oxford Chaucer*, II, 478.

[4] *Ibid.*, p. 479.

By summarizing in a line or two a love-affair of each of the gods, Chaucer shows his perfect familiarity with these stories in the *Metamorphoses*. Moreover, that he should make Troilus recall them at such a moment of emotional anticipation is a subtly executed detail in his general design of a novel with a classical setting.

In iii, 1254–1260, while he is with Criseyde, Troilus acknowledges his obligation to Cupid, Venus, and Hymen for their favor.

In pronouncing a curse upon those who despise the service of love (iii, 1387–1391), Chaucer wishes they had ears as long as Midas and might be forced to drink a potion as hot and strong as did Crassus. The tale of the covetousness of Midas and of his ass's ears is found in *Met.*, xi, 100–193.[1] Chaucer himself tells the story in the *Wife of Bath's Tale*, ll. D 951–982. For the incident of the dead Crassus forced by Orodes, to drink molten gold, Chaucer was no doubt indebted to Boccaccio's *De Casibus Virorum*, vi, vii.[2]

Toward the close of Book iii another emotional climax is reached when, with the coming of day, it

[1] *Oxford Chaucer*, V, 317.

[2] Professor Lowes thinks the dominant influence upon Chaucer here was Dante (*Mod. Phil.*, XIV, 135–137). As the ass's ears are not mentioned in Dante, that information certainly came from Ovid. Dante's reference to Crassus (*Purg.*, xx, 116–117) would be unintelligible without a further knowledge of the story. For this Mr. Lowes suggests Florus. But I show (p. 181) that in the only other place where

is necessary for Troilus and Criseyde to part. Here again Chaucer has recourse to Ovid. For Lucifer in the capacity of "the dayes messager" (iii, 1417), cf. *Amores*, i, vi, 65–66; ii, xi, 55–56; and *Heroides*, xvii, 112. The lover in *Amores*, i, xiii, makes bitter complaint against Day for coming too soon. His situation is exactly that of Troilus and Criseyde. Chaucer has taken Ovid's poem spoken by the one lover, and used from it material for speeches by both lovers, making Criseyde upbraid Night for not staying longer and Troilus reproach Day for coming too soon. Though the lover in *Amores*, i, xiii, does not apostrophize Night as he does Day, he tells how Day by coming too soon deprives man and beast of the advantages that Night gives, for the traveller, however weary, must rise with day and continue his journey, the soldier must wake to his cruel work, and women must rise to their spinning. So, too, the oxen are called again to the plough.[1] Criseyde's idea that men and beasts have just complaints against Night for leaving so soon,

Chaucer has been thought to borrow from Florus, viz., in the *Legend of Cleopatra*, he was using *De Mulieribus Claris* and *De Casibus Virorum*. As all that Chaucer has about Crassus may be found in *De Casibus Virorum*, Mr. Lowes's reference to Jehan de Tuim's *Hystore de Julius Cesar* is also unnecessary. Ovid, Boccaccio, and possibly Dante, contributed to Chaucer in this passage.

[1] *Amores*, i, xiii, 13–24. Professor Kittredge (*Harvard Studies in Classical Philology* XXVIII, 116) has called attention to these lines.

because Day will rouse them to their tasks, was suggested by what the lover says in Ovid's poem.

The speech of Troilus to Day, iii, 1450–1460, is similar in spirit to that of the lover in the *Amores*, who upbraids Aurora for hastening so fast. He calls her "disagreeable" to both men and maidens:

Quo properas, ingrata viris, ingrata puellis.
(*Am.*, i, xiii, 9.)

Troilus calls Day "cruel." The lover in the *Amores* tells Aurora that she is "envious," and that, if she had her Cephalus in her embraces, she would cry, "Run slowly, horses of Night":

Invida, quo properas. (*Am.*, i, xiii, 33.)

At si, quem mavis, Cephalum complexa teneres,
Clamares: "lente currite, Noctis equi."
(*Am.*, i, xiii, 39–40.)

Troilus calls Day "envyous":

Envyous day, what list thee so to spyen. (iii, 1454.)

In the *Amores* the lover asks Aurora what he has done to arouse her animosity:

Cur ego plectar amans, si vir tibi marcet ab annis?
Num me nupsisti conciliante seni.
(*Am.*, i, xiii, 41–42.)

Likewise Troilus asks,

Allas! what han thise loveres thee agilt. (iii, 1457.)

Professor Lowes [1] argues for the *Filocolo* as a source for the addresses to Night and Day by Cri-

---

[1] *Mod. Phil.*, XV, 708–709.

seyde and Troilus. He cites the king in the *Filocolo* as eager for Day to come and invoking Night to hasten. This invocation to Night is then followed by an appeal to Apollo, the Sun, not to delay his coming. But the difficulty here is that the addresses to Night and Day in the *Filocolo* are the very reverse of the desire of the lovers in the *Troilus*, as Mr. Lowes himself notes. On the other hand, the parallelism between Chaucer and the *Amores* is complete — the lover there, as well as Troilus and Criseyde, wishes Night to continue. Additional evidence for the *Amores* is given by Chaucer himself when he makes Criseyde cite the instance:

As longe as whanne Almena lay by Jove (iii, 1428.)

— a circumstance used in the very passage of the lover's appeal in the *Amores:*

Ipse deum genitor, ne te tam saepe videret,
   Commisit noctes in sua vota duas.
                    (*Am.*, i, xiii, 45–46.)

The details of the intrigue Chaucer may have known from *De Genealogia Deorum*, xiii, i. This passage illustrates how thoroughly impregnated Chaucer's mind had become with mythological lore, and how he was thus able to render in specific terms what was suggested to him by an allusion in Ovid.

Book iii, lines 1459–1460:

> For many a lover hastow shent, and wilt;
> Thy pouring in wol no-wher lete hem dwelle.

This passage was probably suggested to Chaucer by Ovid's comment upon Apollo's disclosure of the intrigue of Mars and Venus:

> Primus adulterium Veneris cum Marte putatur
> Hic vidisse deus. Videt hic deus omnia
> Primus.   (*Met.*, iv, 171–173.)

Troilus' reference to Tithonus in this connection (iii, 1464–1469) is significant:

> And eek the sonne Tytan gan he chyde,
> And seyde, "O fool, wel may men thee dispyse,
> That hast the dawing al night by thy syde,
> And suffrest hir so sone up fro thee ryse,
> For to disesen loveres in this wyse.
> What! hold your bed ther, thou, and eek thy morwe.

So the lover in *Amores*, i, xiii, 35–42, taunts Aurora with having Tithonus, an old man whom she no longer loves, for her husband. Though Chaucer does not make use of the sentiments of Ovid's lover, the suggestion for Troilus' derision of Tithonus was evidently due to this passage. In the phrase, "the sonne Tytan" (iii, 1464), Chaucer has confused Tithonus with Titan, a name often used for the sun. Professor Kittredge suggests that this confusion was due to Boccaccio's form "Titon" for Tithonus, in *Teseide*, iv, 72. In fact, Boccaccio seems to have confused the two names constantly.

In *De Genealogia Deorum*, vi, x, he calls Laomedon's son, who was loved by Aurora, Titon instead of Tithonus,[1] and refers to him again as Titon in vi, ix.

Book iii, line 1600,

> Fro Flegeton, the firy flood of helle,

seems to recall Virgil's

> Quae rapidus flammis ambit torrentibus amnis
> Tartareus Phlegeton.   (*Æn.*, vi, 550.) [2]

In iii, 1672, Chaucer preserves the pagan atmosphere by making Troilus, in his joy at the prospect of being with Criseyde again, praise all the gods.

On the occasion of Troilus' second visit to Criseyde (iii, 1702–1708), when morning has come, he upbraids the Sun for rising so early and quotes from Ovid: [3]

> That Pirous and tho swifte stedes three,
> Whiche that drawen forth the sonnes char.

> Interea volucres Pyrois et Eous et Aethon,
> Solis equi, quartusque Phlegon hinnitibus auras.
> (*Met.*, ii, 153–154.)

The concreteness with which Chaucer uses his classical references as compared with Boccaccio is illustrated in iii, 1807–1809. Boccaccio says:

---

[1] Professor Lowes (*Mod. Phil.*, XV, 708–709) has called attention to the same confusion in the *Filocolo*.

[2] *Oxford Chaucer*, II, 482.

[3] *Ibid.*, p. 483.

And thou, Mother of Love, with thy jocund and glad
aspect and thy rapid son, with his darts, potent in every
world, O Castalian sisters, who in Mount Helicon dwell
content![1]

Chaucer, while taking the suggestion, adds some
details on his own account:

> Thou lady bright, the doughter to Dione,
> Thy blinde and winged sone eek, daun Cupyde;
> Ye sustren nyne eek.

Skeat derives this reference to Venus as the daughter of Dione from *Æn.*, iii, 19,

> Sacra Dionaeae matri divisque ferebam.

But Chaucer was also undoubtedly familiar with
Ovid's frequent allusions to Venus under her
mother's name:

> Ite in bella pares: vincant, quibus alma Dione
> Faverit et, toto qui volat orbe, puer.
> > (*Ars Am.*, iii, 3–4.)

> Ulteriora pudet docuisse: sed alma Dione
> "Praecipue nostrumst, quod pudet," inquit, "opus."
> > (*Ars Am.*, iii, 769–770.)

> Illis contulerim, quas quondam nuda Dione
> Pingitur umenti sustinuisse manu.
> > (*Am.*, i, xiv, 33–34.)

> Hoc vetiti vos este! vetat deprensa Dione
> Insidias illas, quas tulit ipsa, dare.
> > (*Ars Am.*, ii, 593–594.)[2]

---

[1] W. M. Rossetti, *Chaucer's Troylus and Crysede, compared with
Boccaccio's Filostrato*, Chaucer Society, 1875, p. 169.

[2] All the details added here by Chaucer were so familiar to him at
this time that one cannot identify the source. Professor Lowes thinks
that they are reminiscences of Dante (*Mod. Phil.*, XIV, 731–733).

Book IV

In the proem to Book iv Chaucer invokes the Furies and Mars as the only ones suitable to aid him in the direful narrative of this book:

> O ye Herines, Nightes doughtren three
> That endeless compleynen ever in pyne,
> Megera, Alete, and eek Thesiphone;
> Thou cruel Mars eek, fader to Quiryne.
>
> (iv, 22–25.)

Both Virgil and Ovid supply information regarding the Furies, calling them "daughters of Night":

> Dicuntur geminae pestes cognomine Dirae
> Quod et Tartaream Nox intempesta Megaeram
> Uno eodemque tulit partu.
>
> (*Æn.*, xii, 845–847.)

> illa sorores
> Nocte vocat genitas, grave et implacabile numen.
>
> (*Met.*, iv, 451–452.) [1]

Virgil gives the names of all three Furies: Megaera (*Æn.*, xii, 846), Allecto (*Æn.*, vii, 324), Tisiphone (*Æn.*, vi, 571).[2] Ovid mentions two by name: Tisiphone (*Her.*, ii, 117) and Allecto (*Her.*, ii, 119). Mr. Wise [3] refers this passage to the *Thebaid*, but nothing is there said of their being daughters of Night. That Mars was supposed to be the father of the Quirini (Romulus and Remus) was known to

---

[1] See Lowes, *Mod. Phil.*, XIV, 720, note 1.
[2] *Oxford Chaucer*, II, 484.
[3] Pages 12–13.

Chaucer probably from *Fasti*, ii, 419.[1] See also
Met., xiv, 772 ff., and xv, 863.[2]

When Calchas is beseeching the Trojans to ask
for his daughter in the exchange of prisoners, he
predicts the doom of Troy and says,

> Appollo hath me told it feithfully. (iv, 114.)

Calchas emphasizes the certainty of his knowledge
by recalling that Apollo and Neptune have always
been hostile toward Troy, because Laomedon, its
first king, had refused to pay these two gods for
assisting him in building the walls of the city (iv,
120–126). This story came from the *Metamorphoses:*

> Inde novae primum moliri moenia Trojae
> Laomedonta (Phoebus) videt, susceptaque magna labore
> Crescere difficili, nec opes exposcere parvas:
> Cumque tridentigero tumidi genitore profundi
> Mortalem induitur formam, Phrygiaeque tyranno
> Aedificat muros, pactus pro moenibus aurum.
> Stabat opus: pretium rex inficiatur, et addit
> Perfidiae cumulum, falsis perjuria verbis.
>
> *(Met.*, xi, 199–206.)

As will be seen, Ovid here gives all the facts of the
building of the walls of Troy that Chaucer uses,
namely, that Apollo and Neptune labored together
to build them and that Laomedon, when the work
was done, refused them their hire.[3] The connection

---

[1] *Oxford Chaucer*, II, 485.

[2] Lowes (*Mod. Phil.*, XIV, 733–734) thinks that Dante's *Paradiso*,
vii, 130–132, was in Chaucer's mind here along with Ovid.

[3] Professor Root (*Chaucer's Troilus and Criseyde*, 1926, p. 503) in
a note on this passage fails to mention Ovid at all. Instead, he cites

that Apollo had with building the walls is also referred to in the Epistle of Paris to Helen:

> Ilion adspicies firmataque turribus altis
> Moenia, Phoebeae structa canore lyrae.
>
> (*Her.*, xv, 181–182.)

In Pandarus' suggestion to Troilus that other ladies in Troy can solace his woes even if he has lost Criseyde (iv, 400 ff.), Boccaccio uses very general terms, which Chaucer, after translating, amplifies concretely. This amplification consists in a brief summary of *Amores*, ii, iv, 10–44,[1] where the poet himself speaks, probably from a personal experience. The appropriateness of sentiment to the lover Troilus, Chaucer did not fail to perceive.

The advice of Pandarus to Troilus for the curing of his love (iv, 421–424) summarizes a good deal of the argument that Ovid makes in the *Remedia Amoris:*

> For also seur as day cometh after night,
> The newe love, labour or other wo,
> Or elles selde seinge of a wight,
> Don olde affeciouns alle over-go.

But Chaucer does not follow Ovid's order.[2] Ovid first suggests "labour":

Benoit, though Benoit says nothing of the withheld wages. Mr. Root also gives the story from Homer, whom of course Chaucer did not know, and quotes from Hyginus and Servius, neither of whom provides a satisfactory source.

[1] *Oxford Chaucer*, II, 487.

[2] Kittredge "Chaucer's Medea and the Date of the Legend of Good Women," *P. M. L. A.*, XXIV, 349, note 2.

Ergo ubi visus eris nostrae medicabilis arti,
Fac monitis fugias otia prima meis.
(Rem. Am., ll. 135–136.)

qui finem quaeris amoris,
(Cedit amor rebus) res age: tutus eris.
(Rem. Am., ll. 143–144.)

See also *Rem. Am.*, ll. 149–150 and 205–206. Next Ovid commends absence (Chaucer's "selde seinge of a wight") as a cure for love:

I procul et longas carpere perge vias.
(Rem. Am., l. 214.)

And later he advises seeking "the newe love" to drive out the old one:

Nunc saltem novus est inveniendus amor.
(Rem. Am., l. 452.)

An instance of Chaucer's rendering Boccaccio's idea in terms of classical mythology is found in iv, 473–474. For Boccaccio's "Down into hell with its utmost pangs," [1] Chaucer has,

but doun with Proserpyne
Whan I am deed, I wol go wone in pyne.

In two passages where Chaucer is following Boccaccio closely he interpolates these references to Jove:

But if that Jove tolde it in thyn ere. (iv, 644.)

Ful bisily to Juppiter bisoughte. (iv, 669.)

---

[1] Rossetti, p. 188.

The story of Orpheus and Eurydice, to which Chaucer refers in iv, 789–791, was well known to him from the accounts in *Met.*, x, 1–85,[1] and xi, 61–66:

> Yet in the feld of pitee, out of pyne
> That hight Elysos, shul we been y-fere,
> As Orpheus and Erudice his fere.

Though Ovid does not use the word "Elysium" in this connection, he does use it elsewhere to refer to the other world.[2] Professor Kittredge (*P. M. L. A.* XXIV, 352, note 14) thinks Chaucer's "feld of pitee" is Ovid's "arva piorum" (*Met.*, xi, 62), and his "Elysos" may have come from a marginal "Campos Elysios."[3] The idea of Elysium as the "feld of pitee" could readily have been suggested by the account in *Met.*, x, 45–48, for according to it neither the Furies, nor the queen nor the king of the lower world, could resist the prayers of Orpheus:

> Tunc primum lacrimis victarum carmine fama est
> Eumenidum maduisse genas, nec regia conjunx
> Sustinet oranti, nec qui regit ima, negare:
> Eurydicenque vocant.
>
> (*Met.*, x, 45–48.)

---

[1] *Oxford Chaucer*, II, 489.

[2] See *Am.*, ii, vi, 49; *Am.*, iii, ix, 59–60; and *Met.*, xiv, 110–112.

[3] Skeat (*Oxford Chaucer*, II, 489) refers to Virgil's *Georgics*, i, 38, and iv, 453–457. But we have no conclusive evidence that Chaucer knew the *Georgics*.

In iv, 1116–1117, Chaucer puts into the mouth of Pandarus a prayer to Juno for aid, which is not in the Italian:

> And blisful Juno, thourgh hir grete mighte
> Shal, as I hope, hir grace unto us sende.

A similar instance occurs in iv, 1149, where Criseyde prays to Jove,

> O Jove, I deye, and mercy I beseche!

The tears of woe that Troilus and Criseyde wept at the prospect of separation (iv, 1138–1139) Chaucer says were more bitter than those of Myrrha, daughter of Cinyras, king of Cyprus, whose tears after she was changed into a myrrh-tree appeared through the bark as myrrh. For the story, see *Met.*, x, 298–502.[1]

In iv, 1188–1208, though Chaucer is here again translating Boccaccio closely, he introduces into the speech of Troilus, when he believes Criseyde to be dead, a reference to Minos as a judge in the lower regions, and another to Atropos, one of the Fates. For the former of these he was probably indebted to *Æneid*, vi, 431–433,[2] or to *Thebaid*, viii, 101–103;[3] for the latter, probably to *Thebaid*, iii, 68.

An appeal to Jove occurs in iv, 1337,

> Or elles, see ich never Joves face.

---

[1] *Oxford Chaucer*, II, 491.   [2] *Ibid.* 492.

[3] Wise, p. 15.

When Chaucer comes to the emotional crisis just preceding the departure of Criseyde from Troy, where the two lovers are vowing eternal fidelity, he inserts from time to time bits of classical lore appropriate to the situation. Troilus, speaking of Calchas, says to Criseyde,

> Your fader is in sleighte as Argus yed. (iv, 1459.)

This is from *Met.*, i, 625.[1]

In iv, 1537–1540, Criseyde prays that Juno may send her to the lower world if she proves false to Troilus:

> Be fals to you, my Troilus, my knight,
> Saturnes doughter, Juno thorugh hir might,
> As wood as Athamante do me dwelle
> Eternally in Stix, the put of helle.[2]

The story of Athamas' madness, caused by Juno, is found in *Met.*, iv, 416–561.[3]

For Boccaccio's simple oath,

> But I swear to thee by these amorous
> Darts which for thee have entered my heart,[4]

Chaucer has substituted the elaborate assemblage of the gods:

> And this on every god celestial
> I swere it you, and eek on eche goddesse.
> On every Nymphe and deite infernal,
> On Satiry and Fauny more and lesse,

---

[1] *Oxford Chaucer*, II, 493.

[2] For Styx as the pit of hell, see Wise, pp. 17–18.

[3] *Oxford Chaucer*, II, 493. See Lowes (*Mod. Phil.*, XIV, 715–717) for a suggestion of Dante's influence here.   [4] Rossetti, p. 226.

That halve goddes ben of wildernesse;
And Attropos my threed of lyf to breste
If I be fals; now trowe me if thow leste.
(iv, 1541–1547.)

With lines 1543–1546, on the "halve goddes of wildernesse," compare the two following passages from Ovid:

Sunt mihi semidei, sunt rustica numina, Nymphae
Faunique Satyrique et monticolae Silvani.
(*Met.*, i, 192–193.)

Illum ruricolae, silvarum numina, Fauni
Et Satyri fratres et tunc quoque carus Olympus
Et Nymphae flerunt. (*Met.*, vi, 392–394.) [1]

Criseyde strengthens her avowal of faithfulness by calling on the Trojan river Simois to bear her witness, and on the day that she shall be "untrewe" to Troilus to return backward to its source:

And thou Simoys, that as an arwe clere
Thorugh Troye rennest ay downward to the see
Ber witnesse of this word that seyd is here,
That ilke day that ich untrewe be
To Troilus, myn owne herte free,
That thou retorne backwarde to thy welle.
(iv, 1548–1553.)

This apostrophe combines parts of the two following passages from Ovid: [2]

Vivet Maeonides, Tenedos dum stabit et Ide
Dum rapidas Simois in mare volvet aquas.
(*Am.*, i, xv, 9–10.)

---

[1] Skeat has given this reference in *Oxford Chaucer*, II, 493.
[2] Fansler, *Chaucer and the Roman de la Rose*, pp. 46–47.

"Cum Paris Oenone poterit spirare relicta,
Ad fontem Xanthi versa recurret aqua."
Xanthe, retro propera, versaeque recurrite lymphae!
Sustinet Oenonen deseruisse Paris.
                                    (*Her.*, v, 29–32.)

The idea of the river turning backward is used by Oenone to recall to Paris his protestation of love for her. The connection here also, as in the *Troilus*, is with Troy. The Xanthus was another stream near Troy often connected with the city in Ovid's poetry. It is mentioned along with the Simois in the following passage:

Ilion et Tenedos Simoisque et Xanthus et Ide
Nomina sunt ipso paene timenda sono.
                                    (*Her.*, xiii, 53–54.)

That Chaucer should substitute the name of the other of these Trojan rivers for the one used by Ovid is of no consequence. He might have been recalling the passage from memory, or more likely he used Simois for the sake of his rhythm. That the Simois was closely associated with Troy elsewhere in his reading of Ovid may be seen from the following passages:

Hac ibat Simois, haec est Sigeia tellus,
Hic steterat Priami regia celsa senis.
                                    (*Her.*, i, 33–34.)

"Haec," inquit, "Troiast" (muros in litore fecit),
Hic tibi sit Simois; haec mea castra puta.
                                    (*Ars Am.*, ii, 133–134.)

Non patrium Simoenta petis, sed Thybridas undas.
(*Her.*, vii, 145.)[1]

Running through Criseyde's passionate protestations of faithfulness are appeals to the gods to bear witness:

I mene, as helpe me Juno, hevene quene.   (iv, 1594.)

Now, for the love of Cynthia the shene.   (iv, 1608.)

And blisful Venus lat me never sterve.   (iv, 1661.)

But Juppiter, that of his might may do
The sorwful to be glad, so yeve us grace.
(iv, 1683–1684.)

Criseyde quotes directly from Ovid when she says that love is full of fear:

Love is thing ay ful of busy drede.   (iv, 1645.)

Res est solliciti plena timoris amor.   (*Her.*, i, 12.) [2]

Book iv thus closes on a high emotional note which is vibrant with reminiscences of the Classics.

Book V

Though the direct sources of the references to "Joves," line 2, "angry Parcas, sustren three," line 3, and "Lachesis," line 7, of the opening stanza

---

[1] Certainly the idea of Criseyde's apostrophizing the Simois came to Chaucer from Ovid rather than from Statius as suggested by Mr. Wise (p. 19), who cites *Thebaid*, viii, 553, "where Tydeus says that the Inachus and Achelous will sooner flow backwards than Eteocles will allow his brother to escape when once in his power within the walls of Thebes." Here there is no connection with Troy.

[2] *Oxford Chaucer*, II, 494.

of Book v cannot be identified, they are, of course, classical in origin.

Where Boccaccio says "the Sun had twice melted," Chaucer uses a specific mythological allusion:

> The *golden-tressed* Phebus heighte on-lofte. (v, 8.)

This epithet is applied to Phoebus by Valerius Flaccus, *Argonauticon*, iv, 92: "Sol auricomus." [1]

Where Boccaccio says,

> He blasphemed the day that he was born,
> And the gods and the goddesses and nature,[2]

Chaucer mentions the gods by name:

> He cursed Jove, Apollo, and eek Cupyde,
> He cursed Ceres, Bacus, and Cipryde.
> (v, 207–208.)

A fitting comparison to use in describing the agony of Troilus was afforded Chaucer in the punishment of Ixion related in *Met.*, iv, 460, and x, 42.[3]

> To bedde he goth, and weyleth there and torneth
> In furie, as dooth he Ixion in helle.
> (v, 211–212.)

In the midst of the passage where Troilus is giving directions about his ashes after death (v, 302–

---

[1] Wise (p. 20) attributes it to Martianus Capella. But see p. 343.
[2] Rossetti, p. 239.
[3] See Kittredge, "Chaucer's Medea and the Date of the Legend of Good Women," *P. M. L. A.*, XXIV, 2, 351, note 9.

322), in which Chaucer is imitating the *Teseide*,[1]
we find him reverting to Ovid:

> The owl eek, which that hight Ascaphilo,
> Hath after me shrighte alle thise nightes two.
>   (v, 319–320.) [2]

How Ascalaphus became an owl, the bird of ill
omen, is related in *Met.*, v, 534 ff.[3] See also *Met.*,
vi, 432; x, 453; xv, 791.

It is probably impossible to say with certainty
what is the source of v, 601–602:

> As Juno was unto the blood Thebane,
> For which the folk of Thebes caught hir bane.

Mr. Wise [4] cites Dante, *Inf.*, xxx, 1, and calls attention to Boccaccio's frequent allusions to Juno's
hatred of Thebes in the *Teseide*. Skeat [5] refers to
Thebaid, i, 12. Ovid, also, furnished sufficient information on this point to account for Chaucer's
reference. In *Met.*, iii, 131–315, there is an account
of Juno's jealousy of Semele, daughter of Cadmus,
the mythical founder of Thebes. Juno in disguise
visits Semele, who was the mother of Bacchus by
Jupiter, and persuades her to ask for a gift from
Jove, which causes her death. Again in *Met.*, iv,

[1] Kittredge, *Harvard Studies in Classical Philology*, XXVIII, 110–
112.

[2] Though Mr. Wise, p. 22, suggests *Thebaid*, iii, 510, and *Æn.*, iv,
462, in connection with these two lines, neither says anything about
Ascalaphus, who was turned into an owl.

[3] *Oxford Chaucer*, II, 496.

[4] Page 23; see also Lowes, *Mod. Phil.*, XIV, 139.

[5] *Oxford Chaucer*, II, 497.

416–542, Juno visits Hades to persuade the Furies
to torment Athamas and Ino, king and queen of
Thebes, because they neglected her shrine. The
Furies, consenting, drive Athamas mad, and he
kills his own son. Ino in despair rushes over a pre-
cipice and would have perished, had not Venus
persuaded Neptune to transform her and her child,
whom she carries in her arms, into sea deities.
Immediately upon Ino's disappearance the Theban
matrons, companions of Ino, lament the unhappy
fate of their mistress and are turned by Juno in her
displeasure into stones and birds.

Charybdis as a devouring monster (v, 644) would
be well known to Chaucer from Ovid,

> Hunc ubi Trojanae remis avidamque Charybdin,
> (*Met.*, xiv, 75.)

and from Virgil,

> Dextrum Scylla latus, laevum implacata Charybdis.
> (*Æn.*, iii, 420.)

Taking Boccaccio's words, "the sun has entered
into new errors," Chaucer translates them,

> And that the sonne went his cours unright. (v, 661.)

He then appends on his own account an effective
allusion to Phaethon's disastrous attempt to drive
Apollo's chariot across the heavens.[1] Troilus says

[1] This story Chaucer has told before in the *House of Fame*,
ll. 941–956.

he dreads always lest the sun's son may still be
alive and drive his father's car amiss:

> . . . . y-wis, me dredeth ever-mo
> The sonne's sone, Pheton, be on-lyve,
> And that his fadres cart amis he dryve.
> (v, 663–665.)

Ovid's account, whence Chaucer's knowledge came,
is found in *Met.*, ii, 34–324.[1]

Boccaccio's "among the dead in hell," Chaucer
has rendered mythologically:

> That Manes, which that goddes been of peyne.   (v, 892.)

For the source of this idea Skeat [2] refers to *Æn.*,
vi, 743. Professor Wise [3] thinks it probably came
from the *Thebaid*, where "the notion that the
Manes torment those who have caused violent
deaths is several times expressed by Statius."

Criseyde appeals to Jupiter in v, 957, and to
Pallas in v, 977 and 999. Troilus thinks his dream
of the boar was sent to him by Jupiter as a warning
(v, 1446), and he prays Jove's curse upon Cassandra (v, 1525).

In v, 1107, the epithet "laurer-crowned" applied
by Chaucer to Phoebus must have come from
Ovid's "laurigo . . . Phoebo" (*Ars Am.*, iii, 389).[4]
"Nisus doughter" in v, 1110, is a reference to the
story of how Scylla, the daughter of Nisus, was

---

[1] *Oxford Chaucer*, II, 497.   [2] *Ibid.*, p. 498.
[3] Pages 23–24.   [4] *Oxford Chaucer*, II, 500.

changed into the bird Ciris, because she aided her father's enemy Minos [1] (*Met.*, viii, 9–151).[2]

As a kind of prologue to his summary of the *Thebaid*, Chaucer gives (v, 1464–1483) the story of Meleager, evidently thinking him the ancestor of Tydeus, who played so important a part at Thebes. The account of Meleager and the Calydonian boar hunt is told at length in *Met.*, viii, 271–546.[3]

For the anger of Diana, who sent the boar (v, 1464–1470), see *Met.*, viii, 273–283.

For Atalanta,

> A mayde, oon of this world the best y-preysed,   (v, 1473.)

see *Met.*, viii, 318–328, and 425–427.

For

> Ther roos a contek and a greet envye, (v, 1479.)

see *Met.*, viii, 430 ff.

For

> But how this Meleagre gan to dye, (v, 1482.)

see *Met.*, viii, 445–525.

In v, 1485–1510, Chaucer gives a rendering of his Latin summary of the twelve books of the *Thebaid*. In v, 1792, he mentions, apparently imitating *Thebaid*, xii, 816, three Latin poets whose works he has made use of in the *Troilus* — Ovid, Virgil, and Statius.[4]

---

[1] Cf. *Legend of Good Women*, ll. 1908–1920.
[2] *Oxford Chaucer*, II, 500.   [3] *Ibid.*, p. 501.
[4] *Ibid.*, p. 503; Wise, pp. 35–36.

The arraignment of the heathen gods in v, 1849–1855, has been the subject of considerable discussion: [1]

> Lo here, of Payens corsed olde rytes,
> Lo here, what alle hir goddes may availle;
> Lo here, these wrecced worldes appetytes;
> Lo here, the fyn and guerdon for travaille
> Of Jove, Appollo, of Mars, of swich rascaille!
> Lo here, the forme of olde clerkes speche
> In poetrye, if ye hir bokes seche.

Whatever the source of these lines, they indicate that Chaucer appreciated the remarkable extent to which the use of local color and the constant appeals by the chief characters to heathen divinities had entered into the poem. He had succeeded so amazingly with his attempt to create an illusion of antiquity that it may be he was anxious lest he be criticized for paganism, and so hastened to announce his adherence to the true religion before the poem was finished.

But there was also danger of the wrath of the Church descending upon him for the tendency to

[1] Professor Hamilton (*Chaucer's Indebtedness to Guido delle Colonna*, pp. 90–92) attributes these lines to the influence of the *Historia Trojana*. Professor Young (*Origin and Development of the Story of Troilus and Criseyde*, pp. 120–121) thinks that they may be due to Benoit's *Roman de Troie*. Professor Kittredge (*Harvard Studies in Classical Philology*, XXVIII, 118) suggests that they may owe something to Emilia's blasphemy in the *Teseide*. Professor Tatlock ("The Epilog of Chaucer's Troilus," *Mod. Phil.*, XLVIII, 128 ff.) thinks that Chaucer was here defending himself against attacks from the Church upon the ground that he had made *Troilus and Criseyde* too pagan.

!echery in the poem. That the authority of the
mediaeval Church in such matters as involved the
deadly sin of *Luxuria* was strong, is clear from the
conversion of Boccaccio, who was a greater sinner
in this way than Chaucer, and whose repentance
seems to have been sincere.[1] In the Prologue to
the *Canterbury Tales* (ll. 654–662), Chaucer indicates his wholesome respect for the archdeacon's
curse:

> He wolde techen him to have non awe,
> In swich cas, of the erchedeknes curs,
> But if a mannes soule were in his purs;
> For in his purs he sholde y-punisshed be.
> "Purs is the erchedeknes helle," seyde he.
> *But wel I woot he lyed right in dede;*
> *Of cursing oghte ech gilty man him drede —*
> *For curs wol slee, right as assoilling saveth —*
> *And also war him of a significavit.*

It was the archdeacon's court, of course, which
would have jurisdiction over cases dealing with
any writings conducive to the sin of lechery.

Though Chaucer has been unwilling to sacrifice
his art upon the ecclesiastical altar, he makes whatever reconciliation he can with the Church in the
end. This is the same spirit that prompted the
"retraction" at the end of the *Canterbury Tales*.[2]
As yet in the *Troilus*, however, through his sense of

[1] See W. E. Farnham, "England's Discovery of the Decameron,"
P. M. L. A., XXXIX, 123–139.

[2] See Tatlock, "Chaucer's Retractions," *P. M. L. A.*, XXVII,
4, 529, note 1.

humor and his natural buoyancy of spirit, he kept
a balanced perspective with regard to literary and
ecclesiastical values. At the end of the *Canterbury
Tales* he was old and poor, so that the Church more
easily secured a hold upon his imagination and
inflamed it unduly.[1]

But gratifying his artistic soul led Chaucer into
another anxiety: namely, for the reception of his
poem at the court on account of its realism. Small
wonder, therefore, that he insists throughout the
poem that he is not responsible for the frailties of
Criseyde, that he is merely telling the story as he
found it in his "auctor Lollius." With this venture
into realism he was running counter to the traditions of both chivalry and the Church.

The Character of Criseyde

It is evident that when Chaucer came to write
the *Troilus and Criseyde* his mind was pretty well

---

[1] I wonder if, after all, Chaucer's failure to mention Boccaccio by
name is the deep dark mystery that we have imagined and given ingenious reasons to explain. It may be nothing more than a desire on
Chaucer's part to avoid any connection with so *risqué* a story-teller as
Boccaccio. See Kittredge, *Harvard Studies in Classical Philology*,
XXVIII, 63, on the *Monk's Tale*. Professor Farnham's argument
(*P. M. L. A.*, XXXIX, 123–139) that the *Decameron* itself was not
known in Engand in Chaucer's day does not preclude the probability
of Boccaccio's having been notorious as a teller of lascivious tales even
among people who had never seen his book. In the days when books
were few, tales were carried by word of mouth. See, for example, the
Man of Law's Tale and the *Clerk's Tale*. I doubt whether Ascham had
ever really read Boccaccio's tales when he inveighed so vigorously
against Italian literature in the *School-master*.

saturated with his reading in the Latin poets. The *Æneid* furnished him some material, though not a great deal. The *Thebaid* is referred to in ii, 83–108, some passages are taken from it, and a summary of it is given in v, 1485–1509. But above all this, his fondness for Ovid pervades the whole poem. From the *Metamorphoses* he knew an abundant supply of stories that were most appropriate for allusion and comparison. This wealth of classical lore enabled him to enrich his poem as compared with Boccaccio's in at least two effective ways: first, by it he produced an impression of greater vividness and reality; and second, he secured the effect of local color, which he desired in order to support the fiction that it was a translation of a Latin work upon the Trojan War by one Lollius.[1]

But as the *Troilus and Criseyde* was to be a love-poem, Chaucer's thoughts were inevitably directed to the love-poetry of Ovid. He borrowed, as we have already seen, from the *Amores*, *Remedia Amoris*, and *Heroides*. But here, as in the *House of Fame*, it was the *Heroides* with its treatment of feminine nature that was most stimulating to his imagination. Ovid's poem was a collection of Epistles dealing with woman and love—six of them especially with Trojan affairs, and three with the

[1] See Kittredge, *Harvard Studies in Classical Philology*, **XXVIII**, 47–133.

cause of the Trojan War itself. These three were Oenone's letter to Paris after he had deserted her for Helen (*Her.*, v), Paris' letter to Helen (*Her.*, xv),[1] and Helen's reply to Paris (*Her.*, xvi). From two of these he took suggestions from which to evolve two of his minor characters. Oenone in her letter to Paris (*Her.*, v, 94) mentions Deiphobus as one of the leaders in Troy, and Paris in his Epistle to Helen (*Her.*, xv, 360), speaks of his brother Deiphobus as one whom he had overcome in a physical contest. This character of Deiphobus Chaucer has used as the central figure of a realistic scene from the family life of the royal house of Troy (*Troilus*, ii, 1394–1708).[2]

Again, both Paris (*Her.*, xv, 279–280) and Oenone (v, 113–114) refer to Cassandra and her prophecies of evil. This conception of Cassandra Chaucer has effectively used in v, 1450–1526, where he makes her tell Troilus how Diomed has supplanted him in Criseyde's affections. Though Boccaccio mentions Cassandra, he makes her more an ill-natured person who twits her brother for loving Criseyde, whom she does not consider worthy of his high lineage.[3]

---

[1] References to the *Heroides* are numbered as in Ehrwald's edition of Merkel.

[2] See Kittredge, *Harvard Studies in Classical Philology*, XXVIII, 52.

[3] Rossetti, p. 287.

But these Epistles in which Ovid reveals the character of the heroine who was the cause of the siege of Troy were to have a greater influence still upon Chaucer's poem. Let us consider the character of Criseyde as Chaucer has portrayed her. She is a new type of woman in mediaeval literature, very different from Boccaccio's Griseida, much more complex in her nature, and in every way more lifelike than any of her prototypes. It is worth observing that Book ii of *Troilus and Criseyde*, which is most distinctly the Criseyde book, as Book i is the Troilus book, shows the least borrowing from Boccaccio of any of the five books of the poem. The percentage of lines borrowed from the *Filostrato* in Book i of *Troilus and Criseyde* is twenty-five; of Book iii, twenty; of Book iv, forty-seven; of Book v, forty-six; while that of Book ii is only thirteen. If Boccaccio furnished little more than the place which Criseyde occupies in the plot of the story, where then did Chaucer find this character? Though we might admit that he was capable of creating her, it does not seem likely, from what we know of the practice of mediaeval writers, that he would ignore a source already familiar and approved. And such a source there was under his very eyes in the Helen Epistles of Ovid. Here was a heroine in much the same position as the heroine of the Troilus story, beloved by both a

Greek and a Trojan, the wife or mistress, first of the one, then of the other. It was inevitable that Ovid's Helen should have been prominently in Chaucer's thoughts while he was shaping the character of his own heroine Criseyde. And a comparison of the two characters reveals, I think, convincing similarities.

1. Helen was a married woman. She was perfectly aware of the end to which Paris' letter was inviting her:

> Quod petis, ut furtim praesentes ista loquamur,
>   Scimus quid captes conloquiumque voces.
> Sed nimium properas, et adhuc tua messis in herba est.
>   (*Her.*, xvi, 261–263.)

Criseyde, who was a widow, knew to what conclusion her yielding to Troilus led:[1]

> With that she gan hir eyen on him caste
> Ful easily, and ful debonairly,
> Avysing hir, and hyed not to faste
> With never a word, but seyde him softely,
> Myn honour sauf, I wol wel trewely,
> And in swich forme as he can now devyse,
> Receyven him fully to my servyse.
>   (*Tr.*, iii 155–161.)

Neither Helen nor Criseyde was blind to the consequences.

2. Helen pretends that she wishes to be let alone by Paris:

[1] See Kittredge, *Chaucer and his Poetry*, pp. 131–132.

Desine molle, precor, verbis convellere pectus,
  Neve mihi, quam te dicis amare, noce
Sed sine, quam tribuit sortem fortuna, tueri,
  Nec spolium nostri turpe pudoris habe.
                              (*Her.*, xvi, 111–114.)

So Criseyde reproaches Pandarus for coming to her
with Troilus' love:

With this he stente, and caste adoun the heed,
And she bigan to breste a-wepe anoon.
And seyde, "Allas, for wo! why nere I deed?
For of this world the feith is al agoon!
Allas! what sholden straunge to me doon,
When he, that for my beste freend I wonde,
Ret me to love, and sholde it me defende? . . .
                              (*Tr.*, ii, 409–427.)

But Helen follows her protest immediately with the
argument that Venus had decreed it as Paris has
said. So Criseyde follows up her disavowal with a
question to Pandarus if Troilus "can wel speke of
love," for a knowledge of this will guide her in her
action. The amorous tendency of both women is
skilfully revealed.

3. Helen insists at first that she cannot forget
her modesty, that so far her fame is unspotted and
hitherto without a fault. Through her no paramour has cause to glory:

Fama tamen clara est, et adhuc sine crimine vixi,
  Et laudem de me nullus adulter habet
                              (*Her.*, xvi, 17–18.)

Criseyde tells Pandarus she will try to please Troilus so far as is consistent with keeping her "honor

safe." And when she reflects that Troilus is no boaster, she says that he will never get a chance to boast of her favors:

> But elles wol I fonde
> Myn honour sauf, plese him fro day to day.
>
> (*Tr.*, ii, 479–480.)

> That he may make avaunt, by juste cause:
> He shal me never binde in swiche a clause.
>
> (*Tr.*, ii, 727–728.)

4. Helen says that men's words are said to be false and women are too credulous:

> Sed quia credulitas damno solet esse puellis.
> Verbaque dicuntur vestra carere fide.
>
> (*Her.*, xvi, 39–40.)

Criseyde says:

> eek men be so untrewe,
> That right anon as cessed is hir lest,
> So cesseth love, and forth to love a newe.
>
> (*Tr.*, ii, 786–788.)

> The treson, that to womman hath be do. (*Tr.*, ii, 793.)

5. Helen argues with herself that she is not made of iron, she cannot resist Paris' love:

> Ferrea sim, si non hoc ego pectus amem.
> Ferrea, crede mihi, non sum.
>
> (*Her.*, xvi, 136–137.)

Criseyde says that there is no reason why she should not love, if she pleases; "I am nought religious."

> Shal I nat loven, in cas if that me leste?
> What par dieux! I am nought religious.
>
> (*Tr.*, ii, 758–759.)

Both again amorous, each in her own way and age, one classical, the other mediaeval.

6. Helen, in replying to Paris' suggestion that others had sinned in the way he was urging her to do, said: "You say others have sinned in this way and few matrons are chaste. Yet if I sin, I shall not be able to say that I was ignorant, and there will be no mistake, as was the case with my mother Leda, to take the fault away":

> At peccant aliae, matronaque rara pudica est.
> (*Her.*, xvi, 41.)

> Nil ego, si peccem, possum nescisse, nec ullus
> Error, qui facti crimen obumbret, erit.
> (*Her.*, xvi, 47–48.)

Criseyde says:

> Al be I not the firste that did amis,
> What helpeth that to do my blame away.
> (*Tr.*, v, 1067–1068.)

7. Helen says there have been rumors about her and Paris, and she advises Paris to dissemble his love:

> .... sensi mala murmura vulgi,
> Et quasdam voces rettulit Aethra mihi.
> At tu dissimula, nisi si desistere mavis.
> (*Her.*, xvi, 149–151.)

Criseyde writes to Troilus that there have been rumors about them and that she will try to dissemble to amend them:

For I have herd wel more than I wende,
Touchinge us two, how thinges han y-stonde;
Which I shal with dissimulinge amende.

(Tr., v, 1611–1613.)

8. Helen is inexperienced in writing:

Nunc quoque, quod tacito mando mea verba libello,
Fungitur officio littera nostra novo.

(Her., xvi, 143–144.)

Criseyde says:

God helpe me so, this is the firste lettre
That ever I wroot, ye, al or any del.

(Tr., ii, 1213–1214.)

9. Chaucer has taken Helen's argument to Paris
about how widely she will be defamed through the
world, if she yields to him, and has put it into the
mouth of Criseyde after she has decided to sur-
render to the advances of Diomed:

Non ita contemno volucris praeconia famae,
Ut probris terras impleat illa meis.
Quid de me poterit Sparte, quid Achaia tota,
Quid gentes Asiae, quid tua Troja loqui?
Quid Priamus de me, Priami quid sentiet uxor,
Totque tui fratres Dardanidesque nurus.

(Her., xvi, 207–212.)

Criseyde says,

Allas! of me unto the worldes ende,
Shal neither been y-writen nor y-songe
No good word, for thise bokes wol me shende,
O, rolled shal I been on many a tonge!
Through-out the world my belle shal be ronge;
And wommen most wol hate me of alle.
Allas, that swich a cas me sholde falle.

(Tr., v, 1058–1064.)

10. Fate plays a large part with both Helen and Criseyde. Paris urges, and Helen accepts it, that the gods decreed her for his wife:

> Namque ego divino monitu, ne nescia pecces,
> Advehor, et coepto non leve numen adest.
> *(Her.,* xv, 17–18.)

> Sic placuit fatis! quae ne convellere temptes
> Accipe cum vera dicta relata fide.
> *(Her.,* xv, 41–42.)

Likewise Diomed urges upon Criseyde that Troy is a doomed city, and for that very reason her father has brought her to the Greek camp:

> What wene ye your wyse fader wolde
> Han yeven Antenor for yow anoon,
> If he ne wiste that the citee sholde
> Destroyed been? Why, nay, so mote I goon!
> He knew ful wel ther shal not scapen oon
> That Troyan is; and for the grete fere,
> He dorste not, ye dwelte lenger there.
> *(Tr.,* v, 904–910.)

> For Troye is brought in swich a Jupartye,
> That, it to save, is now no remedye.
> *(Tr.,* v, 916–917.)

Diomed's argument of Fate prevails with Criseyde,[1] as Paris' does with Helen, for she is convinced that it was of no use for her to return:

> Ritorning in hir soule ay up and doun
> The wordes of this sodein Diomede,
> His greet estat, and peril of the toun,

---

[1] See Kittredge, *Chaucer and his Poetry,* p. 117.

And that she was allone and hadde nede
Of freendes help; and thus bigan to brede
The cause why, the sothe for to telle,
That she tok fully purpos for to dwelle.

(Tr., v, 1023–1029.)

11. The mental processes of Helen and Criseyde
are similar. The first part of Helen's letter is one
long consideration back and forth whether she
shall yield to Paris' entreaties. (See *Her.*, xvi.)
Criseyde is represented by Chaucer as going over
the whole question in her mind, after Pandarus has
gone, whether it is advisable to accept Troilus as
a lover (*Tr.*, ii, 659 ff.). [1]

12. Helen and Criseyde were both untrue, Helen
to her marriage vow and Criseyde to her pledge to
Troilus. [2]

The conclusion is unescapable, I think, that
Chaucer owed much to Ovid's Helen in developing
the character of Criseyde. [3] It is not to be expected
that Chaucer should reproduce the ideas in the
Epistles of Paris and Helen. The circumstances
were in many respects different, and especially the
details. Chaucer's story was pretty definitely
marked out for him in the *Filostrato*. He had no

[1] See W. G. Dodd, *Courtly Love in Chaucer and Gower*, pp. 162–
166.

[2] See *Ibid.*, p. 159.

[3] I had developed this theory of Helen and Criseyde before I was
aware that Professor Kittredge had made the suggestion that possibly
Helen was vaguely in Benoit's mind in his treatment of Briseida. See
Kittredge, *Date of Chaucer's Troilus and Other Chaucer Matters*, p. 72.

desire to alter the main facts of Boccaccio's narrative; he was not interested in creating a new plot; he was concerned with a study of the characters that he found already in the story and of their emotions. To Ovid the climax of the love of Paris and Helen was their union; to Chaucer the climax of the love of Troilus and Criseyde was their separation. Each uses Fate for his chief agent. Paris in the weakness of his case resorts to Fate to bolster up his arguments; Criseyde in the weakness of her case for not returning to Troilus listens to Diomed as he urges the doom of Troy. But, after all, the real argument that prevailed in the mind of both Helen and Criseyde was that she was beloved. The amorous natures of both yielded to the allurements of love. Certainly nowhere else than in the *Heroides* could Chaucer have found so complete an analysis of feminine emotions, and nowhere except in the Helen Epistles a psychological study of a heroine so similar to his own.

THE LEGEND OF GOOD WOMEN

INTRODUCTORY

THE vividness and picturesqueness with which
Chaucer presents his story of Troy in the
Troilus and Criseyde show what release of power
had come to him through his recently acquired
conception of the classical ideal of beauty. The
congeniality of temperament between Ovid and
Chaucer must not be lost sight of. Had he known
all the other Latin poets, they would not have furnished him the inspiration that Ovid did. The results of this inspiration, however, did not come all
at once and full-blown. The truth of the growing
development of Chaucer's genius under the influence of Ovid is evident, I think, in the position
of the *Legend of Good Women*, which stands, as
scholars generally agree, between the *Troilus and
Criseyde* and the *Canterbury Tales*.

The puzzling question will not down: Why
should Chaucer, after having achieved such inde-
pendence from mediaeval convention in the *Troilus
and Criseyde*, revert to the form of poem he presents
in the *Legend of Good Women?*

To attempt an answer to this question necessi-
tates considering the effect of the *Troilus and*

Criseyde upon Chaucer's hearers — for it can be
pretty safely assumed that it was "published" by
being read aloud to the court — and later upon his
readers. When this poem first became known, it
must have created a sensation. It was the most
daring thing that Chaucer or any other mediaeval
poet had ever attempted, and it would be surprising if it had not aroused criticism. It was too advanced for his day. The lords, and particularly the
ladies, of the court had been brought up on the
woman-worship ideas of mediaeval poetry, and
here was their favorite poet setting off a charge of
dynamite under the very foundations of chivalry.
Chaucer had foreseen such criticism of the *Troilus*
and had made an effort to forestall it:

> Bisechinge every lady bright of hewe,
> And every gentil woman, what she be,
> That al be that Criseyde was untrewe,
> That for that gilt she be not wrooth with me.
> Ye may hir gilt in othere bokes see;
> And gladlier I wol writen, if you leste,
> Penelopëes trouthe and good Alceste.
> (*Tr.*, v, 1772–1778.)

Evidence of disapprobation in court circles is not
lacking in the Prologue to the *Legend of Good
Women*. The very censure of the older generation
may have served to render the *Troilus* popular with
the younger set, who, always eager for something
new, would welcome its modernness. Gower's refer-

ences to the poem in the *Confessio Amantis* [1] indicate that it must have been popular, and Lydgate testifies to the delight that lovers found in reading it:

> Gaff it the name of Troilus and Creseyde
> Which for to Redë lovers hem delyte,
> They ha(n) ther-Inne/so greet Devocion.
>
> (*Fall of Princes.*)

The situation was probably not dissimilar to the acclamations with which "stark realism" of our own day has been received by younger readers, much to the dismay and consternation of those who yet linger under the protecting shade of mid-Victorianism. The realistic love-story of *Troilus and Criseyde* in the fourteenth century was no doubt hailed with delight by the rising generation, while the devotees of chivalry of Richard's court were witnessing in it the crumbling of their inherited and carefully cherished ideals.

Such an understanding of the reception of the *Troilus* throws much light upon the Prologue to the *Legend of Good Women*. For after making due allowance for the conventional form of the Prologue as well as for the playful humor of Chaucer, we must admit a certain amount of truth underlying the allegory. Outside the warmth of personal feeling that pervades the Prologue, the very mediaeval

---

[1] Bk. iv, ll. 2794–2797; v, 7597–7602; viii, 2531–2535.

dream-vision and allegorical form of the poem point significantly to criticism of the *Troilus*. It would be contrary to reason to assume that Chaucer was free from criticism by his contemporaries.[1] No author ever is. Hitherto too little attention has been paid to Chaucer's relation to his readers. He has been considered almost wholly from his own point of view as a writer. But a writer's public has a marked influence upon his work. Chaucer was certainly no less sensitive to the praise and blame of his readers than the poets of all the ages have been. To any literary artist popular favor and appreciation are precious. When these are withheld, he is in the Slough of Despond, unless perchance he be endowed with the temperamental robustness of a Browning. And even to him success was sweet. In the *Troilus* Chaucer was engaged in "creating" the taste of his readers, as this educative process is called by Wordsworth:

Every author, as far as he is great and at the same time *original*, has had the task of *creating* the taste by which he is to be enjoyed. . . . The predecessors of an original Genius of a high order will have smoothed the way for all that he has in common with them; — and much he will have in common; but for what is peculiarly his own, he will be called upon to clear and often to shape his own road: — he will be in the condition of Hannibal among the Alps.[2]

---

[1] See Lounsbury, *Studies in Chaucer*, III, 284–288.

[2] *Essay, Supplementary to the Preface*, Oxford ed., 1904, p. 951.

The *Troilus* was creating the taste that was to enjoy the *Canterbury Tales*.

Finding, however, that he had advanced too far for his public of the court with the *Troilus*, Chaucer suddenly reverts to the conventional mediaeval type of poem in the Prologue to the *Legend*. When his imagination had once gone so free in the *Troilus*, would he return to the fetters of the dream-vision of his own accord? Most assuredly, no. The criticism aimed at the *Troilus* was sufficiently strong to make him yield to the demand and write a poem in the accepted form that his critics would applaud.[1]

Though we are generally inclined to accept any testimony from Lydgate with some degree of reservation, it may be that he is right after all and that Chaucer wrote the *Legend of Good Women* at the request of the queen.[2] This view is corroborated by Speght:

For that some ladies of the Court took offence at Chaucer's large speeches against the untruth of women, the Queen enjoyned him to compile this book [*L. G. W.*] in the commendation of sundry maydens and wives, who showed themselves faithful to faithless men.[3]

---

[1] Chaucer, profiting by his previous experience at court, was prudent enough to begin even his *Canterbury Tales* with a romance rather than with a fabliau. And he was wise enough, as someone has observed before, to intersperse among the tales other romances to suit the taste of a large body of readers of his day.

[2] See Tatlock, *The Development and Chronology of Chaucer's Works*, pp. 104–114. On the reliability of Lydgate as a witness, see A. Brusendorff, *The Chaucer Tradition*, pp. 37–43.

[3] *Chaucer's Works*, 1598, Argument to *Legend of Good Women*.

Miss Hammond notes the testimony of Lydgate and Speght, but questions "whether they had any more information than Chaucer's own ambiguous words in the poem." [1] But we must be on our guard against such assumptions. We find that Miss Rickert has established the probable truth of another statement of Speght's, that Chaucer was a student at the Inner Temple, which later biographers ignored or denied on the ground of insufficient proof.[2] Note, too, the guarded position that Speght takes with regard to the presence of Chaucer at the wedding of Lionel with Violante Visconti.[3]

It is necessary to remember that personal matters could be and often were expressed under the guise of symbolism.[4] It is unquestioned that Chaucer has introduced much autobiographical matter into the Prologue to the *Legend* [5] — how he loved

[1] *Chaucer, A Bibliographical Manual*, p. 380.

[2] See Edith Rickert, "Was Chaucer a Student at the Inner Temple?" *Manly Anniversary Papers*, pp. 20–21.

[3] "Some write that he (Chaucer) with Petrarch was present at the marriage of Lionel, Duke of Clarence, with Violante, daughter of Galeasius, Duke of Milan: yet Paulus Jovius nameth not Chaucer, but Petrarch he saith was there. And yet it may well be." Speght, *Chaucer's Works*, 1598. Professor Cook ("The Last Months of Chaucer's Earliest Patron, Lionel, Duke of Clarence," *Trans. Conn. Acad. of Arts and Sciences*, XXI, 6 ff.) has shown that this statement of the case is all that the facts as known will justify.

[4] See Tatlock, *The Development and Chronology of Chaucer's Works*, p. 106.

[5] It makes no difference which Prologue is taken. Fortunately it is not necessary here to try to find our way out of the labyrinth that

books second only to outdoor nature; how many books he had in his library; how he had translated the *Romance of the Rose*, and what it contained; how he had written *Troilus and Criseyde*, in which a woman was unfaithful; how his little arbor was arranged, just the kind of thing that a city-bred man interested in nature would enjoy; how he was indebted to his French predecessors and contemporaries — all this he has told his readers; and besides, he has made some rather pointed comments apparently upon conditions in Richard's kingdom at this time. What is more natural than to believe that he has told us the actual truth about being in literary disfavor with the court for baring the nakedness of the romantic code of chivalry to which they clung so tenaciously? That Chaucer was using in the Prologue the conventionalities of French allegory is no argument against this view. Plainly it would never have done to treat the personal facts of his relations at court seriously and baldly. The popular French manner, therefore, suited him exceedingly well. We can but admire the ingenuity that directed him to the way out of the difficulty, which was through allegory and humor.

If then we agree that Chaucer is telling the truth,

scholars have created to hold the minotaur of the date of the two Prologues to the *Legend of Good Women*.

in part at least, and not indulging wholly in poetic fiction, when he says he was doing penance in the *Legend of Good Women* for offence given, we must see that the *Troilus* had offended because of its divergence from the recognized type. This explanation squares with reason and with the facts as given by Chaucer himself, and obviates the necessity of turning for an interpretation to allegory, that last infirmity of the critical mind.

There was no restriction upon the poet as to subject-matter except that the new poem should show the faithfulness of women in love. There were two reasons why Ovid's *Heroides* should occur to him at this time as offering suitable material for his poem. First, his use of the Classics in the *Troilus* had proved so successful from the point of view of art that it doubtless now seemed to him that a poem could be produced with the substance of it drawn from the Classics, especially from Ovid. Furthermore, Ovid had presented his heroines, not as belonging to the heroic past, but as lovers who might be of any time or age.[1] Modern in spirit and refined in feelings, they were just the thing to suit these ladies of the court.

[1] See Sellar (*Roman Poets of the Augustan Age*, p. 335), who says: "The Epistles [of Ovid] are thoroughly modern: they express the feelings and speak the language of refined women in a refined age."

But there remained the problem of the form for the poem. It must be the love-vision. How to combine the classical substance with the mediaeval type had to be solved. He had tried a blending of the two in the *House of Fame* [1] with unsatisfactory results so far as artistic unity was concerned. Plainly another experiment must be made here. So he adopted the love-vision plan for the Prologue, and followed it by the separate tales, chiefly from Ovid. As it proved, this too was not to satisfy him. Yet at this stage of his literary growth it appealed to his imagination. I do not believe the poet undertook the *Legend of Good Women* in anything but the liveliest spirits. Did he not introduce into English a new poetic form (heroic couplet) for this very poem? [2] Did it not offer him a means of using material from Ovid, the fascination of which was strong upon him? Did it not furnish an opportunity to placate the gossip of the court, which resented his former bold essay? Does not the Prologue display the sprightliness of fancy and the delight that a man takes in revealing the pleasure he finds in his occupations and recreations? Does he not maintain a spirit of banter at the end of several of the legends?

[1] See discussion of this point on p. 117.
[2] Chaucer's constant experimentation in metre and his increasing mastery of metrical form show his development as a metrician.

THE PROLOGUE

Line 503, Skeat has called Chaucer's favorite line:

> But pitee renneth sone in gentil herte.

It recurs in *Knight's Tale*, l. A 1761; *Merchant's Tale*, l. E 1986; *Squire's Tale*, l. F 479; and in *Man of Law's Tale*, l. B 660, where it appears as,

> As gentil herte is fulfild of pitee.

Skeat suggests no source for the line. Professor Lowes [1] refers it to Dante, *Inf.*, v, 100:

> Amor, che al cor gentil ratto s'apprende.

Professor Kittredge, however, has suggested to me the following lines from Ovid, which seem to be the real source of the idea:

> Quo quisque est major, magis est placabilis irae,
> Et faciles motus mens generosa capit.
> *(Tristia*, iii, v, 31–32.)

The objection to Dante's line as the original is that he is talking of *love*, which quickly kindles in the gentle heart. The sentiment is part of the episode of Paolo and Francesca. But Chaucer says and means *pity*, which is quite a different thing. Furthermore, the circumstances in Chaucer's poem correspond in idea with Ovid's. In his letter Ovid is imploring an unnamed friend, who had not deserted him in his disgrace as most of the others

[1] *Mod. Phil.*, XIV, 718.

had done, to use his good offices with Augustus to secure a mitigation of Ovid's punishment, at least to the extent of exile to a more agreeable place. His hope of success lies, as he says, in the nobility of the emperor. And he illustrates from nature,

> Corpora magnanimo satis est prostrasse leoni,
> Pugna suum finem, cum jacet hostis, habet:
> At lupus et turpes instant morientibus ursi
> Et quaecumque minor nobilitate fera.
>
> (*Tristia*, iii, v, 33–36.)

So the God of Love tells Chaucer that it is nobility of soul that moved the "gentil" lady to intercede for him. Ovid's *generosa* means "nobly born," and *placabilis irae* means "pity." *Capit faciles motus* is suitably rendered by "renneth." Chaucer has indeed made an admirable translation and adaptation of the passage. It is noteworthy, too, that in every one of the instances where the line is used by Chaucer, the idea of *major*, "of high station" (Chaucer's "gentil"), is present with the one who shows the pity.

THE LEGEND OF CLEOPATRA [1]

Without doubt it would seem to us moderns that Cleopatra was as notorious and flagrant a violator of the code of the Court of Love as one could

[1] As this is the only one of the Legends which has no material from Ovid or Virgil, it is included with the others here in order to form a complete study of the *Legend of Good Women* in relation to its sources.

imagine. But we must remember that she probably did not appear so to the Middle Ages, especially in her relations with Antony.[1] Even so,
Cleopatra's story as Chaucer gives it was not made
to hand for him, for none of the ancient historians
of her career had ever presented her in the light in
which she appears in the *Legend of Good Women*.
One finds there a story-poem of unusual dramatic
plot: the events move rapidly with little digression,
there is a sharp climax from which the action drops
to a vivid catastrophe, the character of the heroine
is deftly portrayed — and all within one hundred
and twenty-six lines.

For a true appreciation of this achievement, one
must determine, if possible, whence Chaucer knew
the story and consider how he has dealt with his
source.

Among the Latin authors [2] there seems to be
none which could have furnished the basis for
Chaucer's poem. The only proposal of a source

[1] See Lowes, *Journal of English and Germanic Philology*, VIII,
546–566.

[2] Skeat (*Oxford Chaucer*, III, 310) has called attention to Petrarch,
Appian, Dion Cassius, and Orosius as the chief sources for the history
of Cleopatra. Orosius gives merely a very brief summary. Dion
Cassius has a somewhat fuller history, from which alone, however,
Chaucer could not have evolved his legend, and which contains no
distinctive similarities. Appian makes only a few references to the
earlier relations of Antony with Cleopatra, his *De Bellis Civilibus*
breaking off before the declaration of war between Antony and Octavius. Plutarch's Life of Antony is a long and detailed account of

given serious consideration heretofore has been
that of Bech,[1] who suggested Florus for some of
Chaucer's details. Bech attributes to the influence
of Florus Chaucer's description of the sea-fight;
but this has been completely set aside by Professor
Schofield, who shows that Chaucer's battle is a
mediaeval one based upon contemporary accounts
of naval encounters.[2] Bech also refers to Florus for
Chaucer's use of the "purple sail" in describing
Cleopatra's ship. And though he admits that in the
description of Cleopatra's entombment of Antony
and her preparations for her own death Chaucer
appears quite original, he suggests that the ground-
work is from Florus. Professor Lounsbury has
rightly said that Bech's evidence amounts to little
more than the slight detail of the "purple sail"![3]
I think we may eliminate Florus' *Epitome* altogether as a source for Chaucer's poem, when we
consider that Boccaccio has two versions of the

his life and character, which sets forth no circumstance in common
with Chaucer not also found in Boccaccio, while the spirit and style of
Plutarch's narrative seem more foreign to Chaucer's.

Besides these authors I find that Suetonius and Paterculus have
short accounts; Eutropius gives the main facts of the history in a bare
outline; Virgil has a poetic description of the battle of Actium; and in
De Viris Illustribus, attributed usually to Aurelius Victor, there are
very short sketches of Antony and Cleopatra. In none of these, however, is there anything noteworthy in connection with Chaucer.

[1] *Anglia*, V, 314–318.

[2] "The Sea-Battle in Chaucer's Legend of Cleopatra," *Kittredge
Anniversary Papers*, pp. 139–152.

[3] *Studies in Chaucer*, II, 288.

story of Antony and Cleopatra [1] which contain all
that Bech claims for Florus — and much more; in
fact, they furnish all that Chaucer's imagination
needed out of which to produce his Cleopatra.
And just here lies the secret of this Legend. Because it is different from any previous treatment
of Cleopatra, critics have searched in vain for a
source. But it is idle to expect to find that Chaucer is following any older account which portrays
Cleopatra as he does. The *facts* that he uses, however, he obtained from Boccaccio, and he is careful
to assure his readers,

> And this is storial sooth, hit is no fable.

But the *composition* of the facts is all his own, for
he must create in Cleopatra a character fitted to
the company of "Cupid's Saints," who were, of
course, faithful in love. The bantering tone in the
three concluding lines of the poem indicate that
Chaucer was fully aware of the liberty he had taken
with the usual accounts.

It was natural that Chaucer should turn to Boccaccio's Latin works, for these were a storehouse
that he found useful many times. In this case the

---

[1] *De Casibus Virorum,* lib. vi, cap. 15, and *De Claris Mulieribus,*
cap. 86. Skeat (III, xxxvii) makes only this reference to Boccaccio:
"No doubt Chaucer also consulted Boccaccio's *De Claris Mulieribus,*
cap. 86, though he makes no special use of the account there given."
Bech also gives slight consideration to *De Claris Mulieribus* and to
De Casibus Virorum.

gains were doubly rich, for there he found two separate accounts of Cleopatra's career, just as he had used the two stories of Zenobia for his sketch of her in the *Monk's Tale*.[1] The difference between the point of view and purpose of the historian and of the poet is easily discernible in the beginning of Boccaccio's *De Casibus* and Chaucer's *Cleopatra*. The poet dramatically introduces his story with the assumption that Cleopatra was queen of Egypt, a fact which Boccaccio has been at much pains to explain.[2] Then Chaucer brings swiftly into view the great figure of Antony, a Roman senator, fitted by his proud nature and lofty position to be a suitable husband for the Egyptian queen. According to Boccaccio the real power of the whole of Asia seemed to be left to Antony after the death of Brutus and Cassius at Philippi.[3] Chaucer's idea of the success and pros-

[1] See *Oxford Chaucer*, V, 235.

[2] "Cleopatra vero a Ptolomaeo rege Lagi filio, per multos reges originem ducens, testamento patris, una cum fratre (cui nupserat) Aegypti regina successerat. Tandem viro opere suo veneno absumpto, a minore fratre (qui a Pompeio rex factus erat) spoliata regno, et carcere apud Pelusium servata, donec Julius Caesar victor Alexandriam devenit. Cujus, lusis custodibus, cum in conspectum venisset, eumque mira formositate sua coepisset ex concubitu praestito, absorpto jam undis fratre, sola Aegypti regno praeesse promeruit." (*De Casibus Virorum*, lib. vi, cap. 15.)

[3] "Hinc cum magis fortuna jam Caesaris, quam Antonii virtute, Brutus Cassiusque apud Philippos fusi, eidem totius Asiae merum reliquisse videretur imperium redeunte adversus Italiam Caesare, ipse adversus orientem contendit." (*Ibid.*)

perity of Antony in the Orient was suggested by the account in the *De Claris Mulieribus:* how he captured the king of Armenia and with him a great amount of treasure, which he cast into the lap of Cleopatra that he might win her indulgence to his love.[1] Though Chaucer intimates that Antony's martial success prompted him to become a rebel against Rome, he adds that above all this, the chief cause of strife between Antony and Cæsar was Antony's rejection of Octavia and his wedding Cleopatra. That the relation of Antony with Cleopatra meant the repudiation of Octavia, Boccaccio makes clear in both his accounts,[2] and he says the desertion of Octavia, the sister of Augustus, was the cause of the war between Antony and Cæsar.[3]

The representation of Cleopatra as the *wife* of Antony is one of the very striking similarities be-

[1] "Qui quidem Antonius cum fraude Arthabarzanem Armenie regem, olim Tigranis filium cum filiis, et satrapis cepisset, et thesauris permaximis spoliasset, atque argentea cathena victum traheret, ut avidam in suos amplexus provocaret effoeminatus venienti captivum regem cum omni ornatu, ac praeda dejecit in gremium." (*De Mulieribus,* cap. 86.)

[2] "Quo laeta munere cupidissima mulier, adeo blande flagrantem complexa est, ut repudiata Octavia Octaviani Caesaris sorore, illatem totis affectibus sibi uxorem jungeret." (*Ibid.*)

"Et per effusum libidinem conviviis vacans, in tantam trahi se permisit insaniam, ut desponsata Cleopatra repudium Octaviae juberet indici." (*De Casibus,* lib. vi, cap. 15.)

[3] "Sed quid? Jam ob repudium Octaviae, belli seminarium inter Octavianum et Antonium videbatur injectum." (*Ibid.*)

tween Chaucer and Boccaccio. In other versions of the Cleopatra story she is only his mistress, but Boccaccio is very clear upon this point, for he says,

Tandem Antonii primo pellex, inde conjunx effecta est.[1]

Chaucer's reiterated conception of Cleopatra as the wife [2] of Antony serves to give dignity to her character and to ennoble her grief and despair at his death. The description of the regal splendor and extravagance of the wedding, given so fully by Boccaccio,[3] Chaucer omits for the excellent reason that he assigns:

Hit were to longe, lest that I sholde slake
Of thing that bereth more effect and charge.
(*L. G. W.*, ll. 619–620.)

Lines 596–615 of the *Legend of Good Women*, which describe Cleopatra as "fair as is the rose in May" and Antony as a knight, "chivalrous," "gentle," "discreet," and "hardy," have, as Schofield has pointed out, a distinctly mediaeval color.[4] This is a reflection from the courtliness of the love-vision Prologue, which throughout softens and almost obliterates the grossness of the original story. This mediaeval coloring helped too, no doubt, the ladies and knights of Richard's court to visualize

[1] *De Casibus*, lib. vi, cap. 15.
[2] See *L. G. W.*, ll. 594, 615, 632, 663, 691.
[3] *De Mulieribus*, cap. 86.
[4] Schofield, *Kittredge Anniversary Paper*, p. 139.

more clearly as lovers these historical figures. Yet some of Chaucer's mediaeval description is, in point of fact, closely paralleled by passages in Boccaccio, who insists upon the madness and abandon of Antony's love.[1]

As the battle of Actium is not described in either of Boccaccio's accounts, Chaucer took advantage of the opportunity to introduce a sea-fight of a kind that was familiar to him and his readers.[2] For the long duration of the battle, however, ending in the defeat of Antony, and for his and Cleopatra's flight,[3] Chaucer goes back to Boccaccio.[4] The

[1] "Armisque depositis, non aliter, quam si Cleopatrae in sinu decus omne Romanae claritatis consisteret, in luxuriam et segniciem se dejecit. Et per effusam libidinem conviviis vacans, *in tantam trahi se permisit insaniam*, ut desponsata Cleopatra repudium Octaviae juberet indici." (*De Casibus*, lib. vi, cap. 15.)

[2] *L. G. W.*, ll. 624–649; cf. Schofield, pp. 142–151.

[3] *L. G. W.*, ll. 650–662.

[4] "Sed quid? Jam ob repudium Octaviae, belli seminarium inter Octavianum et Antonium videbatur injectum, et ob id actum est, ut congregatis ex utraque parte copiis iretur in illud, verum Antonius cum Cleopatra ornata *purpureis velis*, et aurea classe processere in Epirum, ubi cum obviis hostibus inita pugna terrestri cessere victi, et in classem se recipientes Antoniani in Actium redire, experturi navalis belli fortunam, adversus quos, Octavianus cum Agrippa genero factus obvius, nigenti cum classe mira audatia eos aggressus est, et susceptus acriter, *tenuit aliquandiu mars dubius pugnam in pendulo*." (*De Mulieribus*, cap. 86.)

"Sed postquam diu certatum, cum jam finis stolidae superbiae Antonii propinquaret, proras vertere coepere Aegyptii, fugaeque dux et princeps cum aurata navi, *velisque purpureis*, optatrix imperii, ac postulatrix egregia Cleopatra fuit. Quam continuo tumidus sponsor Antonius, abjecto navis praetore insigni consequutus est." (*De Casibus*, lib. vi, cap. 15.)

"purple sail," which Bech attributed to Florus, occurs in both accounts in Boccaccio. As will be seen, the circumstances in Boccaccio and Chaucer are the same, except that Boccaccio seems to treat satirically the distinguished Cleopatra as the leader of the flight, whereas Chaucer, depicting her as faithful even in battle, does not allow the point that she deserted her colleague. Instead he represents Antony as completely routed and his forces in disaster before the queen takes to flight:

> Til at the laste, as everything hath ende,
> Antony is shent, and put him to the flighte,
> And al his folk to-go, that best go mighte.
> Fleeth eek the queen, with al her purpre sail,
> For strokes, which that wente as thikke as hail;
> No wonder was, she mighte hit nat endure.
>
> (*L. G. W.*, ll. 651–656.)

According to Boccaccio, Antony and Cleopatra, after their defeat at Actium, retired into Egypt, where they made an effort to defend themselves, and finally surrendered in Alexandria. Chaucer, with poetic indifference to the historic consequence of facts, brings about the climax of Antony's suicide during the rout at Actium when he realizes that the day is lost and sees Cleopatra spreading her purple sails in flight. In the *manner* of Antony's death Chaucer agrees with both of Boccaccio's accounts, in which Antony retires into the royal mausoleum in Alexandria and there transfixes himself with a sword.

Cleopatra's unsuccessful efforts (recorded by Boccaccio) to induce Octavius after the death of Antony to become a victim to her charms, Chaucer passes over with the mere statement that she could find no favor with Cæsar.

> His wyf, that coude of Cesar have no grace,
> To Egypte is fled, for drede and for distresse.
>
> (*L. G. W.*, ll. 663–664.)

The portrayal of her as a faithful wife naturally excluded any hope of "grace" for Cleopatra from the brother of Octavia, whom Antony had deserted for the Egyptian.

In no other place in the story do Boccaccio and Chaucer differ so greatly as in the treatment of the catastrophe of Cleopatra's death. Yet they agree as to the manner of her death. With the historian she is a proud woman seeking every possible means to avoid becoming a part of Octavius' triumph in Rome. With the poet she is the builder of a sepulcher for her dead husband as a testimony of her grief for him. The richer the tomb, therefore, the greater proof of her love. Hence it was that she made it

> Of alle the rubies and the stones fyne
> In al Egipte that she coude finde;
> And putte ful the shryne of spycerye.
>
> (*L. G. W.*, ll. 673–675.)

The suggestion for the "spycerye" came no doubt from the passage in the *De Casibus* where Cleo-

patra enters the mausoleum to die surrounded by
many odors:

Eo quo suus jacebat Antonius, pluribus stipata odori-
bus, ac insignibus ornata regiis intrans. (lib. vi, cap. 15).

To emphasize Cleopatra's faithfulness to Antony, Chaucer puts into her mouth a lament (lines
681–695), attesting her loyalty while he was alive
and vowing her determination to die by his side.
From this lament men may see, he says, how true
women can be. The emotional climax of the
Legend is reached with this speech.

But before Cleopatra gives expression to her
"unreprovable wyfhod," she prepares a pit of adders hard by the "shryne," to serve for her own
death. In Boccaccio's versions the serpents are
applied to her veins in the mausoleum where Antony lay dead. Though citations of "pits of
snakes" elsewhere in literature have been made,[1]
none similar to Chaucer's description here has been
found.

His addition of the pit of adders to his story
need not, I think, surprise us. It is in accord with
his method throughout this *Legend* that his imagination has here produced from Boccaccio's simple
recital of fact a bit of subtle characterization,
when, in order to emphasize Cleopatra's deliberate

[1] See Tatlock, *Mod. Lang. Notes*, XXIX, 99–100; C. Brown, *Ibid.*,
p. 108.

intention to die near her husband, he makes her prepare the adders beforehand and hold them in keeping for the event. Boccaccio's bit of moralizing over Cleopatra's end, though quite foreign to Chaucer's conception, was probably sufficient to suggest the description of her entering the pit with naked body for the purpose of being stung to death:

Sic et meretrix foemina, dum non sua forte contenta est, adit a fortuna contracta, ut quae membra summis lenita delitiis in amplexibus libidinosis commendarat pluribus, ea vivente, vidente, ac consentiente a serpentibus lamberentur. (*De Casibus*, lib. vi, cap. 15.)

In the *Legend of Cleopatra* Chaucer's art is a process of selection and — of addition. While following the facts that he uses from the history of Cleopatra fairly closely, yet he deftly throws the emphasis upon the character he has cast for her as one of the women who were loyal in love. The Cleopatra that he has drawn for us is steadfast in devotion, scornful of death, and royal in her end.

The Legend of Thisbe

Chaucer refers the reader to Ovid for the story of Pyramus and Thisbe — "Naso seith thus" (line 725). It is remarkable how closely he follows Ovid's narrative (*Met.*, iv, 55–166), and yet with what pervasiveness his imagination plays upon it and leaves there his own creative impress.

The diverse purposes of the two poets in telling the story account for the difference in treatment. Ovid was intent upon explaining how the fruit of the mulberry tree, once white, became black, the story itself being more or less subsidiary to the metamorphosis:

> an quae poma alba ferebat
> Ut nunc nigra ferat contactu sanguinis arbor.
> (*Met.*, iv, 51–52.)

> Nam color in pomo est, ubi permaturuit, ater.
> (*Met.*, iv, 165.)

Chaucer, whose theme was the constancy of a woman in love, omits all reference to the mulberry tree and concentrates upon the lovers.

Chaucer, following Ovid as to the location in Babylon, gives more prominence to the fathers of the two lovers, one of whom has a splendid son and the other a beautiful daughter. Ovid merely mentions the opposition of the fathers,[1] but Chaucer individualizes them to some slight extent by saying (l. 711),

> Two lordes, *which that were of greet renoun.*

One of Chaucer's most human touches, wholly without suggestion from Ovid, is to be found in the interested and admiring gossip of the neighbor women — whenever the name of the child of one of these two lords was mentioned, it suggested to the

---

[1] "Sed vetuere patres quod non potuere vetare." (*Met.*, iv, 61.)

minds of the women the child of the other and the
suitability of a marriage between them.

> The name of everich gan to other springe
> By wommen, that were neighebores aboute,
>
> (*L. G. W.*, ll. 719–720.)

He adds now and then little explanations of his
own to amplify the ideas. Ovid's *murmure minimo*
(*Met.*, iv, 70), the least murmur of the voices of the
lovers through the cleft they had found in the wall
between their houses, Chaucer has charmingly interpreted by a comparison with the confessional:

> And, with a soun as softe as any shrifte. (*L. G. W.*, l. 745.)

An explanation which Chaucer thought necessary to make to the reader of his day was how the
grave of King Ninus happened to be located alone
in a field:

> For olde payens that ydoles heried
> Useden tho in feldes to be beried.
>
> (*L. G. W.*, ll. 786–787.)

In this same passage Chaucer says the grave of
Ninus was "under a tree," though he omits Ovid's
addition,

> arbor ibi niveis uberrima pomis
> Ardua morus erat.
>
> (*Met.*, iv, 89–90.)

But he includes the rest of the line, *gelido conter-
mina fonti:*

> And faste by this grave was a welle.

With Ovid, Thisbe, having eluded her guardians, arrives first at the meeting-place agreed upon by the lovers. According to Chaucer, it was Thisbe's eagerness to see Pyramus that prompted her early arrival:

> This Tisbe hath so greet affeccioun
> And so greet lyking Piramus to see.
> (*L. G. W.*, ll. 793–794.)

After including what Ovid says about her escape, Chaucer adds,

> Allas! and that is routhe
> That ever woman wolde be so trewe
> To trusten man, but she the bet him knewe.
> (*L. G. W.*, ll. 799–801.)

The sad fate of women who trust in man's faithfulness is one of his favorite topics.[1] To be sure, Pyramus is not faithless, he merely failed to arrive on time. Yet the clear inference from Chaucer is that had Pyramus been as eager and full of "affeccioun" as Thisbe, he would have been there ahead of her, and thus avoided the tragedy.

The sympathetic interest that Chaucer brought to the reading of Pyramus and Thisbe's misfortune is shown in his adding to Ovid's account of the coming of the lioness what the lovers felt and how they acted. After accurately rendering lines 96–104 of the *Metamorphoses*,[2] he describes quite

---

[1] See p. 61.   [2] See *L. G. W.*, ll. 805–813.

tenderly Thisbe's terror as she crouches in the cave:

> And took noon heed, so sore she was a-whaped,
> And eek so glad of that she was escaped;
> And thus she sit, and darketh wonder stille.
>
> (*L. G. W.*, ll. 814–816.)

He also stresses the horror of Pyramus when he comes and finds the tracks of the beast and the bloody wimple. Ovid merely says,

> totoque expalluit ore
> Pyramus.
>
> (*Met.*, iv, 106–107.)

This Chaucer expands:

> And in his herte he sodeinly agroos,
> And pale he wex, therwith his heer aroos,
> And ner he com.
>
> (*L. G. W.*, ll. 830–832.)

In line 842,

> Now what leoun that be in this foreste,

forest is substituted for Ovid's rock or cave (*rupe*):

> O quicumque sub hac habitatis *rupe*, leones.[1]

Chaucer follows minutely the account of the death of Pyramus down to the point where his blood turns the fruit of the mulberry tree from white to black. This, as mentioned above, he omits entirely.[2] It would be hard to find a more

---

[1] *Met.*, iv, 114.
[2] See *Ibid.*, ll. 119–126; *L. G. W.*, ll. 850–852.

charming picture of love's solicitude than Chaucer's in lines 855–857, where he gives the thought
in Thisbe's heart that moves her to come out of the
cave:

> If hit so falle that my Piramus
> Be comen hider, and may me nat finde
> He may me holden fals and eek unkinde.

Ovid merely has

> ne fallat amantem. (*Met.*, iv, 128.)

In depicting the emotions of Thisbe when she
comes upon the bleeding body of Pyramus, Chaucer has added some lines [1] that help to emphasize
her terror-stricken grief,

> And how she lyth and woneth on the grounde. (l. 872.)
> And with his blood herselven gan she peynte. (l. 875.)
> How doth this woful Tisbe in this cas. (l. 877.)

He has improved upon Ovid, as Skeat suggests,[2] by
making Thisbe lift up the head of Pyramus instead
of calling upon him to raise his head and speak to
her (*Met.*, iv, 144).

In place of Thisbe's address to the mulberry tree
that its fruit always be black to commemorate the
double tragedy Chaucer supplies some lines of his
own (ll. 905–912). In these Thisbe prays for better
success to all lovers than she and Pyramus have
had, and says that she, by her death with her own

---

[1] Cf. *Met.*, iv, 137–144, and *L. G. W.*, ll. 869–882.
[2] *Oxford Chaucer*, III, 316.

hand, will show that a woman can "been as trewe and loving as a man."

Lines 916–923, which end the story, are Chaucer's own and serve to lay the emphasis, as we should expect, upon the constancy of Thisbe. Thus he leaves her, a maiden gentle, sweet, loyal, sincere, who could not live after her lover was dead.

In this tale Chaucer exhibits fine craftsmanship in suppressing all reference to the mulberry tree and in introducing delicate touches which enhance the interest of the story. He has lifted this gem of Ovid's out of its setting of mythological alloy, and with a few deft polishing strokes has encased it in pure gold.

THE LEGEND OF DIDO

For the *Legend of Dido* Chaucer tells us that he is indebted to both Virgil and Ovid:

> Glory and honour, Virgil Mantuan,
> Be to thy name! and I shal as I can,
> Folow thy lantern, as thou gost biforn,
> How Aeneas to Dido was forsworn.
> In thyn Eneid and Naso wol I take
> The tenour, and the grete effectes make.
>   (*L. G. W.*, ll. 924–929.)

The facts about Æneas Chaucer knew from the *Æneid*.[1] The tone and spirit of his *Legend* he owes to *Heroides*, vii, the Epistle of Dido to

---

[1] See *House of Fame*, ll. 239–382.

Æneas. This is also true in the case of the story of
Æneas in the *House of Fame*.[1] The points he emphasizes under the influence of Ovid in both instances are the traitorous conduct of Æneas and
the love of Dido, together with her feeling of shame
before her people and neighbors. The anger and
spirit of revenge so marked in Virgil are absent
from both of Chaucer's accounts. The elements of
Virgil's story that Chaucer suppresses as well as
those he uses are instructive in considering his
treatment. It is the first four books of the *Æneid*
that he brings under requisition, but he has
changed the order of Virgil's narrative to suit his
own purposes.

Having no need of a dramatic opening, as Virgil
had for his epic, Chaucer commences his story with
Book ii of the *Æneid*, which gives the account of
the fall of Troy. Lines 930–947 of the *Legend* contain all that Chaucer drew from the eight hundred
lines of the second book of the *Æneid*.[2] A comparison of Chaucer's eighteen lines with Virgil's whole
book shows how Chaucer studiously omitted the
descriptive passages. Virgil was concerned with
heightening the emotional effect upon Dido of the

[1] Lines 256–382.
[2] *L. G. W.*, ll. 930–933, summarizes *Æn.*, ii, 13–267; *L. G. W.*,
l. 934, *Æn.*, ii, 268–298; *L. G. W.*, ll. 935–937, *Æn.*, ii, 437–505;
L. G. W., ll. 938–939, *Æn.*, ii, 531–558; *L. G. W.*, ll. 940–947, *Æn.*, ii,
591–800.

general ruin and destruction of Troy. Chaucer was
interested merely in the principal facts connected
with Æneas' escape from Troy. Moreover, Virgil's
chief character was Æneas, the founder of Rome,
while Chaucer's was Dido, the queen, unfortunate
in love.

The wanderings of Æneas, which he relates to
Dido in *Æneid*, Book iii, Chaucer omits, as irrelevant to his purpose:

> But of his adventures in the see
> Nis nat to purpos for to speke of here,
> For hit accordeth nat to my matere.
> But as I seide, of him and of Dido
> Shal be my tale, til that I have do.
>
> (*L. G. W.*, ll. 953–957.)

In lines 958–1159 — with the exception of lines
1103–1127 — Chaucer reverts to Book i of the
Æneid. This book contained good narration which
could not fail to be entertaining to his mediaeval
readers. As the lines of the *Legend* are so much a
summary of Book i, it will be easier to point out the
omissions, which are very characteristic of Chaucer.
He omits *Æneid*, i, 1–158, in which is given the
cause of Juno's wrath against the Trojan refugees
and the sending of the storm; i, 223–304, containing
the colloquy in Olympus among the gods as to the
fate of the Trojans; and i, 340–366, in which Venus,
disguised, gives to Æneas a brief account of Dido's
previous history. As to this last, Chaucer says:

> Of which as now me lusteth nat to ryme;
> Hit nedeth nat; hit were but los of tyme
> (L. G. W., ll. 996–997.)

But the appearance of Venus to Æneas in the guise of a huntress Chaucer does admit, no doubt because it seemed natural and placed less strain upon his reader's credulity. Two other passages derived from pagan mythology he suggests, but declines to be responsible for. One is Virgil's mention of Venus' enclosing Æneas in a cloud which renders him invisible, but leaves him the power of observation. Of this he says,

> I can nat seyn if that hit be possible,
> But Venus hadde him maked invisible —
> Thus seith the book withouten any lees.
> (L. G. W., ll. 1020–1022.)

The other passage is in *Æneid*, i, 657–688, where Venus instructs Cupid to assume the form of Ascanius, in order to inflame Dido with the pangs of love.

> but, as of that scripture,
> Be as be may, I make of hit no cure.
> (L. G. W., ll. 1144–1145.)

Another of Chaucer's omissions is the description of the banquet scene in *Æneid*, i, 697–747. Ordinarily, no doubt, he would have passed over this scene of feasting as unnecessary,[1] but the lavish entertainment in this case is an integral part of the

---

[1] Cf. *Legend of Cleopatra*, ll. 616–619, and *De Mulieribus*, cap. 86. See also *Canterbury Tales*, l. A 883.

story. So he substitutes for Virgil's Roman banquet a description of a mediaeval festival occasion.[1] The ways of lovers were much the same in all ages and among all peoples, but the social manners and customs must be accommodated to his own times.

With line 1162 of the *Legend* Chaucer begins to follow *Æneid*, Book iv, but not nearly so closely as he has followed Book i. The reason for this is that under the guidance of Ovid he intends to portray Æneas as a traitor to Dido's love because of fickleness, and not because of piety to the gods, which is the motive according to Virgil.

When Dido was aflame with love for Æneas she appealed to her sister Anna for advice about wedding him:

> Now certes, Anne, if that ye rede hit me,
> I wolde fain to him y-wedded be.
>
> (*L. G. W.*, ll. 1178–1179.)

Chaucer says that Anna opposed a little the suggestion of Dido:

> Her suster Anne, as she that coude her good,
> Seide as her thoughte, *and somdel hit withstood.*
> But hereof was so long a sermoning,
> Hit were to long to make rehersing;
> But finally, hit may not been withstonde;
> Love wol love — for no wight wol it wonde.
>
> (*L. G. W.*, ll. 1182–1187.)

---

[1] *L. G. W.*, ll. 1103–1127. Note his introduction of a mediaeval battle in the *Legend of Cleopatra*, p. 186.

In Virgil's account, Anna, after pointing out the difficulties of Dido's position on account of the war-like peoples around her, advises her therefore to accept Æneas for a husband:

Anna refert: "O luce magis dilecta sorori,
Solane perpetua maerens carpere juventa,
Nec dulces natos, Veneris nec praemia noris?
Id cinerem aut Manes credis curare sepultos?
Esto, aegram nulli quondam flexere mariti,
Non Libyae, non ante Tyro; despectus Iarbas
Ductoresque alii, quos Africa terra triumphis
Dives alit: placitone etiam pugnabis amori?
Nec venit in mentem, quorum consederis arvis?
Hinc Gaetulae urbes, genus insuperabile bello
Et Numidae infreni cingunt et inhospita Syrtis;
Hinc deserta siti regio, lateque furentes
Barcaei. Quid bella Tyro surgentia dicam,
Germanique minas?
Dis equidem auspicibus reor et Junone secunda
Hunc cursum Iliacas vento tenuisse carinas.
Quam tu urbem, soror, hanc cernes, quae surgere regna
Conjugio tali! Teucrum comitantibus armis
Punica se quantis attollet gloria rebus!
Tu modo posce deos veniam sacrisque litatis
Indulge hospitio, causasque innecte morandi,
Dum pelago desaevit hiems et aquosus Orion,
Quassataeque rates, dum non tractabile caelum."
(*Æn.*, iv, 31–53.)

From the series of rhetorical questions with which, as will be seen above, Anna introduces her opinion, it would be easy for Chaucer to make the mistake of thinking she appeared to oppose Dido's wishes a little before her imagination begins to see the future which will unite Trojan and Tyrian in a common bond.

The account here in the *Legend* of the episode between the two sisters is different from that in the *House of Fame*. There (ll. 367–371) Dido upbraids Anna with having been the chief cause of her yielding to Æneas:

> And called on hir suster Anne,
> And gan hir to compleyne thanne;
> And seyde, that she cause was
> That she first lovede Aeneas,
> And thus counseilled hir therto.

Chaucer seems to have misinterpreted *leti* in the following passage:

> Ille dies primus *leti* primusque malorum
> Causa fuit.
>
> (*Æn.*, iv, 169–170.)

He renders it,

> This was the firste morwe
> Of hir *gladnesse* and ginning of hir sorwe.
>
> (*L. G. W.*, ll. 1230–1231.)

Skeat and Bech suggest [1] that he mistook *leti* for *letitiae*. It would seem much more probable, I think, that he confused *leti* with the adjective *laetus*, meaning "glad" or "joyous." *Laetum* occurs in *Æneid*, i, 732,

> Hunc laetum Tyriisque diem Trojaque profectis
> Esse volis.

---

[1] See *Oxford Chaucer*, III, 323.

The coming of the storm during the hunt,[1] Chaucer makes a natural event, ignoring the account in the *Æneid* of its prearrangement by Juno and Venus.[2] This is in accord with his usual custom of dispensing with any interference of the pagan gods in the affairs of men.

Chaucer's emphasis upon the falseness of Æneas as a lover is completely at variance with Virgil's treatment of him. In the *Æneid* he is gentle and wishes to spare Dido's feelings as much as possible. He is compelled by the Fates to go to Italy, and he has no intention of taking his leave by stealth.[3] But Chaucer insists that he was false even when declaring his love to Dido in the cave:

> And as a fals lover so wel can pleyne
> That sely Dido rewed on his peyne.
> > (*L. G. W.*, ll. 1236–1237.)

> Have ye swich routhe upon his feined wo.
> > (*L. G. W.*, l. 1257.)

> This Trojan, that so wel her plesen can
> That feineth him so trewe and obeising,
> > (*L. G. W.*, ll. 1265–1266).

He mentions the various ways adopted by Æneas to win Dido:

> Sende her lettres, tokens, broches, ringes.
> > (*L. G. W.*, l. 1275.)

---

[1] *L. G. W.*, ll. 1218–1231.
[2] See *Æn.* iv, ll. 90–128.
[3] See *Ibid.*, ll. 337–346.

Then he adds,

> Now herkneth, how he shal his lady serve.
>
> *(L. G. W.*, l. 1276.)

> This Aeneas, that hath so depe y-swore,
> Is wery of his craft with-in a throwe;
> The hote ernest is al over-blowe.
> And privily he doth his shippes dighte,
> And shapeth him to stele away by nighte.
>
> *(L. G. W.*, ll. 1285–1289.)

That this is a lover's tale and no heroic story of olden times where the gods intervened in human destinies is clear from Chaucer's treatment of Iarbas, the neighbor and lover of Dido. In the *Æneid* [1] Iarbas, aroused by rumor of Æneas' and Dido's love, prays to Jupiter, to whom he has been a loyal devotee, calling attention to Æneas' success in his love, while he himself is spurned and flouted. Jove hears the petition of Iarbas with approval and at once dispatches Mercury to warn Æneas to go on to Italy and leave Dido. This is, therefore, the exciting cause of Æneas' determination to hasten from Carthage and its hospitable queen. In the *Legend* there is no hint of divine intervention; Iarbas is merely a human lover who is unsuccessful in his suit. Chaucer's comment upon Iarbas' fate is very characteristic:

> But as in love, al day it happeth so,
> That on shal laughen at anothers wo;

---

[1] Bk. iv, ll. 196–218.

Now laugheth Eneas, and is in joye
And more richesse than ever he was in Troye.
                    (*L. G. W.*, ll. 1250–1253.)

Though Chaucer makes use of Anchises' ghost
and Mercury's message, which Virgil assigns as the
motives guiding Æneas' conduct, he intimates that
they were mere excuses trumped up by Æneas
to meet the unpleasant situation caused by Dido's
suspicions, and were not the real reason, which was
simple fickleness:

"Certes," quod he, "this night my fadres gost
Hath in my sleep so sore me tormented,
And eek Mercurie his message hath presented,
That nedes to the conquest of Itaile
My destinee is sone for to saile;
For which, me thinketh, brosten is myn herte!"
Ther-with his false teres out they sterte;
And taketh her with-in his armes two.
                    (*L. G. W.*, ll. 1295–1302.)

When Chaucer reaches the climax of his story,
where Dido discovers that Æneas is preparing to
desert her, he turns to Ovid for inspiration to express the emotion of Dido's misplaced love. Virgil
is bent upon showing that thus early in Rome's
history were sown the seeds of hate between the
Romans and the Carthaginians. Though Dido is
angry when she becomes aware of Æneas' purpose
to leave, she appeals to him by every means at her
command to remain.[1] The attitude of Æneas en-

[1] *Æn.*, iv, 304–330.

rages her and she breaks into furious passion.[1]
When she finds that he is resolute and that his
preparations are going forward, she sends her sister
Anna to pray for a delay until she can accustom
herself to the idea of his departure. Finding this of
no avail, she is aroused to fiery denunciation of the
Trojans and predicts future hostility between
Rome and Carthage.[2]

In the *Heroides* Dido is the love-lorn suppliant,
tender toward Æneas and ready to forgive him.
The dominant note is her passionate love:

> Omnia ut eveniant, nec te tua vota morentur,
> Unde tibi, quae te sic amet, uxor erit.
>> (*Her.*, vii, 21-22.)

> Non tamen Aenean, quamvis male cogitat, odi,
> Sed queror infidum questaque pejus amo.
>> (*Her.*, vii, 28-29.)

In line 1323, Chaucer makes Dido use the appeal
of pregnancy,

> I am with childe, and yive my child his lyf.

Virgil intimates that there was no child:

> Saltem si qua mihi de te suscepta fuisset
> Ante fugam suboles, si quis mihi parvulus aula
> Luderet Æneas, qui te tamen ore referret,
> Non equidem omnino capta ac deserta viderer.
>> (*Æn.*, iv, 327-330.)

Ovid, on the other hand, suggests what Chaucer
says directly:

[1] *Æn.*, iv, ll. 365-392.   [2] *Ibid.*, ll. 590-629.

Forsitan et gravidam Didon, scelerate, relinquas,
Parsque tui lateat corpore clausa meo.
Accedet fatis matris miserabilis infans
Et nondum nati funeris auctor eris;
Cumque parente sua frater morietur Juli,
Poenaque conexos auferet una duos.

(*Her.*, vii, 133–138.)

After summarizing the later career of Æneas in two lines,

Thus hath he laft Dido in wo and pyne;
And wedded ther a lady hight Lavyne,

(*L. G. W.*, ll. 1330–1331.)

Chaucer briefly describes the manner of Dido's death. He concludes the story with a translation of the beautifully poetic lines that begin Ovid's Epistle of Dido to Æneas (*Her.*, vii, 1–8), in which she calls her letter a "swan song" such as the white swan sings at the fords of Mæander, when the Fates summon him. She realizes that her appeal is utterly useless, and that she is throwing her words away, but as she has lost her reputation through him, the loss of the words in a letter is of no consequence. For the rest of this letter Chaucer refers the reader to Ovid:

But who wol al this letter have in minde,
Rede Ovide, and in him he shal hit finde.

(*L. G. W.*, ll. 1366–1367.)

In this *Legend* Chaucer stresses more than Virgil the beauty of Dido and the high reputation she enjoyed for character among her own people as well as among those of neighboring kingdoms.[1] By thus emphasizing the high worth of the queen, who was full of interested curiosity, sympathetic and unsuspecting, yet dignified on her funeral pyre, Chaucer makes Æneas' desertion of her the more perfidious. Very skilfully he has woven the two strands of his material from Virgil and Ovid, relying upon one for the facts and upon the other for the interpretation of them.

The Legend of Hypsipyle

The two stories of Hypsipyle and Medea are bound together by Chaucer because both women were deceived by the same man, Jason. For him Chaucer seems to have felt particular dislike.

> Ther other falsen oon, thou falsest two!
>
> .   .   .   .
>
> If that I live, thy name shal be showe
> In English, that thy sleighte shal be knowe.
>
> (*L. G. W.*, ll. 1377–1382.)

But after all it was the faithfulness of the two women and their woeful fate that interested the English poet chiefly.

In the introduction (lines 1368–1395), which is to a large extent original with Chaucer, he addresses Jason thus:

[1] *L. G. W.*, ll. 1004–1014.

Thou madest thy reclaiming and thy lures
To ladies of thy statly apparaunce,
And of thy wordes, farced with plesaunce,
And of thy feyned trouthe and thy manere,
With thyn obeisaunce and thy humble chere,
And with thy counterfeted peyne and wo.

(*L. G. W.*, ll. 1371–1376.)

This conception of Jason as personally so attractive is due to the characteristics given him by Ovid in *Metamorphoses*, vii, 1–158, and *Heroides*, xii. It is his appearance in Colchis that gives Ovid the opportunity to describe so penetratingly (*Met.*, vii, 1–99) the hesitation of Medea between her love for the stranger Jason and her duty to her family and country. This is one of Ovid's finest pieces of analysis of the feminine mind and heart. The personal fascination of Jason is the appeal to Medea. After raising the question of the possibility of his being untrue to her, she replies to herself,

Sed non is vultus in illo,
Non ea nobilitas animo est, ea gratia formae
Ut timeam fraudem meritique oblivia nostri.

(*Met.*, vii, 43–45.)

But when Medea believes that she has conquered her flaming love and the fire is extinct, Jason comes into her presence again, and once more his charm of speech and manner overcome her:

Et casu solito formosior Æsone natus
Illa luce fuit: posses ignoscere amanti.
Spectat, et in vultu veluti tum denique viso

Lumina fixa tenet, nec se mortalia demens
Ora videre putat, nec declinat ab illo.
Ut vero coepitque loqui dextramque prehendit
Hospes et auxilium submissa voce rogavit.

(Met., vii, 84–90.)

Medea also in her letter in the *Heroides* dwells upon the persuasive personality of Jason:

Et decor et linquae gratia ficta tuae. *(Her.*, xii, 12.)

Vidi etiam lacrimas (a! pars est fraudis in illis):
Sic cito sum verbis capta puella tuis.

(Her., xii, 91–92.)

Chaucer cites Guido delle Colonna as his authority for the *Legend of Hypsipyle* and summarizes Guido's narrative in lines 1396 to 1461.[1] This passage is concerned with the history of Jason and his preparations for the journey to the land of Colchis in search of the Golden Fleece. But the allusion to the list of the names of those who accompanied Jason seems to refer, not to Guido, who gives no list, but to the *Argonauticon* of Valerius Flaccus, to which Chaucer refers (ll. 1453–1458). See further discussion in chapter on "Chaucer and Valerius Flaccus," pages 345 ff.

At line 1462 Chaucer leaves Guido and continues the career of Jason in the island of Lemnos. This episode, Chaucer says, is not rehearsed by Guido but is told by Ovid in his Epistles:

---

[1] See Skeat, *Oxford Chaucer*, III, 325.

> So long he sailed in the salte see
> Til in the yle Lemnoun aryved he —
> Al be this nat rehersed of Guido,
> Yet seith Ovyde in his Epistles so.
>
> (*L. G. W.*, ll. 1462–1465.)

That Hypsipyle was the queen of Lemnos and the daughter of Thoas was learned from *Heroides*, vi, 135–136, where Hypsipyle, contrasting herself with Medea, says,

> "Prodidit illa patrem: rapui de clade Thoanta;
> Deseruit Colchos: me mea Lemnos habet."

But the meeting between Jason and Hypsipyle, her entertainment of him and his companions, and his winning her through the help of Hercules are not found in Ovid. Two details in this portion of Chaucer's story seem to come from Valerius Flaccus.[1] Valerius Flaccus' whole story of Jason's visit to Lemnos,[2] where Hypsipyle was queen, has in it many points of similarity to Virgil's account of Æneas' visit to Dido. It is not at all improbable that Chaucer felt the similarity, as any modern reader does,[3] and fell back upon the Dido story for suggestions in developing the relations between

[1] See p. 348.

[2] *Argonauticon*, ii, 311–430.

[3] Bech (*Anglia*, V, 328) cites one line of similarity but no more. Evidently Bech felt the likeness between the two accounts, but did not pursue the subject. Modern students of Valerius Flaccus recognize his indebtedness to Virgil. See W. C. Summers, *A Study of the Argonautica of Valerius Flaccus* (Cambridge, 1894), p. 24; H. G. Blomfield, *The Argonautica of Gaius Valerius Flaccus* (Oxford, 1916), p. 16.

Jason and Hypsipyle. Summarizing the two Latin poems for comparison, we find that:

1. (a) In the *Æneid* Jupiter sends Mercury to dispose the Carthaginians, and especially Dido, to receive the Trojans kindly.

   (b) In the *Argonauticon* Vulcan overcomes Venus' anger against the women of Lemnos, and she sees that they allow the Argonauts to land safely.

2. (a) Dido greets kindly the Trojans, welcomes them, and shows them over the city which she is building.

   (b) Hypsipyle shows the Argonauts the caverns of Vulcan.

3. (a) Dido conducts Æneas to her palace and spreads a banquet for her guests.

   (b) Hypsipyle gives Jason a banquet and asks very much the same questions about the hero's experiences and plans that Dido asks Æneas.

4. (a) In the *Æneid* Juno sends a storm that drives Æneas and Dido into the cave alone where Dido submits to Æneas.

   (b) In the *Argonauticon* Jupiter sends a storm which prevents the Argonauts from returning to their ship, so that Jason has Hypsipyle at his will, as do the other Argonauts have the Lemnian women.

5. (a) Æneas announces his purpose of departure to Dido. She entreats in vain, and is so insistent that Æneas steals away. Dido regrets that there is no little Æneas to comfort her.

   (b) Jason declares his intention of continuing his journey for the Golden Fleece. Hypsipyle weeps and entreats him to remain, and appeals to her pregnancy as a pledge of his return.

As the story of Jason and Hypsipyle in the *Argonauticon* is rather baldly told, with very few descriptive details, it would not be surprising that Chaucer utilized the familiar story of Æneas and Dido in the *Æneid*. The juxtaposition of the stories of Dido and Hypsipyle in Ovid and Chaucer may not be without significance. In the *Heroides* the *Hypsipyle* is VI and *Dido* VII; in the *Legend of Good Women* the *Legend of Dido* is III and *Hypsipyle* is IV. But it was necessary for Chaucer to make proper changes and adaptations. A repetition would be unpardonable and show poverty of creative power. So he represents Jason and Hercules as coming ashore merely to rest and wait for a more favorable wind.

In the *Argonauticon* Hercules does not come ashore at all, and consequently plays no part in Jason's winning of Hypsipyle. But Chaucer's use of Hercules [1] as a faithful ally of Jason in his intercourse with Hypsipyle, suggests the part that Achates plays to Æneas on the occasion of their reception by Dido. In the *Æneid* Achates is despatched to the shore to bring gifts and presents to the queen, and to convey Ascanius to his father. But Venus contrives to send Cupid in the form of

[1] Skeat, after citing Valerius Flaccus, Statius, and Hyginus as possible authorities for Hypsipyle's story, says that Chaucer makes more of Hercules than do these authorities, and seems to be inventing (*Oxford Chaucer*, III, 326).

Ascanius, who fills Dido with all the fires of love.[1] In the *Legend of Hypsipyle*, where the machinery of the gods has been humanized, Hercules praises Jason to Hypsipyle until she is inflamed with love for him:

> This Ercules hath so this Jasoun preysed,
> That to the sonne he hath him up areysed,
> That half so trewe a man ther was of love
> Under the cope of heven that is above;
>
> .   .   .   .
>
> The somme is this, that Jasoun wedded was
> Unto this quene.
>
> (*L. G. W.*, ll. 1524–1560.)

Possibly the messenger service that Achates performs for Æneas may account also for the curious error that Chaucer makes with regard to Hypsipyle's messenger. In the *Argonauticon* the messenger naturally is a woman, since there were only women on Lemnos, and her name is given — Iphinoe.[2] But Chaucer makes the messenger a man (*L. G. W.*, ll. 1479–1486).

In lines 1557–1558 Chaucer refers to an original for this tale:

> Ye gete no more of me, but ye wil rede
> The original, that telleth al the cas.

The reference here is without doubt to *Heroïdes*, vi, for the summary — "the somme is this" —

---

[1] *Æn.*, i, 710 ff.
[2] *Argonauticon*, ii, 326–327.

in the next five lines is in agreement with this Epistle, and immediately following is the line:

A lettre sente she to him certein. (l. 1564.)

In sketching this letter Chaucer has not diverged from the facts as given by Ovid.

That the two children were like Jason save in one thing, that they could not beguile, is translated directly from Ovid: [1]

Felix in numero quoque sum prolemque gemellam,
    Pignora Lucina bina favente dedi.
Si quaeris, cui sint similes, cognosceris illis:
    Fallere non norunt: cetera patris habent.

(*Her.*, vi, 121–124.)

Likewise Hypsipyle's prayer (*L. G. W.*, ll. 1571–1574) that a similar fate to hers might fall upon Medea is due to Ovid:

Quod gemit Hypsipyle, lecti quoque subnuba nostri
    Maereat et leges sentiat ipsa suas;
Utque ego destituor conjunx materque duorum,
    A totidem natis orba sit illa viro.

(*Her.*, vi, 153–156.)

While cleverly combining the material from Guido, Valerius Flaccus, and Ovid, with consistent additions of his own, possibly influenced by Virgil,

---

[1] Valerius Flaccus says nothing of the two children, and Statius, though he mentions the twins, makes Hypsipyle refer to her relation with Jason as compelled and not voluntary. She calls her children "thalami monumenta coacti" (*Thebaid*, v, 463), and justifies herself as follows: "Testor ut externas *non sponte aut crimine* taedas Attegerim" (*Thebaid*, v, 455–456).

Chaucer has contrived to create a distinct character for Hypsipyle. In her kindliness of spirit and innocence she is no match for the carefully planned wiles of Jason and Hercules. Their treacherous behavior serves only to emphasize the dignity and pathos of her position. She looks upon herself as a duly wedded wife, whose purity is not stained by the base desertion of her husband. Loyal and true, it was fitting for her to die of grief.

> And trew to Jason was she al her lyf,
> And ever kepte her chast, as for his wyf;
> Ne never had she joye at her herte,
> But dyed, for his love, of sorwes smerte.
>
> (*L. G. W.*, ll. 1576–1579.)

No suicide's hand would be becoming to her.

THE LEGEND OF MEDEA

The rôle which Chaucer has cast for the heroine in the *Legend of Medea* was determined by her letter to Jason in *Heroides*, xii, though the outline of the story was taken from Guido's *Historia Trojana*.[1] For all that the story is so short, in it as in the other legends, Chaucer's clearness of purpose has produced a very distinct character.

Lines 1580–1655 follow the main trend of Guido's narrative, but Chaucer has transferred the emphasis of culpability from Medea, upon whom Guido places it, to Jason. He applies to Jason the

---

[1] See Bech, *Anglia*, V, 329–330; Skeat, *Oxford Chaucer*, III, 328.

lustful appetite that Guido attributes to all women.[1] Jason appears also in a somewhat different light in the *Medea* from what he seems in the *Hypsipyle*. Hercules in the latter attributes to Jason such qualities as will appeal to Hypsipyle, and so he tells her that, in addition to being wise, bold, secret, and rich, none surpasses him in generosity, he is a gentleman, and will likely become king of Thessaly:

> And he was wys, hardy, secree, and riche. —
> Of thise three pointes ther was noon him liche;
> Of freedom passed he and lustihede,
> Alle tho that liven or been dede;
> Therto so greet a gentil-man was he,
> And of Thessalie lykly king to be.
>
> (*L. G. W.*, ll. 1528–1533.)

But it is a man of fascinating personality [2] that would attract Medea. So as her lover Jason is described as a comely person, royal in looks, affable in speech, and expert in love:

> Now was Jasoun a semely man with-alle,
> And lyk a lord, and had a greet renoun,
> And of his loke as real as leoun,
> And goodly of his speche, and famulere,
> And coude of love al craft and art plenere
> Withoute boke, with everich observaunce.
>
> (*L. G. W.*, ll. 1603–1608.)

Medea is willing to make a clandestine alliance with Jason, and at the last she secretly leaves her father

---

[1] See W. G. Dodd, *Courtly Love in Chaucer and Gower*, p. 224.
[2] This idea is stressed in *Met.*, vii, and *Her.*, xii; see p. 209.

and flees with the hero. Nothing of this sort was possible to Hypsipyle.

In lines 1609–1610, Chaucer adds,

> And as fortune her oghte a foul meschaunce,
> She wex enamoured upon this man.

As Guido has nothing to suggest the idea that fate had anything to do with Medea's love for Jason, the suggestion for it must have come from *Her.*, xii, where Ovid makes Medea say:

> Et formosus eras, et me mea fata trahebant.
>
> *(Her.,* xii, 35.)

From line 1656 to the end Chaucer follows *Her.*, xii. He is indebted to it for the statement that Jason and Medea had two children:

> Per superos oro, per avitae lumina flammae,
> Per meritum et natos, pignora nostra, duos.
>
> *(Her.,* xii, 191–192.)

From the same source he knew that Jason, after deserting Medea, married a third wife, the daughter of Creon:

> Quam tibi tunc longe regnum dotale Creusae
> Et socer et magni nata Creontis erat.
>
> *(Her.,* xii, 53–54.)

This passage is certainly the source of this bit of information rather than *Metamorphoses*, vii, 391–396, referred to by Skeat, where there is only a passing reference to the new wife with no mention of her being the daughter of Creon.

Chaucer closes this *Legend* with a quotation from the Epistle of Medea to Jason and directs the reader to Ovid by name:

> Why lyked me thy yelow heer to see
> More than the boundes of my honestee,
> Why lyked me thy youthe and thy fairnesse,
> And of thy tonge the infinit graciousnesse?
> O haddest thou in thy conquest deed y-be,
> Ful mikel untrouthe had ther dyed with thee!
> Wel can Ovyde her lettre in vers endyte,
> Which were as now to long for me to wryte.
>   (*L. G. W.*, ll. 1672–1679.)

These lines are a very happy translation of *Heroides*, xii, 11–12, and 19–20:

> Cur mihi plus aequo flavi placuere capilli
>   Et decor et linguae gratia ficta tuae?
>
> Quantum perfidiae tecum, scelerate, perisset,
>   Dempta forent capiti quam mala multa meo!

Though Ovid has told the story of Medea at great length in *Metamorphoses*, vii, 1–396, it is his portrayal of her in *Heroides*, xii, that furnished the original for Chaucer's interpretation of her character. According to the *Legend*, Medea is charmed by the physical attractions of Jason. Soft and yielding, she is like Criseyde, to whose type she belongs. As Chaucer leaves her without indicating her end, one can readily believe that she found comfort in another lover. It is excellent art that can within the compass of a scant hundred lines create so definite an image in the reader's mind.

The Legend of Lucretia

The story of Lucretia as told in *Fasti*, ii, 685–852, was dramatic enough in its content. Chaucer found little need to make modifications in it. He opens the *Legend of Lucretia* with a translation of the first line of Ovid's account:

Now must I seyn the exiling of kinges. (*L. G. W.*, l. 1680.)

Nunc mihi dicenda est regis fuga. (*Fasti*, ii, 685.)

Then follow some introductory lines of Chaucer's own, in which he names three previous writers upon the fate of Lucretia (Ovid, Livy, and Augustine)[1] and indicates the theme of his treatment, which is "her wyfhood and her stedfastnesse."

Beginning with line 1694 Chaucer follows Ovid down to line 1778.[2] Two points in this passage

[1] The *Roman de la Rose* (ed. Michel, ll. 9387–9403), *De Claris Mulieribus* (cap. 46), Augustine's *De Civitate Dei* (lib. i, cap. 19), though all known to Chaucer, seem to have contributed practically nothing to his narrative. Livy as a source will be taken up later in the discussion.

[2] Cf. *Fasti*, ii, 721–783. Professor Root ("Chaucer's Legend of Medea," *P. M. L. A.*, XXIV, 146) has pointed out that Chaucer changed the location of the story from Collatia to Rome. Chaucer probably thought he was following Ovid in locating the crime against Lucretia in Rome, for Ovid is very vague as to the location of his story. Certainly the young men ride to Rome:

"tollamur equis, *Urbemque petamus*." (*Fasti*, ii, 735).

After going to the royal household, where they find only idleness and indulgence, they go to seek Lucretia:

"Ecce nurum Regis fusis per colla coronis
Inveniunt posito pervigilare mero.
Inde cito passu petitur Lucretia." (*Fasti*, ii, 739–741.)

have been noted as showing possibly a borrowing from Livy.[1] In line 1705 Chaucer, gives the name of Lucretia's husband as "Colatyne." He could hardly have derived this name from Ovid's

Surgit, cui dederat clarum Collatia nomen. (*Fasti*, ii, 733.)

But Livy (i, 57) calls Collatinus by name,

ubi et *Colatinus* cenabat Tarquinius Egerii filius.

Yet the evidence for Livy as the source of the name is by no means conclusive, for Augustine, whom Chaucer mentions in connection with the story (l. 1690), gives the husband's name twice:

illa scelus improbissimi juvenis marito Collatino et propinquo Bruto, viris clarissimis et fortissimis indicavit. (*De Civitate Dei,* i, 19.)

Collatinum, maritum ejusdem Lucretiae. (*Ibid.*, ii, 17.)

There is no indication here that Lucretia was in another town. Again it was easy for Chaucer, and also for Gower, to have mistaken "Collatia" for an adjective modifying "porta" in line 785,

"Accipit aerata juvenem *Collatia porta.*"

To this summary of Mr. Root's discussion may be added the further point that Brutus, when he became aware of the tragedy, summoned the *Roman citizens* and announced the crime of the prince of the royal family:

"Brutus clamore Quirites
Concitat, et regis facta nefanda refert.
Tarquinius cum prole fugit."   (*Fasti*, ii, 849–851.)

All this seems to take place in Rome. Chaucer, therefore, following Ovid in other respects, was no doubt unaware that he was deviating from him in the location of his story. Livy is careful to locate his account in Collatia.

[1] Skeat, *Oxford Chaucer*, III, 331.

The second point attributed by Skeat without question to Livy is the boast made by Collatinus about the excellent qualities of his wife:

> I have a wyf, quod he, that as I trowe
> *Is holden good* of alle that ever her knowe.
> (*L. G. W.*, ll. 1708–1709.)

But Chaucer's phrase, *is holden good*, is not what Livy says, for he makes Collatinus boast that Lucretia *excels* all the other women:

> paucis id quidem horis posse sciri, *quantum ceteris praestet Lucretia sua.* (*Livy*, i, 57.)

Ovid's words are merely that each one praises his own wife:

> Quisque suam laudat. (*Fasti*, ii, 731.)

The additional statement made by Chaucer that Lucretia's good qualities were recognized by everybody is his own, being neither in Ovid nor in Livy. But the whole context is due to Ovid. For instance,

> Praise every man his owne as him leste.
> (*L. G. W.*, l. 1703.)

> Quisque suam laudat. (*Fasti*, ii, 731.)

> A knight, that highte Colatyne, up-sterte
> And seyde thus, "nay, for hit is no nede
> To trowen on the word, but on the dede.
> (*L. G. W.*, ll. 1705–1707.)

> Surgit, cui dederat clarum Collatia nomen:
> Non opus est verbis, credite rebus! ait.
> (*Fasti*, ii, 733–734.)

Closely as Chaucer follows Ovid, there is one interesting passage where he makes a modification in the story. In lines 1779–1784, he says that Tarquin came secretly into the home of Lucretia:

> Doun was the sonne, and day had lost his light,
> And in he com unto a privy halke,
> And in the night ful theefly gan he stalke
> Whan every wight was to his reste broght
> Ne no wight had of tresoun swich a thoght,
> Were it by window or by other gin.

But Ovid and Livy agree in saying that Tarquin came openly to Lucretia's home where he was hospitably received: [1]

> Hostis, ut hospes, init penetralia Collatina:
> *Comiter excepitur,* sanguine junctus erat.
> Quantum animis erroris inest! parat inscia rerum
> Infelix *epulas* hostibus illa suis
> *Functus erat dapibus:* poscunt sua tempora somnum.
>   (*Fasti,* ii, 787–791.)

> Paucis interjectis diebus, Sex. Tarquinius, inscio Collatino, cum comite uno Collatiam venit. *Ubi exceptus benique* ab ignaris consilii quum *post coenam in hospitale cubiculum deductus esset.* (Livy, i, 58.)

---

[1] Professor Root ("Chaucer's Legend of Medea," *P. M. L. A.*, XXIV, 147, note 1) says, "One wonders whether Boccaccio's *clam* or Livy's *inscio Collatino* may not be responsible for Gower's *privaliche* and Chaucer's *privy halke.*" But these words are used by Boccaccio and Livy with regard to Tarquin's leaving the camp. They both, along with Ovid, say that Sextus came to the home of Collatinus and was hospitably received. Cf. Boccaccio's "a Lucretia comiter susceptus et honoratus," Livy's "ubi exceptus benique," and Ovid's "comiter excepitur."

It seems clear enough why Chaucer has made the change. The Romans — poet and historian — were intent upon showing how Tarquin abused all the recognized laws of kinship and hospitality, as well as how despicable was his deed. Chaucer, who had no interest in the historical facts connected with the overthrow of the monarchy and the establishment of the republic at Rome, is concerned only with the base conduct of Tarquin toward Lucretia. Her perfect chastity and innocence appear in stronger relief when Tarquin enters her house stealthily by night.

The account of the ravishment of Lucretia in the *Fasti* is so vividly told that no change even in detail would improve it.[1] That Chaucer himself felt keenly the violence of the outrage as described by Ovid is seen from his comments in lines 1812–1826, which Skeat says "are original and breathe the spirit of chivalry."

With line 1825,

> But now to purpos: in the story I rede,

he goes back to his account, and describes the feelings of Lucretia after the foul deed. He follows Ovid closely to line 1838,[2] with two slight exceptions. Ovid compares Lucretia to a mother who

---

[1] Cf. *Fasti*, ii, 793–811; *L. G. W.*, ll. 1789–1811.
[2] Cf. *Fasti*, ii, 813–820.

is wont to go to the burial of her child with di-
shevelled hair:

> Passis sedet illa capillis
> Ut solet ad nati *mater* itura rogum.
> *(Fasti*, ii, 813–814.)

Though Chaucer has faithfully preserved the idea
of this passage, he has substituted *women* for
mother and *friends* for *child:*

> And al dischevele, with her here clere,
> In habit swich as women used tho
> Unto the burying of her freendes go.
> *(L. G. W.*, ll. 1829–1831.)

Chaucer includes Lucretia's mother among those
sent for by her, while Ovid says that she sent only
for her aged father and her husband.

> Grandaevum patrem fido cum conjuge castris
> Evocat. *(Fasti*, ii, 815–816).

Chaucer's own are lines 1839–1846, where he
tells of Lucretia's great sorrow and her refusal to
allow her husband to be blamed for her shame.

He then returns to the account in the *Fasti*,
which he follows from line 1847 to line 1870.

Skeat attributes to Livy lines 1847–1849:

> And they answerden alle, upon hir fey,
> That they forgeve it her, for hit was right;
> Hit was no gilt, hit lay nat in her might.

But this attribution seems somewhat doubtful, for
Ovid, whom Chaucer is following closely here, says

the father and the husband of Lucretia condone the
deed because it was committed under compulsion:

> Dant veniam facto genitor conjunxque coactae.
>
> (*Fasti*, ii, 829.)

Naturally when Chaucer has added the mother to
the company, he speaks of them as "alle." Livy
uses "omnes" because he represents Lucretia's
father and her husband as accompanied by P.
Valerius and L. Junius Brutus:

> Dant ordine omnes fidem: consolantur aegram
> animi, avertando noxam ab coacta in auctorem delicti;
> mentem peccare, non corpus: et unde consilium afuerit,
> culpam abesse. (i, 58.)

To be sure "alle," "upon hir fey," "hit was no
gilt" and *omnes fidem . . . culpam abesse* furnish a
rather striking verbal parallel — the best so far as
I know in Chaucer on which to base an argument
for a possible use of Livy. The word "freendes" in
line 1833 does not point decisively to Livy as a
source, for that term might mean only her father,
mother, and husband, whom Chaucer has designated. He refers twice in this *Legend* to Livy
(Titus) by name as an authority for the story of
Lucretia (ll. 1683 and 1873). That fact Chaucer
may have known without having read Livy's history. At any rate there is not unmistakable evidence for his use of Livy in this *Legend*.

Chaucer concludes his account of Lucretia by calling her "a seint" whose day was carefully observed:

> and she was holden there
> A seint, and ever her day y-halwed dere
> As in hir lawe.   (*L. G. W.*, ll. 1870–1872.)

This idea [1] comes from the words of Brutus, who appeared just as Lucretia was dying and swore *through her spirit, which would become a divinity to him,* that he would compel the Tarquins to depart from Rome:

> Per tibi ego hunc juro fortem castumque cruorem,
> Perque tuos manes, qui mihi numen erunt,
> Tarquinium projuga poenas cum stirpe daturum.
>   (*Fasti*, ii, 841–843.)

The suggestion of canonization furnished by Brutus' speech, falling in with Chaucer's general scheme of saints' lives for the whole poem and turning his thoughts at this point into a religious channel, may thus account for the original lines in the conclusion of the tale, in which he erroneously states that Christ himself said He found the greatest faith of all in a woman:

> For wel I wot, that Crist himselve telleth,
> That in Israel, as wyd as is the lond,
> That so gret feith in al the lond he ne fond
> As in a woman.   (*L. G. W.*, ll. 1879–1882.)

---

[1] Skeat's explanation of this point (*Oxford Chaucer*, III, 333) is that Ovid tells her story under a particular date, so that she seemed to have her own day like a saint.

It may be seen how very slightly Chaucer has
modified the account in the *Fasti*. In a story of
such tragic import it required as much real skill to
leave untouched what was supreme in the original
as it would to modify and mold it into greater
form. A bungling hand could easily have spoiled
the effectiveness of this tale.

The Legend of Ariadne

In the *Legend of Ariadne* Chaucer has under-
taken the love-story of a young princess who is still
living in the palace of her father. She is the young-
est, probably, of the women whom he has described so far, unless it be Thisbe, and her case was
a very different one. So it was necessary to give
some account of Ariadne's father in order to secure
the proper background for the daughter. This explains the attention that Chaucer gives to Minos
at the beginning of the story.

As sources for this *Legend* Skeat suggested Ovid,
Met., vii, 456–458, viii, 6–182; *Her.*, x, chiefly
lines 1–74; *Fasti*, iii, 461–516. He says further that
Chaucer consulted other sources also, probably a
Latin translation of Plutarch's Life of Theseus;
Boccaccio's *De Genealogia Deorum*, lib. xi, capp.
27, 29, 30; also Virgil, *Æn.*, vi, 20–30, and perhaps
Hyginus, *Fabulae*, capp. 41–43.[1]

[1] *Oxford Chaucer*, III, 39.

Professor C. G. Child [1] has pursued the suggestion, made by Skeat but not followed up, with regard to Boccaccio's *De Genealogia Deorum* and has shown that where Skeat says "Chaucer here leaves Ovid and seems to have filled in details from some source unknown to me," Chaucer is really indebted to Boccaccio. Professor Lowes [2] has more recently suggested that the source of a part of the *Legend of Ariadne* is to be found in Machaut's *Le Jugement dou Roy de Navarre* and the *Ovide moralisé*.

Our first duty, therefore, will be to endeavor to unravel the different strands that compose this tale and see what relation they bear to one another.

In eight introductory lines (1886–1893), addressed to Minos, Chaucer says that it is not so much for Minos' sake that he tells the story, but to call again to memory the great untruth of Theseus in love. The only lines in this introduction indicating a source are the first and the sixth and seventh. The first line,

> Juge, infernal, Minos of Crete king,

confusing Minos, judge of the infernal regions, and Minos, king of Crete, has been shown by Professor Child [3] to owe its origin to Boccaccio's *De Genealogia Deorum*, xi, 26:

---

[1] *M. L. N.*, XI, 483 ff.

[2] *P. M. L. A.* XXXIII, 320–324.

[3] *M. L. N.*, XI, 483.

Judex ideo apud inferos dictus est: eoque apud mortales: qui respectu habito ad supercaelestia corpora: inferi sumus: componendo leges et jus exhibendo poscentibus judicis officium egit.

In the sixth and seventh lines (1891–1892), Chaucer remarks that the gods were angry with Theseus for his treatment of Ariadne and took vengeance on him for his sin. No comment has ever been made upon these lines, so far as I know, and the idea expressed in them is not to be found in any of the authorities previously cited for this *Legend*. But it occurs in Catullus, lxiv, 188–248. A consideration of the relationship between these two poems is given in connection with the question of Chaucer's knowledge of Catullus on page 367.

Lines 1894–1895, in which Chaucer states that Minos was the ruler of a hundred cities, have the authority of Ovid twice repeated — in *Met.*, vii, from which along with *Met.*, viii, many of the facts for this *Legend* were taken, and in *Her.*, x, from which was drawn the character of its heroine:

That hadde an hundred citees stronge and grete.
(*L. G. W.*, l. 1895.)

Admonitus patrii luctus suspirat et illi
dicta refert rector populorum talia centum.
(*Met.*, vii, 480–481.)

Non ego te, Crete, centum digesta per urbes.
(*Her.*, x, 67.)

Lines 1896–1899, which recount the presence of Minos' son Androgeus in Athens and his having been killed there through envy are from Boccaccio:

> To scole hath sent his sone Androgeus,
> To Athenes: of the whiche it happed thus,
> That he was slayn, lerning philosophye,
> Right in that citee, nat but for envye.

Hic (Minos) autem aetate provectus Pasiphen Solis filiam sumpsit uxorem et ex ea filios filiasque progenuit inter quos Androgeus praeclarae indolis fuit hic ab Atheniensibus et Megarensibus invidia occisus est: eoque caeteros in palestra superaret: in ultionem cujus Minos adversus eos arripuit bellum. (*De Gen.*, xi, 26.)

Androgeus filius fuit Minois et Pasiphis. Juvenis quidem egregiae virtutis: qui cum Athenis in palaestra superaret omnes ab Atheniensibus et Megarensibus invidia occisus est.[1] (*De Gen.*, xi, 27.)

That Minos was seeking to avenge his son's death (line 1901) is explicitly stated by both Ovid and Boccaccio. As this idea is repeated in lines 1938–1939, I shall give the references to Ovid and Boccaccio in the discussion of those lines.

Lines 1902–1921, which tell the fate of Scylla, who betrayed her father for love of Minos, though much condensed, as Chaucer intimates, came from *Metamorphoses*, viii, 6–151. The metamorphosis, which is the motive of Ovid's story, is, as usual, omitted by Chaucer, though in this instance it is alluded to:

[1] Professor Child has cited the latter passage (*M. L. N.*, XI, 484).

> But wikkedly he quitte her kindnesse,
> And let her drenche in sorwe and distresse,
> Nere that the goddes hadde of her pite.
>
> > (*L. G. W.*, ll. 1918–1920.)

Ovid relates that Scylla was turned by the gods into the bird Ciris.

Up to this point it is clear that Chaucer is weaving his story with strands from Boccaccio and Ovid. Interesting evidence of his continuance in the use of these two sources is contained in lines 1921–1947.

The winning of Athens by Minos (line 1922) is indicated definitely by Boccaccio:

> In cujus ultionem (Androgeus) pater insurgens occiso Niso Megarensium rege Athenienses acri bello superavit sibique vectigales facti. (*De Gen.*, xi, 27.)

The victory of Minos over Alcathoe, an ally of Athens, is told by Ovid, as we have just seen above in the story of Scylla. "And other tounes mo" (line 1923) is from *Met.*, vii, 461–466, where there appears a list of cities that Minos secured as allies against the Athenians either by treaty or by conquest.

Chaucer's statement of the result of Minos' war against Athens is in entire agreement with Boccaccio's, except that where Boccaccio specifies the number of young Athenians (seven noble youths) required each year as tribute, Chaucer leaves the

number indefinite, saying that the Athenians must
send their own dear children:

> And this theffect, that Minos hath so driven
> Hem of Athenes, that they mote him yiven
> Fro yere to yere her owne children dere
> For to be sleyn, as ye shul after here.
>
> *(L. G. W.*, ll. 1924–1927.)

Diu tolere Ultimo cum succubuissent in has a Minoe
deducti sunt leges: ut scilicet annis singulis VII nobilis
juvenes ad minotaurum Cretam mitterent. (*De Gen.*, x,
48.)

The parallelism between Chaucer and Boccaccio is striking. But it is just here that Professor
Lowes begins to derive Chaucer's account from
Machaut's *Le Jugement dou Roy de Navarre.* The
corresponding passage from the French is as
follows:

> Quant cil d'Athennes eurent mort
> Androgeus, si grant remort
> En ot Minos, li rois de Crete,
> Que par voie sage et discrete,
> Par force d'armes et de guerre
> Fist essillier toute leur terre;
> Et les mist tous pour cest outrage
> Minos en si mortel servage,
> Que tous les ans li envoioient
> Un homme.
>
> (*Le Jugement*, ll. 2707–2716.)

It will be noticed that Machaut has it that the
Athenians were put in such severe bondage that
they sent every year *a man*, whereas Chaucer,

following Boccaccio, has *children*. He is not concerned with the actual number since he is not writing as an historian but as an artist. There is no
contradiction between these lines and the subsequent ones:

> They casten lot, and, as hit come aboute
> On riche, on pore, he moste his sone take,
> And of his child he moste present make
> Unto Minos, to save him or to spille.
>
> (*L. G. W.*, ll. 1933–1936.)

Professor Lowes,[1] however, interprets these four
lines to mean that only one victim was sent each
year. In this way he discovers a contradiction
in Chaucer's statements and so finds a parallelism
between Chaucer and Machaut's *un homme*. But
I see no conflict between Chaucer's later lines and
his first statement that the Athenians were obliged
to send their *children*. For the context makes it
clear that in these subsequent lines he is explaining
that there was no escape from the decision of the
lot, which was the accepted means of selecting the
children who were to be sent. Each father, whether
he was rich or poor, must send his son when the lot
fell upon him. This explains why even Theseus,
the king's son, could not escape when he was one of
the selected victims. Chaucer's use of the singular
number only serves to give greater concreteness to
the idea and conveys no contradiction to his earlier

[1] *P. M. L. A.*, XXXIII, 323.

statement. On this point of the single victim, therefore, Mr. Lowes fails to be convincing because his
argument rests upon an interpretation of Chaucer's
text which is unjustifiable. This is the first of the
two details upon which he bases his claim for
Chaucer's use in this *Legend* of the *Ovide moralisé*.

Considering as a whole the passage (ll. 1924–
1947) which Mr. Lowes says seems to be derived
from Machaut, we find that Chaucer has followed
Boccaccio in his method of handling the story.
According to Boccaccio there were seven victims
chosen by lot yearly. In the fourth year the lot fell
upon Theseus as one of the seven, and then Boccaccio continues with the story of Theseus, which
he started out to relate. He makes no further
reference to the other victims. Likewise Chaucer
begins by telling that the Athenians must send
yearly some of their children to Minos to be slain.
He interprets the lot by saying that wealth did not
furnish a means of escape. He does not specify the
exact year when the lot fell upon Theseus, as
Boccaccio does (the fourth), any more than he
does the number of children, but merely remarks,

> This wikked custom is so longe y-ronne
> (*L. G. W.*, l. 1943.)

that at last it fell upon Theseus, the son of King
Ægeus. Then he proceeds with the story of Theseus, which was his purpose from the first. The

parallelism of method between Chaucer and Boccaccio is quite clear.

When we consider Machaut's method and purpose, we find that they are very different. Machaut, through the character Franchise, is illustrating the point that women are more loyal than men. He is, therefore, interested only in the story of Ariadne and her treatment by Theseus. So he briefly tells the individual story of these two lovers without any relation to its historical setting. This accounts for the statement that *un homme* was sent each year, who on this occasion was Theseus.

The idea of a *yearly* offering by the Athenians is provided in Boccaccio's *annis singulis* in the passage quoted above.[1] Since Chaucer was here clearly following Boccaccio, who provided him also with much other material for the story, the occurrence of *tous les ans* in Machaut is hardly significant.

In lines 1928–1931, Chaucer has recourse to Ovid for his knowledge of the monster that fed upon human beings:

> This Minos hath a monstre, a wikked beste,
> That was so cruel that, withoute arreste,
> Whan that a man was brought in his presence,
> He wolde him ete, there helpeth no defence.

> Quo postquam geminam tauri juvenisque figuram
> Clausit, et Actaeo bis pastum sanguine monstrum,
> > (*Met.*, viii, 169–170.)

---

[1] Child, *M. L. N.*, XI, 483–484.

Professor Lowes notes that in both Machaut and *Ovide moralisé* the Minotaur is called *un monstre*. When Chaucer had Ovid's *monstrum* [1] before him, however, there is no occasion to seek elsewhere for the source of his use of the word. His amplification of *monstrum* may have been suggested by Boccaccio's description of the Minotaur as "fortissimo, ferocissimo, et furioso animale." [2]

In addition to the statement just quoted from *Metamorphoses* that the monster had twice fed upon Athenian blood, there is in the Epistle of Ariadne to Theseus this reference to the fate of Athenian children who were the victims of the bull-man:

Viveret Androgeos utinam! nec facta luisses
Impia funeribus, Cecropi terra, tuis;
Nec tua mactasset nodoso stipite, Theseu,
Ardua parte virum dextera, parte bovem.
(Her., x, 99–102.)

In these two passages it was manifest to Chaucer that this monster "a man . . . he wolde him ete." [3]

The word Minotaur appears three times in the *Legend of Ariadne* (lines 2104, 2142, and 2145). Ovid does not use it, and it does not occur in either

[1] This word occurs also in *Met.*, viii, 156.

[2] See Child, *M. L. N.*, XI, 486. I have used Professor Child's quotation from Bertussi's translation because I do not happen to have access at this point to Boccaccio's Latin text.

[3] It is unnecessary to refer to Servius for this information. See Lowes, *P. M. L. A.*, XXXIII, 321, note 88.

Machaut or the *Ovide moralisé.*[1] But Boccaccio uses it in chapters 29, 48, and 49 of *De Genealogia,* where without doubt Chaucer found it.[2]

Chaucer does not use the word Minotaur in connection with Minos at all. Note the following lines:

> This Minos hath a monstre, a wikked beste.
> (*L. G. W.*, l. 1928.)

> Unto Minos, to save him or to spille,
> Or lete his beste devoure him at his wille.
> (*L. G. W.*, ll. 1936–1937.)

Nor does he make any of Minos' family, Ariadne or Phaedra, use the word in referring to the monster. He is "this monstre" (l. 1991); "this fend" (l. 1996); "the beste" (l. 1998); "the bestes throte" (l. 2005); "the beste" (l. 2008); "this beste" (l. 2019). In this subtle way Chaucer no doubt intended to indicate a consciousness of the family disgrace on the part of the daughters of Minos, which rendered them reticent about giving the monster a name derived from their father's. That the monster was felt keenly as a scandal to the reputation of Minos' family appears in Ovid, who gives this as a reason for the building of the Labyrinth:

---

[1] Lowes, *P. M. L. A.*, XXXIII, 321, note 88.

[2] Minotaur occurs in Catullus, lxiv, 79, where also Chaucer had probably seen it. See pp. 364 ff.

Creverat opprobrium generis foedumque patebat
Matris adulterium monstri novitate biformis;
Destinat hunc Minos thalamis removere pudorem,
Multiplicique domo caecisque includere tectis.

> (*Met.*, viii, 155–158.)

The delicacy which made Ovid, who was writing
sympathetically with Minos, refrain from connecting his name with the monster, seems to have been
caught by Chaucer here. The fineness of the poetic
nature of Ovid could be no more happily contrasted
with the bald historical method of Boccaccio than
in this instance. Boccaccio refers to the monster as
the Minotaur quite without discrimination. To
neighbors and strangers Minotaur would be a
natural appellation. Chaucer first puts the word
into the mouth of Theseus (l. 2104). To all Athenians the monster was a concrete object of terror,
for which *beast* or *monster* would be too indefinite a
designation. The other two occurrences of the
word Minotaur (ll. 2142 and 2145) are in the
narrative portion of Chaucer's story, where he is
closely following Boccaccio.

Line 1932,

> *And every thridde yeer*, withouten doute
> They casten lot,

is in conflict with line 1926,

> *Fro yere to yere* her owne children dere,

and line 1942,

> *Fro yere to yere*, whyl that he liven shal.

"Fro yere to yere" we have found traceable to Boccaccio's *annis singulis*. Skeat [1] says that Chaucer's
"three year period" is due to Ovid's expression,

Tertia sors annis domuit repetita novenis.

(*Met.*, viii, 171.)

In discussing Skeat's citation of Golding's translation, "the third time at the ninth yeares end,"
and so forth, Professor Child [2] thinks that we are
not "bound to suppose that Chaucer mistranslated
'novenis' because Golding did — that is, as if it
were an ordinal." He then suggests that Chaucer
found his "every thridde yeer" in Boccaccio:

Qui *tribus annis* forte missi sunt, quarto autem fors
cecidit in Theseum. (*De Gen.*, x, 48.)

But there is nothing here about every third year;
the meaning is that the human tribute was sent
yearly for three years and in the fourth year the
lot fell upon Theseus.

Professor Lowes [3] offers the *Ovide moralisé* as
giving "the possible suggestion for 'every thridde
yeer'" in the following passage:

Au tiers terme chei la sort
Dessus le fil au roi d'Athaines
Theseus.

But here again there is no hint of the three-year
period. The phrase in the French poem means that

[1] *Oxford Chaucer*, III, 335.   [2] *M. L. N.*, XI, 485.
[3] *P. M. L. A.*, XXXIII, 323.

on the third occasion the lot fell, and so forth. This disposes of the second of the two points for which Mr. Lowes thought the passage from the *Ovide moralisé* significant.

Now since the third numeral is not used at all by Machaut and since the statements in the *Ovide moralisé* and Boccaccio are totally different from Chaucer's, it will be worth while to examine a little more closely Ovid's expression,

Tertia sors annis domuit repetita novenis.
(*Met.*, viii, 171.)

Though *novenis* is a distributive adjective and would mean ordinarily "nine each," the Roman poets, as a matter of fact, often used the distributive adjectives as cardinals. This is regularly the case among both poets and prose writers where the idea of multiplication is present. Livy, for instance, writes *ter novenae virgines*, that is, "thrice nine maidens" (xxvii, 37). But the use of distributives for cardinals is not entirely restricted to this idiom, for the poets and later prose writers employ them often where the strict grammatical rule would require the cardinal.[1] Ovid permits himself this freedom whenever he chooses. For example, he writes,

quod et aes et proxima rupit
Terga novena boum, decimo tamen orbe moratum est.
(*Met.*, xii, 96–97.)

---

[1] See Gildersleeve-Lodge, *Latin Grammar*, sec. 295, note.

Here the meaning is quite clear that the spear pierced "through nine layers of bull's hide, but was stopped on the tenth."

Again, of the pipe that Apollo carried when he was on the earth, Ovid says that it was made of seven unequal reeds:

Alterius dispar *septenis* fistula cannis. (*Met.*, ii, 682.)

Also in describing Phaeocomes as one who had with knotted thongs bound together six lion hides, he uses the distributive:

qui *sena leonum*
Vinxerat inter se conexis *vellera* nodis.
(*Met.*, xii, 429–430.)

Other examples might be given where it would require the subtlety of modern scholarship to distinguish whether the distributive idea is present or not. Certainly Chaucer could not be expected to make such nice distinctions. And *novenis* being often used by the poets to mean "nine," any general reader would reasonably construe the passage as he did. Instead, therefore, of mistranslating [1] Ovid's

Tertia sors annis domuit repetita novenis,

Chaucer could quite legitimately have understood it to mean *the third lot taken in nine years*, that is, a lot taken every third year.

[1] Professor Lowes concedes that the "three year period" might have come from a misunderstanding of either Boccaccio, Servius, or Ovid (*P. M. L. A.*, XXXIII, 323).

In two passages Chaucer mentions the desire of
Minos to take vengeance for his son's death:

> The grete Minos, of the whiche I speke,
> His sones deeth is comen for to wreke.
>
> (*L. G. W.*, ll. 1900–1901.)

> And this hath Minos don, right in despyt;
> To wreke his sone was set al his delyt.
>
> (*L. G. W.*, ll. 1938–1939.)

This knowledge was abundantly supplied Chaucer
by both Ovid and Boccaccio. He could not know
their stories at all, without understanding this
point. Ovid says that Minos' motive in his preparations for war is to avenge his son's death:

> Bella parat Minos: qui quamquam milite, quamquam
> Classe valet, patria tamen est firmissimus ira
> Androgeique necem justis ulciscitur armis.
>
> (*Met.*, vii, 456–458.)

Again, a few lines farther on in *Metamorphoses*,
vii, Chaucer read that Minos appealed to Æacus
to aid the arms which for his son's sake he had
taken up:

> Admonitus patrii luctus suspirat et illi
> Dicta refert rector populorum talia centum:
> "Arma iuves oro pro gnato sumpta piaeque
> Pars sis militiae; tumulo solacia posco."
>
> (*Met.*, vii, 480–483.)

Boccaccio, too, says plainly that Minos' purpose
is to avenge his son's murder:

Nam inter alia bellum Minois regis Cretensium quod *in vindictam Androgei filii sui indigne occisi moverat.* (*De Gen.*, x, 48.)

Yet in the face of these explicit statements Professor Lowes seeks to account for Chaucer's lines in Machaut's words, *Car peres fu Androgeus!* [1]

In the continuance of his story Chaucer says that in the course of time the lot fell upon Theseus, son of King Ægeus:

> This wikked custom is so longe y-ronne
> Til that of Athenes King Egeus
> Mot sende his owne sone, Theseus,
> Sith that the lot is fallen him upon.
> (*L. G. W.*, ll. 1943–1946.)

Chaucer was familiar with the name of the king of Athens, from both Ovid and Boccaccio. In *Metamorphoses*, vii, 402 ff., is the story of Medea's arrival at Athens, her marriage to the king, Ægeus, and her attempt to poison the king's son, Theseus. In *Metamorphoses*, viii, 174, in the account of Theseus' departure from Crete with Ariadne, he is called the son of Ægeus,

> Protinus *Aegides* rapta Minoide Diam
> Vela dedit.

And in *Heroïdes*, x, 131–132, Ariadne, after her desertion, upbraids Theseus as being the son of the rocks and the sea and not the son of Ægeus:

[1] *P. M. L. A.*, XXXIII, 321.

Nec pater est Aegeus, nec tu Pittheidos Aethrae
Filius: auctores saxa fretumque tui!

Boccaccio likewise names Ægeus in two passages:

quarto autem fors cecidit *in Theseum qui maximo Aegei
patris dolore* navem conscendit iturus. (*De Gen.*, x, 48.)
Aegeus excaelsa turri prospectans nigrum videns
velum Theseum mortuum arbitratus ex turri se dejecit
in mare. (*De Gen.*, x, 48.)

In Machaut's account he is not named, but merely
called "the King of Athens."

Boccaccio is also the authority for the statement
that *the lot* fell upon Theseus:

> *quarta autem fors cecidit in Theseum.*
> (*De Gen.*, x, 48.)

Even without this explicit statement of Boccaccio,
Chaucer would have understood from Ovid that
Theseus had gone to Crete as the result of *the lot*
and not voluntarily:

> Tertia sors annis domuit repetita novenis.
> (*Met.*, viii, 171.)

No other understanding of this line is possible, for
it occurs in the account of Theseus and Ariadne
in *Metamorphoses*, viii. Professor Lowes's note [1] on
this point is misleading. He says:

Chaucer, Machaut, and the *O. m.* agree in the assertion that Theseus was chosen *by lot*, as against the com-

[1] *P. M. L. A.*, XXXIII, 324, note 96.

mon account that he went voluntarily to Crete. Compare Hyginus, Fab. XLI: "Theseus . . . *voluntarie* se ad Minotaurum pollicitus est ire." See Hoepffner, i, lxxvi; de Boer, p. 343. But Boccaccio represents the lot as falling upon Theseus: "septem nobiles juvenes . . . qui tribus annis sorte missi sunt, quarta autem sors cecidit in Theseum" (*De Gen.*, x, 48).

In his first sentence Mr. Lowes implies that the only cases of agreement among authorities for Theseus' having been chosen by lot are Chaucer, Machaut, and the *Ovide moralisé*. His later statement that Boccaccio represents the lot as falling upon Theseus is added as if of slight importance in the consideration of the matter, and the identity of all of these accounts with Ovid, their ultimate source, is ignored altogether.

From the consideration of lines 1924–1947 we have found that in this short passage Chaucer drew from Ovid these facts: the monster that fed upon human flesh, the tribute exacted by Minos every three years, the selection of the victims by lot, the purpose of Minos to avenge his son's death, the name of the Athenian king, Ægeus, and the choice of Theseus by lot.

Some of these details Chaucer found also in Boccaccio, whom he was following along with Ovid. Up to this time the obligation of Chaucer to Boccaccio here has not been fully recognized. Skeat referred to *De Genealogia Deorum*, but, as pointed

out by Child, never followed up his suggestion.
Child, though calling attention to some of the borrowings from Boccaccio, failed to complete the list.
From Boccaccio Chaucer was cognizant of the conditions fixed by Minos upon the Athenians, of the
yearly offering of victims, of a number of Athenian
children being offered at one time, of the selection
by lot, of Minos' desire to take vengeance for his
son's death, of the name of the Athenian king,
Ægeus, and of the falling of the lot upon Theseus.
In addition to these points we have seen that Chaucer follows Boccaccio's method in developing his
story.

It is probable that Chaucer knew Machaut's
poem [1] and possibly also the *Ovide moralisé*. But
if there is any influence from either on the *Legend
of Ariadne*, it is of necessity very slight. Machaut's
version leaves untold the part of the story concerning Minos, which occupies the first thirty-six
lines of Chaucer's *Legend*, and only briefly summarizes (in sixty-two lines) the relationship between
Ariadne and Theseus, which, based upon Ovid's
Epistle in the *Heroides*, is in Chaucer developed to
a length of 267 lines. Boccaccio's *De Genealogia
Deorum*, also, which Professor Lowes neglects practically altogether, is of far greater influence on

[1] See Kittredge, *Mod. Phil.*, VII, 471–474; *P. M. L. A.*, XXX, 3–4,
14–15.

Chaucer's *Legend* than Machaut's version could possibly be. In fact, so far as the details in Professor Lowes's carefully italicized arrangement of parallel passages are concerned, *Le Jugement dou Roy de Navarre* and the *Ovide moralisé* might as well never have been written. If Chaucer got anything from Machaut, it might much more likely have been the suggestion of using the Theseus and Ariadne story from Franchise's speech on woman's greater loyalty than man's. But there is no reason to suppose that Chaucer was dependent upon Machaut for such an idea when the Ariadne story was included, along with most of the others that Chaucer has used in the *Legend of Good Women*, in the great model for the design of his series of stories upon the faithfulness of women, the *Heroides* of Ovid.

The comparison of Chaucer's story of Theseus and Ariadne in both the *House of Fame* and in the *Legend of Good Women* and Machaut's in *Le Jugement dou Roy de Navarre* with Ovid's in the *Heroides* makes it clear that Chaucer has caught the mood of Ovid, as he has so constantly done in his adaptations from the *Heroides*, and has rendered it much more artistically than has Machaut. This is probably due, aside from Chaucer's superior genius, to Machaut's having got his knowledge of Ovid very largely from the *Ovide moralisé,* as Professor de

Boer thinks,[1] whereas Chaucer got his, with a few additional facts from Boccaccio, at first hand from Ovid himself.[2]

Lines 1960–2122, giving the account of Theseus in prison in Crete and the pity felt for him by Ariadne and her sister, serve to bring the two young people, prince and princess, together, a circumstance which Chaucer did not find provided for in *Heroides*, x, *Metamorphoses*, vii, or *De Genealogia Deorum*. Professor Lowes has pointed out the influence of the *Teseide* upon these lines. Chaucer would naturally turn to the *Teseide* when treating of Theseus. In seeking some means of introducing Theseus to the young Ariadne, he could have thought of no more romantic way of bringing it about than to portray Theseus as a prince in distress, whom Ariadne out of pity for his fate sought to assist, and then to let him offer to prove his gratitude by becoming her servant and living in disguise. That Ariadne was a romantic young princess is shown by her remarks to her sister when Theseus promises to marry her and so make her queen at Athens:

> This lady smyleth at his stedfastnesse,
> And at his hertly wordes, and his chere,
> And to hir sister seide in this manere,

---

[1] See Lowes, *P. M. L. A.*, XXXIII, 320.
[2] For further discussion of Chaucer's relation to the Old French adaptations of Ovid, see p. 282.

Al softely, now sister myn, quod she,
Now be we duchesses, bothe I and ye,
And sikered to the regals of Athenes,
And both here-after lykly to be quenes.

(*L. G. W.*, ll. 2123-2129.)

In line 2075, Theseus is said by Chaucer to be twenty-three years of age.[1] Yet in lines 2096-2100, Ariadne proposes that Theseus take Phaedra along with them to be wedded to his son. This is, of course, a bit of carelessness on Chaucer's part, due to his plan of making Theseus a young knight suitable for Ariadne.[2] The idea of wedding Phaedra to Theseus' son, Hippolytus, comes from Boccaccio:

Ariadne filia fuit Minois ex Pasiphe: ut saepe testatur Ovidius.   Haec Theseum ab Atheniensibus Cretam missum amavit: et ejus clam usa contubernio sumpta fide: que eam in conjugem et Phaedram sororem suam pro Hippolyto asportaret. (*De Gen.*, xi, 29.)

Lines 2146-2149 are from Ovid:

And by the teching of this Adriane
He overcom this beste, and was his bane;
And out he cometh by the clewe again
Ful prevely, whan he this beste hath slain.

Cum tibi, ne victor tecto morerere recurvo,
Quae regerent passus, pro duce fila dedi.

(*Her.*, x, 71-72.)

---

[1] See the chapter on Chaucer and Catullus, p. 366.

[2] This carelessness is similar to his speaking of the human sacrifice sent to the Minotaur as going yearly in line 1926 and line 1941, and every third year in line 1932. Though there are these inconsistencies in the *Legend of Ariadne*, they are, as Professor Tatlock has said (*The Development and Chronology of Chaucer's Works*, p. 125), due to a lack of care and do not amount to artistic defects.

Nec tibi, quae reditus monstrarent, fila dedissem.
(*Her.*, x, 103.)

Utque ope virginea nullis iterata priorum
Janua difficilis filo est inventa relecto.
(*Met.*, viii, 172–173.)

Professor Child, after calling attention to the passage in *Met.*, viii, but saying nothing of the two passages in *Her.*, x, suggests that Boccaccio's words, "Theseo poi per consiglio d'Arianna restato vittorisos," may have been also in Chaucer's mind along with the *Metamorphoses*. But it will be observed that Boccaccio does not provide for the method of escape by the "clewe" after Theseus has vanquished the Minotaur, as does Ovid in *Metamorphoses*, viii, and particularly in the passages from *Heroides*, x, which are here for the first time pointed out in detail in connection with this passage.[1]

In lines 2155–2162, Chaucer represents Theseus as stopping at "Ennopye" on his way home to Athens with Ariadne and Phaedra:

And to the contree of Ennopye him dighte
Ther as he had a frend of his knowinge.
(*L. G. W.*, ll. 2155–2156.)

Chaucer's knowledge of this island and the friendship that existed between its inhabitants and the Athenians came from Ovid's account in *Met.*, vii,

[1] Skeat gives the general reference to *Her.*, x.

472–511. Here we are told that the ancients called the island Oenopia — hence Chaucer's "Ennopye":

> Oenopiam veteres appellavere. (*Met.*, vii, 473.)

To this island Minos went to enlist support for his war against Athens on account of the death of his son Androgeus, but Æacus, because of his friendship for Athens and his treaty with that city, declined to give Minos aid. (See *Met.*, vii, 472–489.) Quite different was the response of Æacus to the messenger from Athens who came sailing into the harbor of Oenopia just as Minos was leaving. After Cephalus, the Athenian messenger, had made known the request of his countrymen for help against Minos, Æacus replied that they need not ask aid; just take it, for everything that the island possessed was theirs:

> Ne petite auxilium, sed sumite, dixit, Athenae
> Nec dubie vires, quas haec habet insula, vestras
> Ducite.
>
> (*Met.*, vii, 507–509.)

Such a place as "Ennopye" would be a suitable refuge for the Athenian prince fleeing from King Minos, and Chaucer makes use of it.[1]

But the gist of the story lies in Theseus' desertion of the generous young Ariadne, the material for which Chaucer found in *Heroïdes*, x. The de-

[1] See Child, *M. L. N.*, XI, 486.

scription of the island on which Ariadne was left
is from this source:

> And in an yle, amid the wilde see,
> Ther as ther dwelte creature noon
> Save wilde bestes, and that ful many oon,
> He made his ship a-londe for to sette.
>
> *(L. G. W.,* ll. 2163–2166.)

> Vacat insula cultu
> Non hominum video, non ego facta boum,
> Omne latus terrae cingit mare, navita nusquam,
> Nulla per ambiguas puppis itura vias.
>
> *(Her.,* x, 60–63.)

> Jam, jam venturos aut hac aut suspicor illac
> Qui lanient avido viscera dente, lupos.
> Forsitan et fulvos tellus alat ista leones.
> Quis scit, an haec saevas tigridas insulas habet?
>
> *(Her.,* x, 83–86.)

The substance of lines 2171–2174 is found in two
passages in *De Genealogia:*

> When Adriane his wyf a-slepe was,
> For that hir suster fairer was than she,
> He taketh her in his hond, and forth goth he
> To shippe, and as a traitour stal his way.

Minotaurum interemit et Athenas a turpi servitis
liberavit Ariadnam atque Phedram Minois filias patri
subripuit et Ariadna relicta Phedram sibi conjugio copulavit. *(De Gen.,* x, 49.)

Qui cum perfecisset omnia noctu Ariadna et Phaedra
navi positis clam discessit et in Chium Insulam (ut dicit
Ovidius) seu Naxum, (ut ait Lactantius) nocte discedens
dimisit Ariadnam ibidem dormientem. *(De Gen.,* xi, 29.)

The source for lines 2175–2176, which repeat
that Theseus deserted Ariadne while she was asleep

and add that he sailed away to his own country, is
amply supplied by Ovid.

> Whyl that this Adriane a-slepe lay,
> And to his contree-ward he saileth blyve.

> Incertum vigilans a somno languida movi.
>> (*Her.*, x, 9.)

> Crudeles somni, quid me tenuistis inertem.
>> (*Her.*, x, 111.)

> Quae legis, ex illo, Theseu, tibi litore mitto
> Unde tuam sine me vela tulere ratem.
>> (*Her.*, x, 4–5.)

> Ibis Cecropios portus patriaque receptus
> . . . .
> Me quoque narrato sola tellure relictam.
>> (*Her.*, x, 125–129.)

Lines 2176–2178 came from Boccaccio's account
of the death of Ægeus when he saw the black sail on
the returning ship:

> And to his contree-ward he saileth blyve —
> A twenty devil way the wind him dryve —
> And fond his fader drenched in the see.

Et cum omnia navigii ornamenta nigra essent et navis
velum habuit in mandatis a patre ut si contingeret in
agendis eum felicem obtinere exitum; rediens navi album
ponere velum ammota nigro ut a longe fortunium suum
noscere. Theseus autem Ariadnae consilio victorum
mandatorum immemor non ammoto nigro velo redibat.
Aegeus excaelsa turri prospectans nigrum videns velum
Theseum mortuum arbitratus ex turri se dejecit in mare
et mortuus ab Atheniensibus liberatis et Neptunni
filius et marinus deus in solatium Thesei consecratus
est. (*De Gen.*, x, 48.)

From the awakening of Ariadne almost to the
end of the *Legend* (ll. 2185–2220), Chaucer is making close use of Ovid's epistle. He describes how
she groped in the bed for Theseus and then realized
that she had been deserted:

> Right in the dawening awaketh she,
> And gropeth in the bedde, and fond right noght.
> "Allas!" quod she, "that ever I was wrought!
> I am betrayed!" and her heer to-rente,
> And to the stronde bar-fet faste she wente.
> (*L. G. W.*, ll. 2185–2189.)

> Tempus erat, vitrea quo primum terra pruina
> Spargitur et tectae fronde queruntur aves;
> Incertum vigilans, a somno languida, movi
> Thesea prensuras semisupina manus:
> Nullas erat, referoque manus, iterumque retempto,
> Perque torum moveo bracchia, nullus erat.
> (*Her.*, x, 7–12.)

She cried out pathetically to Theseus, only to be
answered by the echo of the hollow rocks:

> And cryed, "Theseus! myn herte swete."
> . . . .
> The holwe rokkes answerde her again.
> (*L. G. W.*, ll. 2190–2193.)

> Interea toto clamanti litore "Theseu!"
> Reddebant nomen concava saxa tuum,
> Et quotiens ego te, totiens locus ipse vocabat.
> (*Her.*, x, 21–23.)

When she mounted upon a high rock and saw his
ship sailing away, her heart grew cold:

And hye upon a rokke she wente sone,
And saw his barge sailing in the see.
Cold wex her herte, and right thus seide she.
(L. G. W., ll. 2195-2197.)

Mons fuit, apparent frutices in vertice rari;
Nunc scopulus raucis pendet adesus aquis:
Ascendo, vires animus dabat, atque ita late
Aequora prospectu metior alta meo.
Inde ego — nam ventis quoque sum crudelibus usa —
Vidi praecipiti carbasa tenta noto.
Aut vidi, aut tamquam quae me vidisse putarem,
Frigidior glacie semi animisque fui.
(Her., x, 25-32.)

The wild beasts even she finds milder than Theseus:

Meker than ye finde I the bestes wilde.
(L. G. W., l. 2198.)

Mitius inveni quam te genus omne ferarum.
(Her., x, 3.)

She cried to him to return and stuck her "kerchief" upon a pole, hoping that he might see it:

She cryed, "O turne again, for routhe and sinne!
Thy barge hath not al his meiny inne!"
Her kerchef on a pole up stikked she,
Ascaunce that he sholde hit wel y-see,
And him remembre that she was behinde,
And turne again, and on the stronde her finde
But al for noght: his wey he is y-goon.
(L. G. W., ll. 2200-2206.)

"Quo fugis?" exclamo, "scelerate revertere Theseu,
Flecte ratem! numerum non habet illa suum."
(Her. x, 35-36.)

Candidaque imposui longae velamina virgae,
Scilicet oblitos admonitura mei.
(Her., x, 41-42.)

She kissed his footprints and spoke to the bed
which had held them both:

> And up she rist, and kiste, in al her care,
> The steppes of his feet, ther he hath fare,
> And to her bedde right thus she speketh tho: —
> "Thou bed," quod she, "that hast receyved two,
> Thou shalt answere of two, and nat of oon!
> Wher is thy gretter part away y-goon?"
>
> (*L. G. W.*, ll. 2208–2213.)

> Saepe torum repeto, qui nos acceperat ambos,
>   Sed non acceptos exhibiturus erat,
> Et tua, quae possum pro te, vestigia tango,
>   Strataque quae membris intepuere tuis
> Incumbo, lacrimisque toro manante profusis
>   "Pressimus" exclamo "te duo, redde duos.
> Venimus huc ambo, cur non discedimus ambo?
>   Perfide, pars nostri, lectule, major ubi est?"
>
> (*Her.*, x, 51–58.)

She would not now be received at her home, even if
she found a means of returning:

> Allas! wher shal I, wrecched wight, become!
> For, thogh so be that ship or boot her come,
> Hoom to my contree dar I nat for drede.
>
> (*L. G. W.*, ll. 2214–2216.)

> Finge dari comitesque mihi ventosque ratemque,
>   Quid sequar? Accessus terra paterna negat.
>
> (*Her.*, x, 63–64.)

The vividness of this pathetic picture Chaucer saw
no reason to change from Ovid, to whom he refers
the reader for her whole "compleining."

> What shal I telle more her compleining?
> Hit is so long, hit were an hevy thing.
> In her epistle Naso telleth al.
>
> (*L. G. W.*, ll. 2218–2220.)

The gods in pity placed her crown among the stars:

> The goddes have her holpen, for pitee;
> And in the signe of Taurus, men may see
> The stones of her coroun shyne clere.
>
> (*L. G. W.*, ll. 2222–2224.)

> desertae et multa querenti
> Amplexus et opem Liber tulit; utque perenni
> Sidere clara foret, sumptam de fronte coronam
> Inmisit caelo, tenues volat illa per auras,
> Dumque volat, gemmae nitidos vertuntur in ignes
> Consistuntque loco, specie remanente coronae,
> Qui medius Mixique genu est, Anguemque tenentis.
>
> (*Met.*, viii, 176–182.)

> Dicta facit, gemmasque novem transformat in ignes:
> Aurea per stellas nunc micat illa novem.
>
> (*Fasti*, iii, 515–516.)

Chaucer cannot restrain a curse at the end upon the man who could repay Ariadne's generosity with such base ingratitude:

> The devil quyte him his whyle!

THE LEGEND OF PHILOMELA

The *Legend of Philomela* is the portrayal of a young woman who is the victim of the basest outrage by one who should have been her protector. Tereus is a betrayer within the family circle. Philomela is the only one of the victims of man's infidelity in the *Legend of Good Women* who is mutilated, and that too in so horrible a way. But unlike Lucretia, who can hardly endure to tell her shame,

Philomela doggedly sets about revealing it to her sister.

After an introduction of sixteen lines Chaucer takes up the thread of his story, the original for which he found, as pointed out by Skeat and others, in *Met.*, vi, 424–605. So closely do the two accounts agree that they may be compared by scenes rather than by lines. The first of these is given by Chaucer in lines 2244–2269. He here tells of the marriage of Tereus and Progne, which was celebrated under the influence of the Furies instead of under the favor of Juno and Hymenæus, and the revel of song and dance which lasted about two weeks. After five years of wedded life Progne longs to see her sister and requests her husband to let her return to her home or to send for her sister to visit her.

In order to see what Chaucer has added and what he has omitted from Ovid's account, it is necessary to quote the corresponding passages from the two authors:

> Of Trace was he lord, and kin to Marte,
> The cruel god that stant with blody darte;
> And wedded had he, with a blisful chere,
> King Pandiones faire doghter dere,
> That highte Progne, flour of her contree,
> Thogh Juno list nat at the feste be,
> Ne Ymeneus, that god of wedding is;
> But at the feste redy ben, y-wis,
> The furies three, with alle hir mortel brond.
> The owle al night aboute the balkes wond,
> That prophet is of wo and of mischaunce.
> (*L. G. W.*, ll. 2244–2254.)

Threicius Tereus haec auxiliaribus armis
Fuderat, et clarum vincendo nomen habebat:
Quem sibi Pandion opibusque virisque potentem
Et genus a magno ducentem forte Gradivo
Conubio Prognes junxit; non pronuba Juno,
Non Hymenaeus adest, non illi Gratis lecto.
Eumenides tenuere faces de funere raptas;
Eumenides stravere torum, tectoque profanus
Incubuit bubo thalamique in culmine sedit.

(*Met.*, vi, 424–432.)

Professor Lowes,[1] who suggests that Chaucer
used the *Ovide moralisé* along with the *Metamorphoses* in the *Legend of Philomela*, offers verbal
parallelisms for some of these details as follows:
"with a blisful chere" of the bridegroom; "that
god of wedding is" with regard to Hymenaeus; "al
night" and "prophet is of wo and of mischaunce"
of the owl. It would require no source to suggest to
Chaucer that a bridegroom would have "a blisful
chere." Moreover, as Professor Lowes says, "If the
hint is taken from the *O. m.*, Chaucer has transformed the joy from Pandion to Tereus." [2] It is
Pandion in the *Ovide moralisé* who rejoices because
he is marrying his daughter to a king, and there is
nothing about the bridegroom's having a joyful
countenance. Chaucer knew from many passages
in the *Heroides* and *Metamorphoses* that Hymenæus was the God of Wedding, and that the owl,
which was a bird of ill omen, cried all the wedding-

[1] *P. M. L. A.*, XXXIII, 303–305.
[2] *Ibid.*, 304.

night. "Prophet is of wo and of mischaunce" is an
excellent translation of Ovid's "profanus," that is,
"ill boding." Chrétien includes the owl among the
five different kinds of birds as omens of ill on this
occasion:

> Chanta sus la chanbre lidus
> Et li huaz et li cucu
> Et la fresaie et lie corbiaus.[1]

Huaz, however, does not necessarily mean "owl"
here, because the word is not restricted to that bird
alone. Ovid, like Chaucer, mentions only the owl,
and insists upon the ill-boding nature of this bird:

> Hac ave conjuncti Progne Tereusque, parentes
> Hac ave sunt facti.
> (*Met.*, vi, 433–434.)

The evidence that Chaucer was following Ovid on
these points, supplemented with phrases of his
own, is strengthened by his use in this same passage of "that stant with blody darte" with regard
to Mars, and of "faire doghter dere and flour of
her contree" with regard to Progne, neither of
which is found in the *Ovide moralisé*.

Following Ovid's order of narrative strictly,
Chaucer next says that; when Tereus and Progne
had been married five years, she greatly longed to
see her sister.

> Five yeer his wyf and he togeder dwelle.
> (*L. G. W.*, l. 2259.)

---

[1] *P. M. L. A.*, XXXIII, 305.

These words are the simplest rendering of Ovid's mythological phrasing which Chaucer so often discarded:

> Jam tempora Titan
> Quinque per autumnos repetiti duxerat anni.
> (*Met.*, vi, 438-439.)

Though it is true that there is some verbal resemblance between Chaucer and the *Ovide moralisé* with regard to Tereus and Progne's having been married five years,[1] it is of little significance. Chaucer and Chrétien, the author of this portion of the *Ovide moralisé*,[2] are both translating from Ovid, and it is not surprising that they should phrase the idea somewhat similarly. But Chrétien's "plus de," *more than* five years, is in neither Ovid nor Chaucer.

According to Chaucer, Progne has such an intense longing to see her sister that she requests her husband to let her go to see her or send for her sister to visit her. And this was her constant prayer to her husband, made with all wifely humility:

> Til on a day she gan so sore longe
> To seen her suster, that she saw nat longe,
> That for desyr she niste what to seye.
> But to her husband gan she for to preye,
> For goddes love, that she moste ones goon
> Her suster for to seen, and come anoon,
> Or elles, but she moste to her wende,
> She preyde him, that he wolde after her sende;

---

[1] See *P. M. L. A.*, XXXIII, 305.
[2] See *Ibid.*, pp. 302-303.

And this was, day by day, al her prayere
With al humblesse of wyfhood, word, and chere.
(*L. G. W.*, ll. 2260–2269.)

It is this intensity of her desire that Ovid expresses
when he describes how Progne said *coaxingly* to her
husband, "*If I have found any favor in your sight,
either send me to visit my sister or let my sister
come hither. . . . In giving me a chance to see my
sister you will confer upon me a great boon*":

> Cum blandita viro Progne "si gratia" dixit
> "Ulla mea est, vel me visendam mitte sorori,
> Vel soror huc veniat: redituram tempore parvo
> Promittes socero; magni mihi muneris instar
> Germanam vidisse dabis."
(*Met.*, vi, 440–444.)

In the *Ovide moralisé* there is no description of the
longing of Progne such as Ovid and Chaucer express. Chrétien merely says that she has a desire
to go to see her sister Philomela. When she speaks
to her husband about it she promises to return
quickly and not to sojourn. And if he denies her
this, then she prays that he will seek her sister and
lead her to their land.[1] In the French account the
emphasis is upon Progne's promise that she will not
be gone long. In Progne's prayer that she be allowed to visit her sister, or that her sister be allowed
to come to her, Chaucer has translated Ovid's

[1] *P. M. L. A.*, XXXIII, 305–306.

words, *Vel me visendam mitte sorori, Vel soror huc veniat.*

In line 2269, describing Progne's wifely humility, Chaucer has happily rendered Ovid's

> Cum blandita viro Progne "si gratia" dixit
> "Ulla mea est."

In attributing this line to Chaucer himself, Professor Lowes [1] apparently overlooked Ovid's words.

The next scene of the *Legend* opens with the rapid narration of the departure of Tereus for Greece, his arrival there, and his petition to Pandion to let Philomela return with him:

> This Tereus let make his shippes yare
> And into Grece himself is forth y-fare
> Unto his fader-in-lawe.
> *(L. G. W.*, ll. 2270–2272.)

These lines aptly render the terseness of Ovid's sentence:

> Jubet ille carinas
> In freta deduci veloque et remige portus
> Cecropios intrat Piraeaque litora tangit.
> *(Met.*, vi, 444–446.)

Very different is the French, in which Tereus commands his vessel to be fitted out with food, masts, and sails, and which, Professor Lowes says, "gives a brief account of the voyage and elaborates at considerable length (86–105) the reception accorded Tereus by Pandion." He adds that Chau-

---

[1] *P. M. L. A.*, XXXIII, 306.

cer "agrees with Ovid in the absence of these details, and condenses even Ovid's brief account." [1]

In presenting the request to Pandion, Tereus prays that Philomela might

> On Progne his wyf but ones have a sighte
> "And she shal come to you again anoon."
> > (*L. G. W.*, ll. 2275-2276.)

In these words Tereus is repeating *verbatim* what in the *Metamorphoses* Progne had said to him at home:

> Vel me visendam mitte sorori
> Vel soror huc veniat: redituram tempore parvo
> Promittes socero.
> > (*Met.*, vi, 441-443.)

Ovid, in describing Tereus' meeting with Pandion, adds that Tereus promised Philomela's speedy return:

> Coeperat, adventus causam, mandata referre
> Conjugis et celeres missae spondere recursus.
> > (*Met.*, vi, 449-450.)

In Tereus' speech to Pandion Chaucer includes several points that are not to be found in Ovid or the *Ovide moralisé*. For instance, he promises that Philomela shall be gone "for a month or tweye," "myself with her wol bothe come and goon," "and as myn hertes lyf I wol her kepe." Had he been following the *Ovide moralisé*, he would surely have taken at least some of his additions from Chrétien,

[1] *P. M. L. A.*, XXXIII, 306.

who puts an eloquent speech into Tereus' mouth.
In it Tereus promises that she shall not remain a
single day or even an hour. On this point Professor
Lowes notes, "Tereus elsewhere limits the time to
'tant solemant trois jourz on quatre' (line 515),
or 'quinzainne' (line 535). Chaucer more carefully observes the demands of verisimilitude." [1]
The only place in this passage where there is a suggestion of similarity between Chaucer and the
Ovide moralisé is in Tereus' statement that he will
bring her back quickly,

> Que je tantost ne la ramaingne.[2]

But this is not a verbal parallelism to Chaucer's

> Myself with her wol bothe come and goon.

If Chaucer had been using the *Ovide moralisé* to
assist him in interpreting Ovid, there must have
been something more indicative of it than this.

Up to this point Chaucer has followed the order
of Ovid's narrative exactly. But in describing the
scene between Pandion, Philomela, and Tereus
(*L. G. W.*, ll. 2279–2301) he changes the arrangement somewhat, though the details, with some additions of his own, are quite in agreement with
Ovid's. (See *L. G. W.*, ll. 2279–2287, *Met.*, vi, 475–
476; *L. G. W.*, ll. 2288–2294, *Met.*, vi, 455–482;

---

[1] *P. M. L. A.*, XXXIII, 307, note 40ᵃ.
[2] *Ibid.*, p. 308.

L. G. W., ll. 2296–2299, *Met.*, vi, 494–501, and 507–
508.) Interestingly enough, the details which
Chaucer adds, Philomela's tears (l. 2284) and
Pandion's request that Progne be given leave to
visit him sometime (ll. 2300–2301), are not taken
from the 524 lines of the *Ovide moralisé* detailing
this scene.[1] In Ovid, Philomela is represented as
entering while Tereus is begging Pandion to allow
her to accompany him home, and as arousing immediately Tereus' lustful nature.[2] The burning
flame of his passion, which he had so suddenly
conceived, makes him more eloquent than ever.
Chaucer more effectively describes the inception
of Tereus' mad infatuation when he observes Philomela entreating her father to let her go, weeping
and embracing him before Tereus. It was then

> He caste his fyry herte upon her so
> That he wol have her, how so that it go.
> > (*L. G. W.*, ll. 2292–2293.)

In describing Philomela's entrance upon the
dialogue between Pandion and Tereus, Ovid says
that Philomela enters rich in her apparel but richer
still in beauty:

> Ecce venit magno dives Philomela paratu,
> Divitior forma.
> > (*Met.*, vi, 451–452.)

---

[1] *P. M. L. A.*, XXXIII, 309.
[2] See *Met.*, vi, 451–474.

Chaucer, after first saying,

> That, whan that Tereus saw her beautee,
> (*L. G. W.*, l. 2289.)

adds literally from Ovid,

> And of array that ther was noon her liche
> And yit of beautee was she two so riche.
> (*L. G. W.*, ll. 2290–2291.)

Though all the Chaucer MSS have *beautee* in this last line, except B and F, which have "*bountee*," Skeat has adopted the reading of the latter inferior MS., evidently thinking *beautee* must be wrong because Chaucer had used that word just two lines above.[1] Clearly Chaucer repeated *beautee* because he was translating Ovid so closely. Professor Lowes, though noting the evidence of the MSS,[2] retains *bountee*, presumably because it seems to suggest a parallel with a word in the *Ovide moralisé*. But there the statement is that she was not less *wise* than beautiful:

> Ne fu pas mains sage que bele.

Chaucer uses from Ovid the detail of Pandion's weeping, but he assigns it to the time when the old king gives his consent for Philomela to go (ll. 2279–2281).

At the end of Pandion's speech of farewell in lines 2305–2307, Chaucer explains that the king

[1] See *Oxford Chaucer*, III, 160, bottom.
[2] *P. M. L. A.*, XXXIII, 310, note 44.

brought them down to the sea and then returned
home without thinking of any malice being intended against Philomela:

> And him conveyeth through the maister-strete
> Of Athens, and to the see him broghte,
> And turneth hoom; no malice he ne thoghte.

There is a verbal similarity between "conveyeth"
and "to the see him broghte" and the words of
Chrétien,

> Au port l'an mainne Tereus
> Et Pandions les i convoie.[1]

Forty lines farther on in the *Philomena*, Chrétien
remarks that Pandion will never see his daughter
again, nor will she return to her land, but of this he
does not think:

> Car ja mes la reverra
> N'an sa terre ne ranterra.
> Mes de tot ce ne panse il.

Though this might conceivably be the source of
Chaucer's "no malice he ne thoghte," [2] that phrase
expresses the connotation of Ovid's lines far more
delicately than Chrétien's does. Ovid makes Pandion begin his speech of farewell with tears (*Met.*,
vi, 495), and at the close describes him as scarcely
able to speak for his sobs, and fearful of the fore-
bodings of his mind:

> Vix dixit, timuitque suae praesagia mentis.
>
> (*Met.*, vi, 510.)

---

[1] *P. M. L. A.*, XXXIII, 310.   [2] See Lowes, *Ibid.*

Pandion, who was timid because he was old and was saying farewell to his beloved daughter, was fearful of never seeing her again. He was afraid of what might happen to her on the sea. But with all his fears of danger for Philomela, he never once thought of *malice* against her. Had this idea entered his mind, he would not have entrusted Philomela into Tereus' hand.

How Tereus rejoiced over having Philomela in his power as given in the *Metamorphoses*, Chaucer omits altogether. But in the account of the rape of Philomela he follows Ovid very closely even to details. Immediately after the arrival in Thrace, according to Ovid, Tereus takes Philomela to a forest:

> Cum rex Pandione natam
> In stabula alta trahit silvis obscura vetustis.
> *(Met.*, vi, 520–521.)

Chaucer renders this,

> And up into a forest he her ledde,
> And to a cave privily him spedde;
> And in this derke cave, yif her leste,
> Or leste noght, he bad her for to reste.
> *(L. G. W.*, ll. 2310–2313.)

That Chaucer had the Latin in mind here is evident from his choice of words: "forest," *silvis;* "ledde," *trahit;* "derke," *obscura.* He has rendered *stabula alta,* "a cave," the transition from the meaning of a "lair" or "haunt of wild beasts" to that of a "cave" being easy.[1] Virgil has a line in the *Æneid*, which would easily contribute to such a conception:

Itur in antiquam silvam, stabula alta ferarum.

(*Æn.*, vi, 179.)

Every other detail that follows in this scene (ll. 2315–2338) is derived from the *Metamorphoses*.[2] But Chaucer, as he often does, changes the exact order of Ovid's narrative for better dramatic effect. For instance, here Ovid says that Tereus overcame Philomela by force, and compares her in the hands of Tereus, *after* his violation of her, to a lamb in the power of the wolf, or to a dove at the mercy of an eagle. Chaucer, however, uses these same figures to describe Philomela *before* Tereus' attack and then brings forward to this point Ovid's vivid account of the rape, with Philomela calling for aid upon her sister, her father, and all the gods.

Ovid's lines 531–548, telling of the rage of Philomela when she recovers her senses after Tereus' attack, Chaucer omits. But they supply the motive that he assigns for Tereus' cutting out Philomela's tongue. In Ovid, she upbraids him for his baseness, and says that, if the gods see these things, he will pay dearly for this act, that she will proclaim his deed to the people, or if that opportunity

[1] If Chaucer had been very dependent upon French translations of Ovid, he would surely have adopted Chrétien's word here, "meison."

[2] See *Met.*, vi, 519–530.

is denied her, she will fill the woods with her story
and move the rocks to pity, the air of heaven shall
hear it, and, if there is any god in heaven, he shall
hear it too:

> Si tamen haec superi cernunt, si numina divum
> Sunt aliquid, si non perierunt omnia mecum,
> Quandocumque mihi poenas dabis! ipsa pudore
> Projecto tua facta loquar: si copia detur,
> In populos veniam; si silvis clausa tenebor,
> Implebo silvas et conscia saxa movebo;
> Audiet haec aether et si deus ullus in illo est.
>
> *(Met.*, vi, 542-548.)

These words of Philomela both angered Tereus and
made him realize the danger in her tongue, which
he forthwith cut out:

> Talibus ira feri postquam commota tyranni
> Nec minor hac metus est, causa stimulatus utraque.
>
> *(Met.*, vi, 549-550.)

Disregarding Tereus' anger at Philomela's words,
Chaucer puts the reason for Tereus' next step
upon his fear of the shame that her tongue may
bring upon him. Therefore he says,

> And yet this false theef
> Hath doon this lady yet a more mischeef,
> For fere lest she sholde his shame crye
> And doon him openly a vilanye
> And with his swerd her tong of kerveth he.
>
> *(L. G. W.*, ll. 2330-2334.)

False theef is an excellent rendering of Ovid's *feri
tyranni*. In addition to the motive supplied by

Philomela's reproaches of Tereus, Chaucer has taken Ovid's very words, *metus* (l. 550) and *tua facta loquar* [1] (l. 545), and put them into his line,

> For fere lest she sholde his shame crye.
>
> (*L. G. W.*, l. 2332.)

And the succeeding line,

> And doon him openly a vilanye,

reflects very patently the threats that Philomela had made to Tereus, that she would proclaim his baseness. With the fact of the cutting out of her tongue and the motive for it both supplied by Ovid immediately after Tereus' violation of Philomela, it seems unlikely that Chaucer resorted to the *Ovide moralisé* for this circumstance, especially since in the preceding scene he is not following the *Ovide moralisé*, which elaborates for nearly one hundred lines Tereus' efforts to win Philomela's consent.[2] In spirit and method, as well as in the translation of words, Chaucer's procedure is in keeping with Ovid's narrative rather than Chrétien's. The minute description which Ovid gives of the cutting out of Philomela's tongue [3] Chaucer summarizes in a line,

> And with his swerd her tong of kerveth he.

Ovid states that Tereus often returned to Philomela's mutilated body to gratify his foul lust,

---

[1] *Facta* could mean in this connection only "shameful deeds."
[2] *P. M. L. A.*, XXXIII, 312.   [3] *Met.*, vi, 551–560.

though it is scarcely credible (*vix ausim credere*). This Chaucer has used, and, in the same connection, says that Tereus enclosed her in a castle:

> And in a castel made her for to be
> Ful privily in prison evermore,
> And kepte her to his usage and his store.
> (*L. G. W.*, ll. 2335–2337.)

This detail of the castle, as well as the return of Tereus to his wife with the report that Philomela was dead (*L. G. W.*, ll. 2342–2348), came from *Met.*, vi, 563–567.

Ovid's question, "Quid faciat Philomela?" (*Met.*, vi, 572), as every interrogation does, focusses attention. Philomela is enclosed in a castle; escape is impossible; her mute tongue prevents an explanation of the crime against her:

> fugam custodia claudit:
> Structa rigent solido stabulorum moenia saxo:
> Os mutum facti caret indice.
> (*Met.*, vi, 572–574.)

But great is the ingenuity of grief, and her skill (*sollertia*) comes to her rescue in the midst of her miserable state; she can weave into tapestry the story of her wrongs:

> grande doloris
> Ingenium est, miserisque venit sollertia rebus.
> (*Met.*, vi, 574–575.)

So she sets up her loom and weaves an account of the crime:

Stamina barbarica suspendit Pallade telae,
Purpureasque notas filis intexuit albis,
Indicium sceleris.
(*Met.*, vi, 576–578.)

Ovid assumes without explanation that Philomela knew how to weave. As Chaucer often makes additions of his own, either to amplify the narrative or possibly only to fill out the line, so here he explains that Philomela learned this art of weaving in her youth and that this is the common accomplishment of women. Though Chaucer and the *Ovide moralisé* agree in describing Philomela as skilful in weaving, nothing is said in the French poem of her having learned it in youth. This accomplishment is ascribed to her in lines 188–193 of the *Philomena* in the midst of a long list of others that she possessed. Not until nearly nine hundred lines later (ll. 1086 ff.) does Chrétien introduce the web, the device of which he has made Philomela hit upon in a very different way from Chaucer's. In other words, Chrétien did not specifically connect her accomplishment of weaving with her need at this time. But Ovid and Chaucer both do. Ovid says in the immediate connection with her setting up the loom that her skill (*sollertia*, the synonym for which is *scientia*) came to her assistance in her miserable condition of imprisonment. Chaucer explains that Philomela was unable to write with a pen:

> But with a penne coude she nat wryte;
> But lettres can she weven to and fro.
>
> (*L. G. W.*, ll. 2357-2358.)

This inability to use a pen, which is his own addition, Chaucer assigns as a reason for Philomela's weaving her story upon the tapestry.[1] Chaucer's specific statement that Philomela had food and clothing as much as she desired was possibly suggested by Chrétien's general one, that nothing was forbidden to her except to go out of the house:[2]

> And shortly for to seyn she hath her fille
> Of mete and drink, and clothing at her wille.
>
> (*L. G. W.*, ll. 2354-2355.)

> Ne ja ne li fust contredite
> Nule chose granz ne petite
> Fors l'issue de la meison.

Chaucer says that after a year Philomela had finished the web, and he then gives a summary of what was contained in it:

> So that, by that the yeer was al a-go
> She had y-woven in a stamin large
> How she was broght from Athenes in a barge
> And in a cave how that she was broght;
> And al the thing that Tereus hath wroght,
> She waf it wel, and wroot the story above.
>
> (*L. G. W.*, ll. 2359-2364.)

The statement that Philomela was a prisoner for a year came from Ovid:

---

[1] "On the other hand, Chrétien has skilfully motivated in quite different fashion the manner in which Philomela hit upon the web." Lowes, *P. M. L. A.*, XXXIII, 313, note 62[b].

[2] *Ibid.*, 314.

Signa deus bis sex acto lustraverat anno.

(*Met.*, vi, 571.)

The "stamin" in line 2360 is clearly Ovid's *stamina* (l. 576). The verbal closeness of Chaucer to Ovid all through this scene is illustrated by the use of "clooth," which Ovid describes as *vestes* when Progne unfolds the web:

Unto the quene and beren her that clooth.

(*L. G. W.*, l. 2368.)

Evolvit vestes saevi matrona tyranni.

(*Met.*, vi, 581.)

Chrétien uses "cortine," [1] a word which one cannot help feeling would have been intriguing to Chaucer had the French poet been much in his mind at this time. Chaucer includes her being taken to "a cave," which is, as we have found, probably his interpretation of what Ovid meant. And of Ovid's *indicium sceleris* Chaucer has made a good rendition with his line,

And al the thing that Tereus hath wroght.

The suggestion of a summary of the contents of the web may have come from Chrétien. Chaucer's summary is very brief: Philomela was brought from Athens in a barge, taken to a cave, and the rest is condensed into a single line. Chrétien, on the other hand, recapitulates in detail: that she

[1] *P. M. L. A.*, XXXIII, 315, note 66ª.

wove a picture of the ship on which Tereus crossed the sea when he went to Athens; and that she wrote how he conducted himself there, how he brought her away, how he abandoned her after he had cut out her tongue; and that she wove a picture of the house and garden where she was imprisoned.

But in a more significant way the English and the French accounts differ. Chaucer's summary is simple narrative and shows no indication of direct portrayal having been combined with it. The use of "lettres" that she wove is clear evidence of this:

> But lettres can she weven to and fro.
> (*L. G. W.*, l. 2358.)

This corresponds to Ovid's line,

> Purpureasque notas filis intexuit albis.
> (*Met.*, vi, 577.)

Notas is a very common designation for the characters used in writing, especially among the poets.[1] Chaucer recapitulates "lettres" with his tautological line,

> She waf it wel, and wroot the story above.[2]

"Waf" and "wroot" are synonymous terms here. "Above" means "as told above" by Chaucer himself. The repetition of his "a cave" indicates that this is the correct interpretation of "above." So

---

[1] See *Harpers' Latin Dictionary.*

[2] The reader of Chaucer will recall many another tautological expression in his poetry.

when Chaucer says that she wove in "lettres" how she was brought from Athens in a barge, he intends nothing but that the story was told by means of the letters that she wove in the web. Chrétien, however, uses direct portrayal along with narrative.[1] He says Philomela wove a picture of the ship on which Tereus crossed the sea, and a picture of the house and garden where she is confined. The rest is told apparently in narrative form. Since the dissimilarity of result between Chaucer and Chrétien is so great, it makes one skeptical after all as to the suggestion of a summary having come to Chaucer from the *Ovide moralisé*.

The circumstance of giving "a knave" a ring and praying him by signs to bear to Progne the web on which she had woven her pitiful tale comes from Ovid, with the exception of the ring:

> And to a knave a ring she yaf anoon,
> And prayed him by signes, for to goon
> Unto the quene, and beren her that clooth.
> (*L. G. W.*, ll. 2366–2368.)

> perfectaque tradidit uni:
> Utque ferat dominae gestu rogat: ille rogata
> Pertulit ad Procnem; necscit quid tradat in illis.
> (*Met.*, vi, 578–580.)

In both Chaucer and Ovid it is a man messenger who is employed by Philomela. *Uni*, to be sure, is non-committal as to gender, but *ille* is masculine.

---

[1] Lowes, *P. M. L. A.*, XXXIII, 315.

Though some of the MSS and editions of Ovid read *illa rogata*, the best, and by far the majority, read *ille*, and it is evident that Chaucer was following a MS. in which *ille* was used. On Chaucer's calling the messenger "a knave," Professor Lowes says, "Chaucer has diverged from both Ovid and the *Ovide moralisé*. In Ovid the web is given to her attendant, who is a woman (578–580); and in the *Ovide moralisé* the messenger is the old woman's daughter (1145, 1220 ff.; cf. 867–73); in Chaucer she gives it to 'a knave' (2366)." [1] But the critical text of Ovid, that is, "Magnus," which Professor Lowes is following, has *ille rogata*,[2] and he quotes it so in discussing another point.[3] Besides, Ovid's use of *illis* in the next line is conclusive that *rogata* is the accusative plural neuter of the participle and not the nominative singular feminine.

The point as to the verbal similarity to *Ovide moralisé* in Chaucer's use of "to the quene" (lines 2363 and 2371) rather than to Ovid's *dominae* and *ad Procnem* seems inconsiderable as evidence.

Chaucer's use of "by signes" in line 2367 and again in line 2369 comes from Ovid:

> Utque ferat dominae gestu [4] rogat.
>
> (*Met.*, vi, 579.)

---

[1] *P. M. L. A.*, XXXIII, 315–316.

[2] *Ibid.*, 314, note 10.

[3] *Ibid.*, 317.

[4] That this detail is also in the *Ovide Moralisé*, does not signify that Chaucer was following that source.

The suggestion of a reward to the "knave" seems to be Chaucer's own:

> And by signes swor him many an ooth,
> She sholde him yeve what she geten mighte.
> (*L. G. W.*, ll. 2369–2370.)

Though in the *Ovide moralisé* Philomela offers the excuse for sending the web, that she will receive something for the work, there is no suggestion that the messenger is to obtain a reward.[1] Besides, tipping for service, I suppose, was as common a practice in the "Merry England" of Chaucer's day as it is at the present time, so that it required little originality to add that suggestion, even though Ovid had said nothing of any remuneration.

The closing scene, lines 2371–2382, Chaucer takes from *Met.*, vi, 582–587, and 603–605, up to the point where Progne finds Philomela. Here his *Legend* ends. He has characteristically omitted the Bacchic rites which Ovid gives. Nor is he concerned with the vengeance of Progne and Philomela upon Tereus, and later with the transformation of the two sisters into the swallow and the nightingale. Having brought the story to the dramatic meeting of the two sisters, he has finished:

> Allas! the wo, the compleint, and the mone
> That Progne upon her dombe suster maketh!
> In armes everich of hem other taketh,
> And thus I lete hem in hir sorwe dwelle.
> (*L. G. W.*, ll. 2379–2382.)

---

[1] *P. M. L. A.*, XXXIII, 316.

After consideration of the evidence for Chaucer's use of Machaut or the *Ovide moralisé* in the story of Theseus and Ariadne in the *House of Fame* and in the *Legend of Good Women*, and of the *Ovide moralisé* in the *Legend of Philomela*, it seems clear that the claims for any large use of French translations of Ovid by Chaucer are unjustifiable.[1] However much court circles in France or in England may have found it helpful to call in the aid of French translations of Latin authors,[2] this practice was not necessary to Chaucer in dealing with Ovid's poems. Though it may be conjectured that in Chaucer's early acquaintance with Ovid he knew also the French adaptations, his complete familiarity with Ovid's language and art of narration precludes any dependence upon the French by the time he wrote the *House of Fame*, *Troilus*, and the *Legend of Good Women*. His literal renderings, some involving points of textual variations which have been discussed in this volume, are sufficient proof that his knowledge was at first hand. As we have seen in these Legends, he characteristically interpreted Ovid in terms of his own art, and any use he may have made of the French poets who had followed Ovid was of minor consequence. In addition to the accuracy of his knowledge of Ovid, Chaucer's mood

[1] J. L. Lowes, *Nation* (Dec. 21, 1916), Supplement, CIII, No. 2686, 2).

[2] *P. M. L. A.*, XXXIII, 319.

and spirit as well as methods of narration are more
closely akin to the Latin with its unity of thought
and precision of expression than to the psychologiz-
ing habits of the Old French writers. His interest
is in human relationships realistically and dramatically portrayed. It is apparent that the Old French
translations and allegorizations of the Classics
weighed virtually nothing either in the extent of
Chaucer's knowledge or the shaping of his art.

The Legend of Phyllis

The *Legend of Phyllis*, though separated from the
Legend of Ariadne by that of *Philomela*, belongs
with the *Ariadne*, much as the *Legend of Medea* belongs with the *Hypsipyle*.[1] The latter are bound
together by one man, Jason; the legends of *Phyllis*
and *Ariadne* are bound together by Theseus and
Demophoon, father and son. In fact, Chaucer
constantly refers in the *Phyllis* to the *Ariadne*.
The contrast between the two heroines here is as
striking as that between Hypsipyle and Medea.
As we have seen, Ariadne was young and romantic.
She was deserted immediately and suddenly. She
woke to find over night an empty bed. Phyllis, on
the other hand, is already queen of her land, calm
and full of dignity. She trusted Demophoon, who

[1] See Tatlock, *Development and Chronology of Chaucer's Works*,
p. 128.

came in weariness to her shores, and gave him her love. He left her openly, promising to return in a month and take her to Athens as his wife. She, after waiting four months, became convinced that she had been deceived. In the Epistle of Ovid from which Chaucer took this story, the emotion is less passionate than in the others which he has used.

To supplement the story in *Heroides*, ii, Chaucer had recourse to Boccaccio's *De Genealogia Deorum*. Boccaccio furnished him with the facts about how Demophoon came to Thrace and how he happened to leave.[1] From the *Heroides*, he knew and had already used in the *House of Fame* the information that Demophoon was duke of Athens, that Phyllis was daughter to the Thracian king, and that Demophoon foreswore himself.[2] He added from the same source two details that are lacking in the former poem: that Phyllis is the daughter of Lycurgus and that she lived in Rhodope:

> Wherof that Phillis lady was and quene,
> Ligurgus doghter, fairer on to sene.
>
> > (*L. G. W.*, ll. 2425-2426.)

> Quae tibi subjeci latissima regna Lycurgi.
>
> > (*Her.*, ii, 111.)

---

[1] See C. G. Child, "Chaucer's Legend of Good Women and Boccaccio's De Genealogia Deorum," *M. L. N.*, XI, 480-482.

[2] Kittredge, "Chaucer's Medea and the Date of the Legend of Good Women," *P. M. L. A.*, XXIV, 250.

And lyth in Rodopeya him for to reste.

>   (*L. G. W.*, l. 2438.)

Hospita, Demophoon, tua te Rhodopeia Phyllis.

>   (*Her.*, ii, 1.)

Qua patet umbrosum Rhodope glacialis ad Haemum.

>   (*Her.*, ii, 113.)

That Demophoon was driven to Rhodope by a storm [1] was probably suggested to Chaucer by Ovid, who makes Phyllis recall to Demophoon that it was she who refitted his shattered ships and gave him the oars by which he was enabled to flee from her:

>   At laceras etiam puppes furiosa refeci —
>   Ut qua desererer, firma carina foret! —
>   Remigiumque dedi, quod me fugiturus haberes.
>   (*Her.*, ii, 45–47.) [2]

The description of the storm Chaucer may have invented, or he may have recalled *Æneid*, i, 85–90, 102, 142, which has been suggested by Bech,[3] who is quoted by Skeat. If the *Æneid* was the source, Chaucer has adapted Virgil's lines rather freely. Bech and Skeat are probably correct in citing *Æneid*, v, 823–825, as the source for line 2422,

>   And Thetis, Chorus, Triton, and they alle.

This impression is strengthened by the preceding line, which calls to mind Virgil's account of Neptune's calming the sea for Æneas,

---

[1] *L. G. W.*, ll. 2411–2440.   [2] Cf. also *Her.*, ii, 107 ff.
[3] *Anglia*, V, 345.

Til Neptune hath of him compassion.
(*L. G. W.*, l. 2421.)

Child has suggested that "Chorus" in line 2422
came from the *De Genealogia Deorum.*[1] The promise
to return in a month (l. 2477) Chaucer found in
Heroides, ii, 1–4:

> Hospita, Demophoon, tua te Rhodopeia Phyllis
> Ultra promissum tempus abesse queror.
> Cornua cum lunae pleno semel orbe coissent,
> Litoribus nostris ancora pacta tua est.

After weaving together the details from Ovid and
Boccaccio in the first part of his account, Chaucer
begins with line 2496 to follow Ovid closely. In
fact, the first seventeen lines of this passage, down
to line 2512, are a translation of the first eight lines
of *Heroides*, ii. Then, with the acumen that he has
manifested so constantly, Chaucer realizes that the
Epistle of Phyllis is too full of repetition of her
plaint of having loved too well but not wisely to
appeal to his reader, and he determines to use from
it only pertinent selections. He characteristically
offers as a reason that it is too long, but it is not so
much weariness or limitation of time that guided
him as literary expediency. He takes his reader
into his confidence and says plainly that he will
select here and there where he thinks Ovid has well
expressed the feelings of Phyllis:

[1] *M. L. N.*, XI, 477–478.

But here and there in ryme I have hit laid
Ther as me thoughte that she wel hath said.
(L. G. W., ll. 2516–2517.)

Though we have found Chaucer practising this art previously in many instances, it is interesting now to hear the master explaining his own method.

The first lines he selects from Ovid are,

Vela queror reditu, verba carere fide.
Dic mihi, quid feci, nisi non sapienter amavi.
(Her., ii, 26–27.)

These Chaucer has fittingly rendered,

She seide, "thy sailes comen nat again,
Ne to thy word ther nis no fey certain;
But I wot why ye come nat," quod she;
"For I was of my love to yow so free."
(L. G. W., ll. 2518–2521.)

Phyllis in her Epistle next calls Demophoon's attention to his swearing by the gods falsely, and tells him that he will not be able to bear the pain that they will inflict upon him (*Her.*, ii, 35–44). Ovid has named many of the divinities, — the sea, his grandsire, Venus, and Juno, — to whom Chaucer refers by the one word, "goddes."

Phyllis reminds Demophoon that she trusted too much to his noble birth, his smooth tongue, and his false tears:

Credidimus blandis, quorum tibi copia, verbis:
Credidimus generi numinibusque tuis:
Credidimus lacrimis: an et hae similare docentur.
(Her., ii, 49–51.)

These lines Chaucer has translated almost literally:

"To moche trusted I, wel may I pleyne,
Upon your linage and your faire tonge,
And on your teres falsly out y-wronge.
How could ye wepe so by craft?" quod she.
May ther swiche teres feyned be.
(*L. G. W.*, ll. 2525-2529.)

In Ovid, Phyllis next tells Demophoon that it is no glory to deceive a trusting maiden, and prays that this may be the highest praise to which he may attain:

Fallere credentem non est operosa puellam
Gloria.   (*Her.*, ii, 63-64.)

Di faciant, laudis summa sit ista tuae.
(*Her.*, ii, 66.)

In Chaucer this idea appears thus,

Now certes, yif ye wolde have in memorie,
Hit oughte be to yow but litel glorie
To have a sely mayde thus betrayed!
To god, quod she, preye I, and ofte have prayed,
That hit be now the grettest prys of alle,
And moste honour that ever yow shal befalle!

Phyllis prays in *Heroides*, ii, that when Demophoon's statue is erected among those of his ancestors who have distinguished themselves by various exploits, he may be indicated as the man who betrayed the hostess that loved him:

Hoc tua post illos titulo signetur imago:
Hic est, cujus amans hospita capta dolo est.
(*Her.*, ii, 73-74.)

Though Ovid mentions the ancestors by name, Theseus, Scyron, Procrustes, Sinis (*Her.*, ii, 67–74), because they carried some connotation to readers of antiquity, Chaucer, realizing that none of them except Theseus would mean anything to his readers, omitted them, merely calling them "auncestres" (*L. G. W.*, ll. 2536–2542). But he makes much of Demophoon's relationship to his false father, Theseus.

In the *Heroides*, Phyllis says that Demophoon has chosen to imitate his father, whose one great fault was falseness in love:

> De tanta rerum turba factisque parentis
> Sedit in ingenio Cressa relicta tuo.
> Quod solum excusat, solum miraris in illo.
> Heredem patriae, perfide, fraudis agis.
> (Her., ii, 75–78.)

This feature of inherited unfaithfulness in love in Demophoon's character, more than any other, seems to have impressed Chaucer, for the basis of his attack upon him is like father, like son. It runs with constant iteration all through the *Legend of Phyllis*, as the following references show: lines 2399–2400; 2446–2447; 2459–2464; 2492–2493; 2543–2547.

Ovid makes Phyllis threaten to throw herself into the sea that Demophoon may soon see her dead body floating in the bay at Athens; and she adds that, though he is harder than iron or ada-

290 THE LEGEND OF GOOD WOMEN

mant, he will say that this was not the way he
should have been followed:

> Ad tua me fluctus projectam litora portent,
> Occurramque oculis intumulata tuis,
> Duritia ferrum ut superes adamantaque teque,
> "Non tibi sic," dices, "Phylli, sequendus eram."
>
> (*Her.*, ii, 135–138.)

Chaucer has made use of all this except the last
line, which he omitted, probably feeling that it was
off the key for the serious tone of his *Legend*. At
any rate, he has incorporated Ovid's comparison
"harder than any stoon," without completing the
sentence to which it belongs in the Latin or sub-
stituting any other for it. It thus becomes a "non
sequitur" to the preceding thought and is left
dangling in the air. If he appreciated the incongruity of Ovid's witticism, he nevertheless seems
to have imitated him in indulging in a bit of pleas-
antry at the very end of this *Legend*. Ovid puts his
into the mouth of Phyllis herself at the moment
when she is contemplating suicide, while Chaucer's
is his own and only incidentally belongs to the
story. Whatever artistic blemish there may be, it
is greater in the *Heroides* than in the *Legend*.

Though Ovid in *Heroides*, ii, makes Phyllis
suggest at least three other methods of death —
the sword, poison, and hanging — besides that of
drowning, he does not say which one she employed.[1]

[1] *Her.*, ii, 133–148.

Chaucer likewise contents himself with the statement,

> She for dispeyr fordide herself, allas!

though earlier in the *Legend* (ll. 2484–2485), he stated that she hanged herself.[1]

Though this tale is less interesting than some of the others and makes a weaker emotional appeal, in form and finish it shows little indication that Chaucer is growing weary of the series. In three of the stories Chaucer has selected — Hypsipyle, Philomela, and Phyllis — Ovid has used the figure of the Furies as presiding at the nuptials instead of the usual Juno and Hymenæus.[2] Chaucer retains it only in the story of Philomela, where it is used of Progne and Tereus with telling effect. The care taken by Chaucer to avoid the repetition of such a detail indicates his appreciation of the relation of each separate tale to the unity of the poem, and his desire to introduce variety into the treatment of heroines whose fates were so similar.

THE LEGEND OF HYPERMNESTRA

The problem of Hypermnestra is unlike that of any of the other heroines portrayed in the *Legend of Good Women*. She is required by her father to slay her husband on their wedding-night. Here is a

---

[1] For a discussion of this point, see p. 64.
[2] Cf. *Her.*, vi, 45–46; *Met.*, vi, 64, 428–432; *Her.*, ii, 117–120.

conflict between two imperative duties — obedience to a father to save his life and loyalty to a husband whom she loves.

As sources for the *Legend of Hypermnestra* Chaucer seems to have followed *De Genealogia Deorum* and *Heroides*, xiv.[1] Skeat attributes Chaucer's use of "Lino" instead of *Lynceo* for the husband's name to Boccaccio, and suggests that Chaucer's "Hypermistra" is closer to the *Hypermestra* of Boccaccio than to the forms in Ovid. But these two names hardly furnish conclusive proof that Chaucer was indebted to Boccaccio. Boccaccio does give, to be sure, the name as *Lino seu Lynceo*. But most likely *Linus* was the form of the name in Chaucer's MS. of Ovid, for Palmer in his edition of the *Heroides* says that in the chief MS. the title of this Epistle is *Hypermestra Lyno*.[2] *Linus* being then probably the familiar form to Chaucer from his reading of Ovid, he was moved to use it when Boccaccio offered a choice between *Lino* and *Lynceo*. In a note upon the name *Hypermestra*, Palmer says, "so always in the best MSS in Latin,

---

[1] Skeat, *Oxford Chaucer*, vol. III, p. xl.

[2] P. Palmer, *Ovidi Nasonis Heroides* (Oxford, 1898), pp. xxxiii and 85. See also Nic. Heinsius, *Commentarius in Ovidi opera* (Lipsiae, 1758), p. 110; and J. C. Jahn (*P. Ovidii Nasonis Opera Omnia*, Lipsiae, 1828, I, 113), who says that many books in the inscription of this Epistle exhibit *Lino* for *Lynceo*. Boccaccio himself says, "Lyncaeus quem *Linum* appellat Ovidius, filius fuit Aegypti" (*De Genealogia*, lib. ii, cap. 28).

and so Clytaemestra." [1] Again, the Latin of Ovid
and Boccaccio coincided.

Instead of representing Hypermnestra as writing
a letter to Lynceus after he has gone, as Ovid does,
Chaucer chooses to portray her emotions at the
dramatic moment when she is prompted to allow
her husband to escape. With unerring instinct for
the effectiveness of the story, Chaucer has concen-
trated upon Hypermnestra and Lynceus and disregarded the other ninety-eight brothers and
sisters, though he suggests in passing that the two
fathers, Danao and Egiste, must have been false
lovers to have had so many sons and daughters
each. For some reason, which is of no consequence,
Chaucer has made Danao the father of Lino and
the other sons, and Egiste the father of Hypermnestra and the other daughters, whereas in Boccaccio and Ovid, Danao is the father of the daughters and Egiste of the sons. Chaucer passes over
Lino with no other comment than that he was the
best-beloved son of Danao. Upon Hypermnestra,
as we should expect, he lavishes his attention. In
order to explain her disposition and her fate, he has
recourse to the mediaeval belief in astrology as
the dominating influence in men's lives (ll. 2576–
2599). [2] Very briefly, he says that the marriage

---

[1] Palmer, *op. cit.*, p. 411.
[2] W. C. Curry, *J. E. G. P.*, XXII, 347–352.

between the favorite son and daughter is arranged by their fathers, and the wedding is celebrated.

For the description of the wedding-feast Chaucer is indebted to Ovid,[1] but in the interview between Egiste and his daughter, he seems to be inventing. Boccaccio merely says that the daughters, at the command of their father, entered their bridal chambers, each with a hidden sword, and at the appointed time slew their husbands, all except Hypermnestra. Ovid is more specific, for Hypermnestra says that she would not under any circumstances obey the command of her father to slay her husband:

> Me pater igne licet, quem non violavimus, urat,
> Quaeque aderant sacris, tendat in ora faces
> Aut illo jugulet, quem non bene tradidit ensem,
> Ut, qua non cecidit vir nece, nupta cadam.
> *(Her.*, xiv, 9–12.)

The reason that Egiste gives to Hypermnestra (*L. G. W.*, l. 2569), that he was warned in a dream that his nephew would be his destruction, came from Boccaccio's statement that Danao was warned by the oracle that he would die by the hand of a son-in-law. The drink that Egiste tells her to give to her husband was suggested by Ovid:

[1] Cf. *Her.*, xiv, 25–34; *L. G. W.*, ll. 2610–2622. The probable reason that Chaucer avoided the description of the feast in the *Legend of Dido* and included this one is that here the description in the Latin is very brief and general and quite intelligible to a reader of any age or time.

> ipse jacebas
> Quaeque tibi dederam, vina soporis erant.
>
> (*Her.*, xiv, 41–42.)

Most of the description of Hypermnestra as she hesitates to commit the murder Chaucer took from Ovid:

> She rist her up, and dredfully she quaketh.
>
> (*L. G. W.*, l. 2680.)

> Erigor, et capio tela tremente manu.
>
> (*Her.*, xiv, 44.)

> As doth the braunche that Zephirus shaketh.
>
> (*L. G. W.*, l. 2681.)

> Ut leni zephyro graciles vibrantur aristae
> Frigida populeas ut quatit aura comas.
>
> (*Her.*, xiv, 39–40.)

> And hushed were alle in Argon that citee.
>
> (*L. G. W.*, l. 2682.)

> Securumque quies alta per Argos erat.
>
> (*Her.*, xiv, 34.)

> As cold as any frost now wexeth she.
>
> (*L. G. W.*, l. 2683.)

> Sanguis abit, mentemque calor corpusque relinquit,
> Inque novo jacui frigida facta toro.
>
> (*Her.*, xiv, 37–38.)

Lines 2684–2686 are evidently Chaucer's adaptation of Ovid's lines in which he says her hand let fall the uplifted sword three times, because fear and duty opposed the crime:

> For pite by the herte her streyneth so,
> And dreed of deeth doth her so muche wo,
> That thryes doun she fil in swiche a were.
>
> (*L. G. W.*, ll. 2684–2686.)

ter acutum sustulit ensem,
Ter male sublato reccidit ense manus;

. . . .

Sed timor et pietas crudelibus obstitit ausis.

(*Her.*, xiv, 45–49.)

And on her handes faste loketh she.
Allas! and shul my handes blody be.

(*L. G. W.*, ll. 2688–2689.)

Sic manus haec aliquam posset committere caedem,
Morte foret dominae sanguinolenta suae.

(*Her.*, xiv, 59–60.)

I am a maid, and, as by my nature,
And by my semblant and by my vesture,
My handes been nat shapen for a knyf,
As for to reve no man fro his lyf.

(*L. G. W.*, ll. 2690–2693.)

Femina sum et virgo, natura mitis et annis:
Non faciunt molles ad fera tela manus.

(*Her.*, xiv, 55–56.)

Quid mihi cum ferro? Quo bellica tela puellae.

(*Her.*, xiv, 65.)

"Now, certes," quod she, " sin I am his wyf,
And hath my feith, yet it is bet for me
For to be deed in wyfly honestee
Than be a traitour in my shame."

(*L. G. W.*, ll. 2699–2702.)

Quod manus extimuit jugulo demittere ferrum,
Sum rea: laudarer, si scelus ausa forem
Esse ream praestat, quam sic placuisse parenti.

(*Her.*, xiv, 5–7.)

And weep ful tenderly upon his face.

(*L. G. W.*, l. 2706.)

dumque queror, lacrimae sua verba sequuntur
Deque meis oculis in tua membra cadunt.

(*Her.*, xiv, 67–68.)

Til she was caught and fetered in prisoun.

(*L. G. W.*, l. 2722.)

Abstrahor a patriis pedibus, raptamque capillis
(Haec meruit pietas praemia!) carcer habet.

(*Her.*, xiv, 83–84.)

In this last of the Legends Chaucer has treated the matter from Boccaccio and Ovid with the greatest freedom. He has confined his story to Hypermnestra and Lynceus, disregarding the murder of the other sons of Danaus by the daughters of Egiste. He has heightened the emotional effect of Hypermnestra's situation by emphasizing strongly Egiste's command to her to kill her husband in the interview between father and daughter on her wedding-night. He has chosen to portray the emotions of Hypermnestra at her nuptial couch in direct narrative rather than to recall them afterwards in a letter from prison, as Ovid has done. The failure of this *Legend* to measure up to the standard of most of the others lies in the weakness of the story told by Ovid. With all his art Chaucer could not make it pulsate with genuine emotion. It appealed to him perhaps only because of the variation that it offered upon the general theme of his poem.

CRITICAL COMMENT UPON THE LEGENDS

The charm of the Prologue to the *Legend of Good Women* has so obscured the merit of the various tales that they have not, I think, been accorded their full meed of praise.[1] The critic cannot afford to condemn a poem because of a few apparent blemishes. Rather he must strive to enter into the spirit of a master and determine the quality of his art as he sees him dealing with his materials. To estimate a work of a genius like Chaucer or Shakspere it is necessary to compare it with the original from which it was derived.

The foregoing study of the *Legend of Good Women* in relation to its sources has convinced me that this poem is of real artistic excellence. Chaucer has put into it much of the creative imagination that characterizes his best work, even though the merit of the separate legends is not "always after oon." His purpose of portraying various types of women under the stress of strong emotion in a series of short stories, he has achieved with poetic insight and skill. The poem as a whole constitutes the first comprehensive treatment of the sex problem in English literature. No less interesting than the heroines is the roll call of the "villains": Antony mad with love, Pyramus true but

[1] Skeat, of course, annotated the *Legend of Good Women*, indicating sources and borrowings. Mr. Dodd (*Courtly Love in Chaucer and Gower*, pp. 208–232) has considered them, with a view to showing "that Chaucer was following in the *Legend* a plan based on medieval ecclesiastical ideas." His discussion of the tales is colored by this preoccupation. Others, like Professor Tatlock (*The Development and Chronology of Chaucer's Works*, p. 112), have seen in the *Legend* "a sense of haste and weariness" more than in any of his other works.

dilatory, Æneas driven by the Fates, Jason wily
with Hypsipyle and seductive with Medea, Tarquin proud and lustful of Lucretia, Theseus perfidious toward Ariadne, Tereus brutal with Philomela, Demophoon hereditarily false, and Lino
making good his own escape and leaving his bride
to her fate.

That Chaucer was familiar with all the stories of
the *Heroides* may be safely assumed, for he mentions a great many of them in the two lists that he
gives of faithful women.[1] It may be, as Skeat has
conjectured, that from these two sources we can
compile the list of stories of women which appealed
to him most and which he intended to include in the
Legend of Good Women. But even of these that he
has mentioned, the Epistles in the *Heroides* vary
greatly in dramatic power. Penelope, Briseis, Her-
mione, Deianira, Canace, Laodamia, Helen, and
Hero are not provoked to passionate action as the
heroines are whom Chaucer has depicted in the
Legend. His realization of this may have had something to do with his failure to complete the series.
As his interest lay in the stories in the *Metamorphoses*, *Heroides*, or *Fasti* not chiefly as tales of the
heroic past, but as a means of portraying vital
human emotion in an essentially dramatic setting,

[1] The *balade* in the Prologue to the *Legend of Good Women* (ll.
A 203–223; B 249–269) and the contents of the "Saintes Legende of
Cupyde" in the Introduction to the *Man of Law's Prologue*, ll. 59–76.

he no doubt realized, what is true, that for his purpose he had already chosen the best of them by the time he had finished the *Legend of Phyllis*.

However this may have been, Chaucer's work on the *Legend* had carried him forward in his poetic development. He emerged from writing the *Legend of Good Women* with a heightened precision, lucidity, and finish of style. From this time forward he is a master of his art. Ovid had done his work well in instructing him. If Chaucer was in the future diffuse, it was for some dramatic purpose and by no means due to a lack of knowledge of the technique of narration. Ovid had furnished him, too, a God's plenty of classical information and material; but far above and beyond all this he had shown him that human nature with its passions and foibles was a subject of unfailing concern to a poet. Under the stimulus of this idea Chaucer's imagination conceived its greatest purpose — to make types of the various social groups of his own England troop into action for all succeeding generations to enjoy. Fortunate he was in the swiftly moving events of his time — serf and landowner pitted against each other, chivalry in decay, the middle class beginning to emerge, the nobility struggling to curb the power of the king, and the Church itself, with all its traditions of service, showing vast discrepancies between its avowed aspirations and its manifest practices. For the depiction of this far-richer content than Ovid could boast — because Ovid described a decadent civilization and Chaucer one that was just being born — Chaucer brought to his task a nobler genius than Ovid's. More sensitive, delicate, and refined than Ovid, he would inevitably produce a greater masterpiece.

THE CANTERBURY TALES

THE very nature of the classical influence upon Chaucer, that is, the broadening of his intellectual and artistic horizon, meant that the direct borrowings from the Latin should decrease as he advanced into the extensive field of contemporary life. The conception of the *Canterbury Tales* excluded the employment of any large body of material from the Classics, yet something of classical matter enters into its patterns here and there. Chaucer's study of the Roman poets inevitably colored his thought and his imagination, for no man ever rises from a reading of the Classics the same man as before.[1]

THE KNIGHT'S TALE

Though Chaucer was mainly following Boccaccio in the *Knight's Tale*, he has enriched his account from his extensive knowledge of Ovid.

Lines A 1385–1390, which describe Mercury as he appeared before Argus and put him to sleep, are taken from Ovid's account of this episode in the *Metamorphoses*. In both Chaucer and Ovid the description of Mercury occurs in immediate connec-

[1] See Henry Osborn Taylor, *The Mediaeval Mind*, vol. II, chap. 31, "The Spell of the Classics," especially pp. 162–175.

tion with the blinding of Argus. In *De Raptu Proserpinae*, I, 76, which Skeat suggests in his note as the source of the description of Mercury,[1] it is Pluto who summons the winged god to bear a message to Jove, a circumstance which has no relation to the story of Argus. Every detail of Mercury's equipment in the *Metamorphoses* is given by Chaucer:

> Him thoughte how that the winged god Mercurie
> Biforn him stood, and bad him to be murye.
> His slepy yerde in hond he bar uprighte;
> An hat he werede up-on his heres brighte.
> Arrayed was this god (as he took keep)
> As he was whan that Argus took his sleep.

> Parva mora est alas pedibus virganique potenti
> Somniferam sumpsisse manu tegumenque capillis.
> > (*Met.*, i, 671–672.)

> Arge, jaces, quodque in tot lumina lumen habebas,
> Exstinctum est, centumque oculos nox occupat una.
> > (*Met.*, i, 720–721.)

Line A 1761,

> For pitee renneth sone in gentil herte,

came from Ovid's *Tristia*, iii, v, 31–32.[2]

In discussing the temple of Venus in the *House of Fame*,[3] I have shown that the temple of Venus in the *Knight's Tale* (l. A 1918) was also in its function a classical conception. That is, the temple was shrine of the god, such as Juno's temple at Carthage

[1] *Oxford Chaucer*, V, 70.
[2] See discussion of *L. G. W.*, l. 503, p. 178.   [3] See p. 104.

in the *Æneid*, on the walls of which a story was
portrayed. The suggestion for the portraiture on
the wall in the temple of Venus in the *House of
Fame* came from the *Æneid*, and Chaucer found it
convenient to use the idea again here in the
Knight's Tale. In fact, the painting on the walls
occurs in connection with all of the three temples
built by Theseus to Venus, Mars, and Diana.[1] The
descriptions of this portraiture came from a variety
of sources.[2] The temple of Diana is the only one
that shows clearly material from the Classics.[3] The
story of Callisto (lines A 2056–2061), who was
changed into the bear when Diana was angry with
her, came from *Fasti*, ii, 153–192. That this reference is from Ovid and not from Boccaccio is made
clear by Chaucer's addition that Callisto's son
Arcas became a star. While Boccaccio tells of Callisto's metamorphosis (*Teseide*, vii, 61), he makes
no mention of Arcas. The story of Daphne (ll.
A 2062–2064), who was turned into a laurel tree
when she was pursued by Apollo, came from *Met.*,
i, 450–567. That Actaeon was transformed into a
stag is mentioned in *Teseide*, vii, 79; but Chaucer
gives the details (ll. A 2065–2068) which he could
have got only from *Met.*, iii, 155–252: how Actaeon
was changed into a stag out of vengeance by Diana,

[1] See *Knight's Tale*, ll. 1918–1919, 1975, 2054.
[2] See Skeat's notes.
[3] On Medea and Circe as enchantresses (l. A 1944), see p. 89.

whom he had observed in her bath, how his dogs pursued him and devoured him because they did not recognize him. Likewise from Ovid (*Met.*, viii, 271–545) came the story of the Calydonian boar hunt in which were engaged Atalanta and Meleager (ll. A 2069–2171). Though Boccaccio (*Teseide*, vii, 61) mentions Atalanta as swift in running, he says nothing of the boar hunt.

Lines A 2083–2086, which represent Lucina as the Goddess of Childbirth, are probably due to Ovid, who has many references to her in this capacity. See *Fasti*, ii, 449, iii, 255; *Her.*, vi, 122, xi, 55; *Ars Am.*, iii, 785; *Met.*, v, 304, ix, 294, 698, x, 507–510.[1]

The story of the discovery of the intrigue of Venus and Mars by Vulcan (ll. A 2388–2390) was well known to Chaucer from the *Ars Amatoria*, ii, 561–600, and *Metamorphoses*, iv, 171–189. The *Romance of the Rose* also tells the story at length.[2] Chaucer was familiar with both sources.

In lines A 2925–2928, Chaucer evidently recalls passages in the *Metamorphoses:*

> Ne how the goddes ronnen up and doun,
> Disherited of hir habitacioun,
> In which they woneden in rest and pees,
> Nymphes, Faunes, and Amadrides.

---

[1] See Fansler, *Chaucer and the Roman de la Rose*, p. 53 (Columbia Univ. Press, 1914). Skeat's note referring to Virgil, *Ecl.*, iv, 10, seems unnecessary in the light of the passages cited from Ovid, particularly as there is no certainty that Chaucer knew the *Eclogues*.

[2] See Fansler, *Chaucer and the Roman de la Rose*, p. 60.

Compare the following:

> Sunt mihi semidei, sunt rustica numina nymphae
> Faunique Satyrique et monticolae Silvani.
> > (*Met.*, i, 192–193.)
>
> Inter hamadryadas celeberrima Nonacrinas
> Naias una fuit, nymphae Syringa vocabant.
> > (*Met.*, i, 690–691.)

Chaucer's idea of the habitation of the gods as one of rest and peace seems to have been suggested by Ovid's description of the places where the hamadryads and nymphs lived:

> Neque enim pecori fecundior ullo
> Herba loco est, aptamque vides pastoribus umbram.
> > (*Met.*, i, 680–681.)
>
> "Arcadiae gelidis in montibus," inquit
> "Inter hamadryadas."
> > (*Met.*, i, 689–690.)

From Ovid's "rich grass for the flocks and shade agreeable to shepherds," and "in the cool mountains of Arcadia," where these nymphs, fauns, and hamadryads dwelt, the inference is easy that the place was one of rest and peace.[1]

Chaucer's reference to "the vale of Galgopheye" (l. A 2626) points to Ovid,[2] who calls Gargaphie a valley:

---

[1] Mr. Wise suggests (p. 54) that this idea came from Statius, but the connection seems rather to indicate Ovid.

[2] *Oxford Chaucer*, V, 90.

Vallis erat piceis et acuta densa cupressu,
Nomine Gargaphie succintae sacra Dianae.
(*Met.*, iii, 155–156.)

This passage occurs in Ovid's story of Actaeon, to which Chaucer has made reference earlier in this tale. Though *Gargaphye* is used by Statius in *Thebaid*, vii, 273–274, there it is the name of a spring.

INTRODUCTION TO THE MAN OF LAW'S PROLOGUE

Lines B 50–93 in the Introduction to the *Man of Law's Prologue*, containing Chaucer's list of his writings upon lovers, which he puts into the mouth of the Man of Law, have been the subject of interested speculation, especially in connection with the *Legend of Good Women*. Some of the stories mentioned here he wrote, and others he intended to write. His list includes fourteen of the Epistles in the *Heroides*. In addition to these he cites the stories of Ceys and Alcyone and Thisbe from the *Metamorphoses* and Lucretia from the *Fasti*.

Pierides (l. B 92) refers to the story of the daughters of Pierus, who dared to contest with the Muses and for their effrontery were changed into magpies (*Met.*, v, 298–678). Chaucer adds the reference, "*Metamorphoseos* wot what I mene" (*C. T.*, l. B 93).

For the use of the Greek genitive singular *Metamorphoseos* instead of the plural *Metamorphoseon* in referring to Ovid's *Metamorphoses*, no explanation, I think, has hitherto been offered. Skeat says: "It was common to cite thus, by a title in the *genitive case*, since the word *Liber* was understood. There is, however, a slight error in this substitution of the singular for the plural; the true title being P. Ovidii Nasonis Metamorphoseon Libri Quindecim." [1]

This "slight error" was not Chaucer's alone, but was a common one in the MSS and early editions of Ovid.

In the lists of MSS taken from the catalogues of the libraries of the Middle Ages there are four of Ovid with the title *Metamorphoseos*. As these lists often refer to the *Metamorphoses* as *Ovidius Magnus* or *Major*, we have now no means of telling how many others had this title, *Metamorphoseos*.[2]

One of the oldest and best extant MSS of the *Metamorphoses* is an eleventh-century MS. known as the Codex Marcianus Florentinus 225, formerly in the Bibliotheca Dominicanorum S. Marci, but now preserved in the Bibliotheca Laurentina. This MS. is given by Riese [3] as having the title *Metamor-*

---

[1] *Oxford Chaucer*, V, 141.

[2] Manitius, *Rheinisches Museum*, N. F., p. 47. *Philologisches aus alten Bibliothekskatalogen*, pp. 31–36.

[3] *Carmina P'Ovidii Nasonis* (Lipsiae, 1872), vol. II. Metamorphoses, Praefatio, p. x.

phoseos. Otto Korn [1] also cites this same Codex Marcianus Florentinus 225 as beginning, *P'Ovidii Nasonis Metamorphoseos Liber I cum suis narrationibus incip.* [2]

Another MS., known as Codex Amplonianus prior Erfurtanus Numero I, of the twelfth or thirteenth century, is cited by Grau [3] as having the title, *Incipit I Liber Ovidii Metamorphoseos.*

Moreover, in a MS. of Guido delle Colonne's (Guido de Columna) *Liber de Casu Trojae* preserved in the library of Harvard University, Ovid's work is referred to as *Methamorphoseos.* [4] It is interesting to note that the copyist of this MS. says he copied it between April and September, 1353, a date within Chaucer's lifetime. It is, of course, well established that Chaucer was familiar with Guido's work.

The frequent use of the title *Metamorphoseos* caused considerable discussion among the com-

[1] *P. Ovidii Nasonis Metamorphoseon Libri XV* (Berlin, 1880), p. i, note.

[2] Hugo Magnus, in his edition of the *Metamorphoses* (Berlin, 1914), describes this MS. and gives the title as reading *P'Ovidii Nasonis Metamorphoses Liber I cum suis narrationibus incip.* But *Metamorphoses* here is apparently an oversight on the part of the proof-reader, for the grammatical construction would not allow this reading.

[3] *De Ovidii Metamorphoseon codice Amploniano Priore,* Diss. (Halle, 1892), p. 35.

[4] Lydgate also in his *Troy Book,* i, 567–568, has:

> That Ovyde lyst recorde hym silve
> Methamorphoseos, his famus dedis twelve.

mentators as to what was the true title of the book.
Burmann quotes from three of these.[1] The first,
Raphael Regius of the fifteenth century, argues for
using the title *Metamorphoseos*, urging that the
theme of the whole work is "transmutation,"
though of many kinds.

The second commentator whom Burmann quotes
is Micyllus (ll. 1503–1558), who, though admitting
the weight of the arguments for the plural, decides
to let the title stand as in former editions, *Metamorphoseos*.

Farnaby (ll. 1575–1647), the third commentator
quoted by Burmann, says that on account of the
unity of the work it is often written *Metamorphosis*.
But he argues that there are many transformations
and that the title is frequently written *Metamorphoses;* furthermore, that certain MSS prefer the
title in the plural.

Nicolaus Heinsius (ll. 1620–1681)[2] gave the
weight of his authority to the reading *Metamorphoseon* as follows:

METAMORPHOSEON LIBER PRIMUS. Nihil verius hac
lectione, quam optimus liber Berneggerianus, alter codicum splendidissimi Equitis ac Baroneti Rogerii Twisden,
et Patauinus Sancti Joannis in Viridario agnoscunt sub
finem quoque voluminis ex Balthasaris Moreti V, Cl.
codicibus unus, et initio libri septimi Mediceus primae

---

[1] *Ovidius II, Notis Burmanni* (Amsterdam, 1727), pp. 7–8.
[2] *Heinsii Commentar, in Ovidium*, II (Lipsiae, 1758), 425.

notae sic exhibebant. Neque aliter Graeca horum libro-
rum Metaphrasis Planudae. Reliqui METAMORPHOSEOS,
perperam: uti Farnabius quoque iam vidit. Genuina
huius poëmatis inscriptio extat apud Senecam patrem
Epitome Controuers. lib. III, cap. VII, etc.

It will be noticed that Heinsius, after citing several authorities to establish the soundness of the
title *Metamorphoseon*, says that *the rest* wrongly
have *Metamorphoseos*.

Further evidence of numerous early editions with
the title in the singular is to be found in an "Index
Editionum" prefixed to the first volume of an edition of Ovid's works in the Studiis Societatis Bi-
pontinae. In this index are listed thirteen editions
with the title *Metamorphoseos* and twelve with
Metamorphosis.[1] The first of these editions bears
the date of 1479 and the last 1543. The persistence
of the singular form appears in an edition at Frankfort in 1601,[2] where the Greek letters ΩΣ are used
with the rest of the word in Latin spelling, *Meta-
morphose* ΩΣ. J. C. Jahn in his edition (1832),[3] gives
the following explanation of the title of the poem:

Poëma inscriptum est Graeco vocabulo *Metamorphoses* cum Latinum *transformationum* vocabulum, ut
videtur, nondum inventum esset, sed Quintiliani tem-

---

[1] *Publii Ovidii Nasonis Opera* cum notitia Literaria, volumen
primum (Argentorati, 1807), pp. xlii ff.

[2] *Ovidii Opera*, Tom. I, Frankfort, 1601.

[3] *P. Ovidii Nasonis Opera Omnia* (Lipsiae, 1832), vol. II, Tom. I,
Introductio, p. 4.

pore demum novaretur. V. Bähr, Geschichte der Roem. Literatur, p. 118. Atque hanc inscriptionem cum scriptores veteres, Seneca, Quintilianus, Tertullianus, Fulgentius, Servius et Priscianus, tum Planudes et optimi libri MSS agnoscunt et confirmant. In deterioribus recentioribusque codicibus minus apte singulari numero *Metamorphosis* totum opus nuncupatur.

From the foregoing it would appear that Chaucer's use of *Metamorphoseos* [1] was in accord with the best scholarship of his time.

THE MAN OF LAW'S TALE
Line B 660,

As gentil herte is fulfild of pitee,

is a slight variation of Chaucer's usual adaptation of Ovid's *Tristia*, iii, v, 31–32.[2]

THE MONK'S TALE

In lines B 3293–3294, Chaucer has confused the two episodes of Busiris and Diomedes. Skeat [3] explains the confusion as follows:

Here Chaucer has confused two stories. One is that Busiris, a king of Egypt, used to sacrifice all foreigners who came to Egypt, till the arrival of Hercules, who slew him. The other is "the eighth labour," when Hercules killed Diomedes, a king in Thrace, who fed his

---

[1] This discussion of the form, *Metamorphoseos*, has been previously published in *M. L. N.*, XXXV, 5, 288–291.

[2] See *L. G. W.*, l. 503, and *Knight's Tale*, l. A 1761.

[3] *Oxford Chaucer*, V, 232.

mares with human flesh, till Hercules slew him and gave his body to be eaten by the mares, as Chaucer *himself* says in his translation of Boethius. The confusion was easy, because the story of Busiris is mentioned elsewhere by Boethius, Book ii, pr. 6, in a passage which Chaucer thus translates: "I have herd told of Busirides, that was wont to sleen his gestes that herberweden in his hous; and he was sleyn himself of Ercules that was his gest."

This confusion might more naturally have arisen from a misunderstanding of the following passage in *Heroïdes*, ix, 67–70:

> Non tibi succurrit crudi Diomedis imago,
> Efferus humana qui dape pavit equas,
> Si te vidisset cultu Busiris in isto,
> Huic victor victo nempe pudendus eras!

Every reader of Ovid knows that he must be on the watch if he is always to recognize a character under the various names which the poet gives him. So in this passage, the two statements might seem to bear a close relationship, the second confirming the thought suggested in the first and referring to the same person under a different name. Confusion of names was not uncommon in the Middle Ages. A notable instance is that of Walter Burley (1275–1345?), a commentator on Aristotle and a scholar of great fame, who in his *De vita et moribus philosophorum* confused Livius Andronicus with Livy, the historian, and Horatius Flaccus, the poet, with Horatius Pulvillus. That Chaucer, who was not a professional scholar, should have made such mistakes is therefore not surprising.

Though Chaucer's selection of the name Busiris rather than Diomedes may have been mere chance, it is probable that the choice was made designedly to avoid confusion with Diomedes, the Grecian hero, whom Chaucer knew in Benoit and whom he afterward used in his own story of *Troilus and Criseyde*.[1] It is unlikely that Chaucer was acquainted with the name Busiris in any connection which would necessarily indicate that he could not be the same person as the tyrant Diomedes mentioned in the *Heroides*. Of all the other works in classical and mediaeval literature containing references to Busiris,[2] there is no probability that Chaucer knew any except the *Metamorphoses* and *Ars Amatoria* of Ovid and the *De consolatione philosophiae* of Boethius. In none of these three is the story of Busiris given in detail. The references to him are as follows:

[1] See G. L. Kittredge, *The Date of Chaucer's Troilus and Other Chaucer Matters*, Chaucer Society, 1905, p. 67.

[2] For a list of such references, see Roscher, *Ausführliches Lexikon der griech. u. röm. Mythologie*, under "Busiris." It is possible that Chaucer may have known the following works in which there are references to Busiris, though there is no evidence of any knowledge of these works in his writings: Virgil, *Georgics*, iii, 5; *Claudianus in Rufinum*, i, 255; *in Eutropium*, i, 159; Macrobius, *Saturnalia*, vi, 7; Hyginus, *Fab.*, 31, 56, 157. In regard to Chaucer's knowledge of these writers, see Lounsbury, *Studies in Chaucer*, II, 250, 255, 277, 278, 287.

Ergo ego foedantem peregrino templa cruore
Busirin domui?
　　　　(*Met.*, ix, 182–183.)

Dicitur Aegyptos caruisse iuvantibus arva
Imbribus atque annos sicca fuisse novem,
Cum Thrasius Busirin adit monstratque piari
Hospitis adfuso sanguine posse Iovem.
Illi Busiris "fies Iovis hostia primus"
Inquit "et Aegypto tu dabis hospes aquam."
　　　　(*Ars Amatoria*, i, 647–652.)

I have herd told of Busirides that was wont to sleen
his gestes that herberweden in his hous; and he was
sleyn himself of Ercules that was his gest. — Chaucer's
Translation of Boethius, Book ii, pr. 6.

Chaucer might have read the passages and still
not have realized that Busiris was any other than
the tyrant whom Hercules fed to his own mares.
The similarity of the two stories easily tends to
confusion: both are labors of Hercules; both are
instances of tyrants slain for ruthlessly murdering
human beings. If Chaucer mistook the two names
in the *Heroïdes* as referring to one person, his recollection of the passages in the *Metamorphoses*, the
Ars Amatoria, and Boethius would not correct his
error. So, as he knew of another Diomedes with
whom this one might be confused, and did not
know of another Busiris, he would naturally choose
the distinctive name.

This supposition that Chaucer would choose a
name about which he thought there could be no

confusion is not merely a fanciful one. We have evidence of what he did under circumstances where there might be uncertainty as to identity. In the *Knight's Tale*, ll. 2062–2064, he stops in the midst of his story to explain that in referring to Daphne, who was turned into a tree, he does not mean the goddess Diana:

> There saugh I Dane, y-turned til a tree,
> I mene not the goddesse Diane,
> But Penneus doughter, which that highte Dane.

Skeat [1] mentions the confusion of names in the story of Hercules as evidence that Chaucer must have written part of the *Monk's Tale* before 1380, for in his translation of Boethius the name is given correctly:

> He overcomer, as it is seyd, hath put an unmeke lord foddre to his cruel hors; *this is to syen that Hercules slowh Diomedes and made his hors to freten him.* — Boethius, Book iv, metre 7.[2]

But, even if Chaucer had failed to notice the name in this passage in a previous hasty reading, he

---

[1] *Oxford Chaucer*, III, 430, note.

[2] The name Diomedes in this passage does not belong to the text of Boethius, but is given, as will be noticed, in the gloss. As the explanations in Chaucer's translation are, however, probably not his own notes, but translations of glosses on the MS. of Boethius which he used, or some MS. which he had seen, this is of no consequence in the present discussion. For further information on the glosses, see the *Globe Chaucer*, Introduction, p. xi; Skeat, *Oxford Chaucer*, vol. II, Introduction, pp. xxiv and xxxviii.

could not fail, when he came to make his translation, to note that the king who fed his mares on human flesh is here called Diomedes. If we assume, however, that Chaucer thought both names belonged to that tyrant, the occurrence of the name Diomedes would still, even when he considered the passage carefully, have had no significance to him in the way of pointing out his error in the tragedy of Hercules.[1]

THE NUN'S PRIEST'S TALE

Lines B 4546–4549, which tell how Priam was slain by Pyrrhus, are from the *Æneid*, ii, 550–554.[2] Chaucer refers the reader to Virgil's poem ("as saith us *Eneydos*"). Mock-heroically Chaucer compares the uproar in the barnyard when Chauntecleer was carried off to the supposedly historical account of King Priam's death.

THE PHYSICIAN'S TALE

Line C 14, which contains a reference to Pygmalion, seems to be from Ovid, who devotes considerable space (*Met.*, x, 245–297) to Pygmalion and his art. Though he is mentioned in the *Roman de la Rose*, it would seem more likely that Chaucer was

[1] This note upon Busiris was published in *Mod. Phil.*, XI, 227–230.

[2] *Oxford Chaucer*, V, 257.

thinking of the fuller account in the *Metamor-phoses*.

Lines C 59 and C 65–66, which mention the effect of wine and revels upon youth, were probably suggested by *Ars Amatoria*, I, 229 ff., and 243.[1]

THE WIFE OF BATH'S PROLOGUE

In line D 680, the wife of Bath refers to *Ovydes Art* as included among the manuscripts possessed by her fifth husband. This is, of course, the *Ars Amatoria*. In Chaucer's poetry there are more direct references to Ovid by name, and to his works, than to any other single author.

Lines D 724–726 refer to the story of Hercules and Deianira, which Chaucer has told in the *Monk's Tale*.

THE WIFE OF BATH'S TALE

Lines D 952–982 refer to Ovid by name and relate the story of Midas and his ass's ears. In *Met.*, xi, 174–193, it is Midas' barber who discovers the secret and, being unable to keep it, digs a hole in the ground and whispers his secret into it. In the *Wife of Bath's Tale* it is Midas' wife who betrays the secret. The conclusion of the story — how the. secret was revealed — Chaucer does not give, but

[1] *Oxford Chaucer*, V, 262.

refers the reader to Ovid. Possibly the wife's per-
version of the tale was due to her having heard it in
this form from her fifth husband, Jankin the clerk,
who irritated her immeasurably by the accounts of
vicious wives which he read from a book he had.
Color is lent to the probability of this because the
wife refers her hearers to Ovid, apparently in bliss-
ful ignorance of the modification she is working
upon the original.[1]

THE FRIAR'S TALE

Line D 1519 in the *Friar's Tale* refers to Virgil
by name as a writer along with Dante upon the
lower world. Book vi of the *Æneid* recounts the
visit of Æneas to Hades.

THE MERCHANT'S TALE

Lines E 1715–1717 refer to Orpheus and Amphion of Thebes as famous musicians. Orpheus as
a musician was well known to Chaucer from two
accounts of him in *Metamorphoses*, x, 1–85, and xi,
1–66. From Ovid, too, Chaucer learned of the
fame of Amphion with the lyre. In the story of
Niobe in *Metamorphoses*, vi, she is represented as
boasting of her position in Thebes. She says she
is the queen, and her husband, Amphion, by whose
lyre the walls of Thebes have risen, is the king:

---

[1] I am indebted for this suggestion to a student in my Chaucer
course in 1926-27, Mr. A. Warren Pierpont.

Me gentes metuunt Phrygiae, me regia Cadmi
Sub domina est, fidibusque mei commissa mariti
Moenia cum populis a meque viroque reguntur.
                                (*Met.*, vi, 177–179.)

Though Skeat refers to lines 221, 271, and 402 of
Metamorphoses, vi, and to line 427 of *Metamorphoses*, xv, where Amphion's name occurs, he
appears to have overlooked the important passage
quoted above about Amphion's being a musician,
and seems to rely upon Hyginus for the information about Amphion.[1] But the reference in the
Manciple's Tale (ll. H 116–117) to Amphion as
king of Thebes as well as a magic musician shows
that Chaucer was familiar with the story in *Metamorphoses*, vi, where both ideas occur.[2] Further
evidence of Chaucer's knowledge of the story of
Niobe and Amphion is to be found in *Troilus*,
i, 699.[3]

Lines E 2034–2035, which refer to Priapus as the
God of Gardens, are from *Fasti*, i, 415.

Lines 2111–2113, about the blinding of Argus,
refer to the story in *Metamorphoses*, i, 625–721.

In lines E 2125–2131 Chaucer calls upon Ovid
by name as having shown in the story of Pyramus
and Thisbe how love will overcome all difficulties.

[1] *Oxford Chaucer*, V, 359.
[2] Mr. Wise (p. 59) refers the suggestion as to Amphion's being a
musician to the *Thebaid*, and, as to his being king of Thebes, he says,
"It is probably due to mediaeval sources." But the passage from the
Metamorphoses accounts for both points.   [3] See p. 123.

THE SQUIRE'S TALE

Lines F 220–223 describe the ways of ignorant people in dealing with matters beyond their comprehension:

> Of sundry doutes thus they jangle and trete,
> As lewed peple demeth comunly
> Of thinges that been maad more subtilly
> Than they can in her lewednes comprehende.

These lines, though characteristically Chaucerian, were probably suggested by Ovid:

> Quorum pars causas et res et nomina quaeret
> Pars referet, quamvis noverit illa parum.[1]
>   (*Tristia*, iv, ii, 25–26.)

The reference in lines F 238–240 to Thelopus, who was wounded and healed by the spear of Achilles, was most probably recalled from the numerous references to this circumstance in Ovid.[2] See *Tristia*, v, ii, 15; *Rem. Am.*, 1. 47; *Met.*, xii, 112, xiii, 171; *ex Ponto*, ii, ii, 26.

On line F 479,

> That pitee renneth sone in gentil herte,

see p. 178.

THE FRANKLIN'S TALE

Lines F 951–952,

> And dye he moste, he seyde, as dide Ekko
> For Narcisus, that dorste nat telle hir wo,

---

[1] I am indebted to Professor Kittredge for this reference.
[2] *Oxford Chaucer*, V, 378.

Skeat attributes to *Roman de la Rose*, but he also suggests *Met.*, iii, 407.[1] The latter reference is the correct source. In Ovid's account Echo does not tell her woe, for when spurned she lurks in the woods, keeps herself hidden, and lives in lonely caves. It is someone else (*Met.*, iii, 403–404) who prays for vengeance of the gods upon Narcissus. In the *Roman*, Echo herself prays that Narcissus may feel the torture of loving and not being loved.[2]

For line 1077 with its reference to Delphi,

> Thy temple in Delphos wol I barefoot seke,

Skeat has cited *Met.*, x, 168, and xi, 414. See *Her.*, xxi, 232, and especially *Met.*, xv, 630–631, where the form Delphos occurs:

> Auxilium caeleste petunt, mediamque tenentes
> Orbis humum Delphos adeunt, oracula Phoebi.

The Manciple's Tale

The story of how the crow was changed from white to black, which Chaucer tells in the *Manciple's Tale*, he found in *Metamorphoses*, ii, 534–632. There it is the raven (*corvus*), instead of the crow, which belonged to Phoebus. As the raven is on the way to report the unfaithfulness of Coronis to Apollo, he is intercepted by the crow (*cornix*), who tells *his* story of how his feathers became black, and warns the raven. But to no purpose, for

---

[1] *Oxford Chaucer*, V, 390.

[2] See Fansler, *Chaucer and the Roman de la Rose*, pp. 54–55.

with a curse for the crow, the raven goes on his way. Though the two stories carry the same moral in Ovid, it is the narrative of the raven that Chaucer tells, calling him the crow.

The *Manciple's Tale* begins:

> Whan Phebus dwelled here in this erthe adoun,
> As olde bokes maken mencioun.
> (ll. H 105–106.)

In two passages not cited before, Ovid refers to Apollo's dwelling on the earth. The first tells that Apollo was said to have fed the cattle of Admetus and lived in a small house:

> Cynthius Admeti vaccas pavisse Pheraei
> Fertur et in parva delituisse casa.
> (*Ars Am.*, ii, 239–240.)

The second amplifies this same story with details of how Apollo wore a shepherd's cloak, carried a stout stick in his hand, and allowed his cattle to stray while his thoughts were all upon love:

> Elin Messeniaque arva colebas.
> Illud erat tempus, quo te pastoria pellis
> Texit, onusque fuit baculum silvestre sinistrae,
> Alterius dispar septenis fistula cannis.
> Dumque amor est curae, dum te tua fistula mulcet,
> Incustoditae Pylios memorantur in agros
> Processisse boves.
> (*Met.*, ii, 679–685.)

Ovid's account, too, of the slaying of the Python [1] by Phoebus would be sufficient ground for Chau-

<hr>

[1] *Oxford Chaucer*, V, 439.

cer's statement that Phoebus lived at one time on
the earth. The Python, Ovid relates, was a terror
to the inhabitants of the earth, and to commemorate its death Phoebus established the famous
Pythian games (*Met.*, i, 438–447). In this passage
Ovid represents Apollo as an archer, calling him
"deus arquitenens," and speaking of his quiver as
almost exhausted — "exhausta paene pharetra."
It seems quite clearly indicated that Chaucer was
thinking of this incident, when he says in the same
connection with Apollo's living upon the earth,

> He was the moste lusty bacheler
> In al this world, and eek the best archer.

In spite of being derived from classical mythology,
Chaucer's Phoebus is after all a mediaeval knight:

> He was therwith fulfild of gentilesse,
> Of honour, and of parfit worthinesse.
> This Phebus, that was flour of bachelrye,
> As wel in freedom as in chivalrye.
>   (ll. H 123–126.)

The reference to Amphion as king of Thebes
(ll. H 116–117) has been discussed in connection
with lines E 1715–1717 in the *Merchant's Tale*.[1]

In the *Manciple's Tale* Chaucer has modified
Ovid's story in some respects. He does not mention the name of Coronis, Phoebus' wife, and he
represents the crow in his cage at the house of

[1] See p. 319.

Phoebus telling his master on his return home of his wife's adultery. In Ovid, the raven went on a journey to tell his master of the circumstance. Chaucer's account is more realistic than Ovid's. In the *Manciple's Tale*, the wife sent for her "lemman" while Phoebus was away from home. Ovid says nothing of this. Chaucer follows Ovid pretty closely in describing the conduct of Phoebus after he is convinced of the truthfulness of the crow's report, but he omits the appeal of Coronis to Phoebus for her unborn child, and adds some reflections upon too hasty suspicions. Though the metamorphosis in this tale is slight, — the mere changing of the color of the bird's feathers, — Chaucer's use of it is noteworthy. The change in the color of the fruit of the mulberry tree in the Pyramus and Thisbe story is just as slight, and yet he rejects it in the *Legend of Thisbe*, and habitually, in borrowing from the *Metamorphoses*, he omits the transformation of persons into birds or animals.

The emphasis of the two poets in telling this tale is very different. Ovid is intent upon showing the punishment of the raven for his loquacity. Chaucer, true to his usual purpose of interpreting Ovid's fables in terms of the life of men, stresses the propensity of human nature, exemplified by Phoebus' wife, to follow its own bent, even without a justifiable excuse.

II

CHAUCER AND THE OTHER ROMAN POETS

STATIUS

STATIUS was a well-known and popular poet in the Middle Ages.[1] His *Thebaid* existed in a large number of manuscripts, and the *Achilleis* was easily accessible, though the number of manuscripts was far fewer than those of the *Thebaid*. His *Silvae* was practically unknown until Poggio's discovery of a MS. of this work at St. Gallen in 1416. (See p. 21.) The *Thebaid* seems to have been the only poem of Statius known to Chaucer. At least he indicates no knowledge of the *Achilleis*,[2] though he refers to it by name as one of Statius' poems in the *House of Fame*, line 1460.

As Professor Wise has made so thorough a study of the relation of Chaucer to Statius, it would seem a work of supererogation for me to restate his findings in detail. For the sake of completeness it will be necessary to discuss some of the passages cited by Mr. Wise, where my own investigations and those of other scholars have rendered advisable some modification of his statements.

[1] J. E. Sandys, *History of Classical Scholarship*, pp. 642–643; A. Graf, *Roma nella memoria et nelle imaginazione del medio evo* (Torino, Ristampa, 1915), pp. 612–614; Teuffel-Schwabe, *History of Roman Literature*, trans. by G. C. W. Warr, 321.6; Manitius, *Rhein. Mus.*, XLVII, 60–63.

[2] A. B. Wise, *Influence of Statius upon Chaucer*, pp. 137–138; for the *Silvae*, see also pp. 139–140.

COMPLEYNT UNTO PITE

Line 92,

> Have mercy on me, thou Herenus quene,

Skeat refers to *Thebaid*, xi, 457–496. But Mr. Fansler [1] with better reason attributes it to Dante, and his suggestion has been amplified by Professor Lowes.[2]

THE BOOK OF THE DUCHESS

Lines 153–165, which describe the habitation of the God of Sleep, have generally been accepted as Chaucer's adaptation of both *Metamorphoses*, xi, 592 ff., and the *Dit de la Fontaine Amoureuse*. Mr. Wise [3] suggests that Chaucer had also in mind *Thebaid*, x, 84 ff. His citation of line 156 as coming from Statius does not seem warranted when we consider Machaut's lines quoted by Skeat.[4]

In attributing Chaucer's line 164,

> That was under a rock y-grave,

to Statius, Mr. Wise failed to take into account *Metamorphoses*, xi, 591, which indicates the location of the cave of sleep, to which Iris came:

> Tecta petit jussi sub rupe latentia regis.

---

[1] *Chaucer and the Roman de la Rose*, p. 51.
[2] *Mod. Phil.*, XIV, 722–724.
[3] Pages 41–42.
[4] *Oxford Chaucer*, I, 467.

Chaucer's "under a rock" corresponds more exactly with Ovid's *sub rupe* than with Statius'
subterque cavis rupibus.[1]

TROILUS AND CRISEYDE

Troilus, iii, 722–723, which recall the love of
Jupiter for Europa, Mr. Wise [2] refers to *Thebaid*,
vii, 191. As I have shown in the discussion of this
passage (p. 132), the clear indication of the mood
and connection is that it came from *Metamorphoses*,
ii, 843–875.

Troilus, iii, 1427–1428, the address of Criseyde to
Night, and iii, 1450 ff., the address of Troilus to
Day, which Mr. Wise [3] attributes to the *Thebaid*
and Lactantius, unquestionably, I think, were inspired by *Amores*, i, xiii. (See p. 134.)

Troilus, iv, 22–24, naming the Furies, Mr. Wise [4]
attributes to *Thebaid*, xi, 57 ff. As Statius does not
call them "daughters of night," and both Virgil
and Ovid do, in addition to providing the names,
the passage must be referred to the latter poets.[5]

Troilus, iv, 1548–1554, where Criseyde swears
her oath of faithfulness by the Simois, Mr. Wise [6]
refers to *Thebaid*, viii, 553. But much more similar
and probable sources are to be found in *Amores*, i,
xv, 9–10, and *Heroides*, v, 29–30, as indicated in the
discussion of this point, on page 147.

---

[1] For a discussion of the text of Ovid's line, see p. 6.   [2] Page 11.
[3] Pages 11–12.   [4] Pages 12–13.   [5] See p. 140.   [6] Page 19.

For *Parliament of Fowls*, l. 343, *Troilus*, v, 318 f. and v, 380, and *Legend of Good Women*, ll. 2253 f., all of which refer to the owl as a bird of ill omen, Mr. Wise [1] cites *Thebaid*, iii, 510, and Lactantius, and *Æneid*, iv, 462. Though the *Thebaid* and the *Æneid* refer to the ill-boding prophecies of the owl, neither mentions the transformation of Ascalaphus into that bird. Lactantius, to be sure, furnished information on both points, but it is much more probable that Chaucer owed his knowledge of the owl to Ovid. (See p. 151.)

As Mr. Wise's study shows, Chaucer was intimately acquainted with the *Thebaid*. His direct borrowings from it are greatest in the *Troilus and Criseyde*. But even with regard to that poem, it cannot be said that Statius exerted any influence upon the structure or upon the conception of the characters. There is no central love-story in the *Thebaid*, nor is there any character in the poem that appealed to Chaucer for treatment. The whole epic in its historical setting no doubt seemed to him too far removed from the affairs of ordinary men to furnish any interest to his readers. The style, too, of Statius, with its elaborate descriptions and similes and eloquent orations, would make little appeal to Chaucer. However great intellectual pleasure he may have found in the *Thebaid*,[2] his chief debt to it lies only in poetic enrichment of thought or phrase.

[1] Page 22.   [2] Wise, p. 36.

LUCAN

IN Chaucer's works there are four references to
Lucan [1] by name: one in the *Troilus and Criseyde*, one in the *House of Fame*, one in the *Tale of
the Man of Lawe*, and the fourth in the *Monk's
Tale*.

In *Troilus and Criseyde* there is only the line
giving the names of the poets,

> Virgile, Ovyde, Omer, Lucan, and Stace.
> <div align="right">(<i>Troilus</i>, v, 1792.)</div>

Here Lucan's name is joined with one, Homer,
whose work Chaucer evidently did not know at
first hand, and with three whom he did know, Virgil, Ovid, and Statius. This line, therefore, cannot
justify any inference about Chaucer's acquaintance with Lucan.

In the *House of Fame* there is apparently a little
more to go upon (ll. 1497–1502):

> Tho saugh I, on a piler hy,
> Of yren wrought ful sternely,
> The grete poete, daun Lucan,
> And on his shoulders bar up than,
> As highe as that I mighte see,
> The fame of Julius and Pompee.

It is evident from this passage that Chaucer knew
that Lucan in the *Pharsalia* had much to say about

[1] See Skeat, *Oxford Chaucer*, III, 279.

Cæsar and Pompey. Whether he knew this from his own reading of the Latin poet or got his information from someone else, this passage does not indicate.

In the *Tale of the Man of Lawe* (ll. B 400–401), Chaucer refers to Lucan as describing a great triumph of Julius Cæsar:

> Noght trowe I the triumphe of Julius
> Of which that Lucan maketh swich a bost.

Apparently the same idea is in Chaucer's mind when he says in the *Monk's Tale* (ll. B 3909–3910):

> To Rome agayn repaireth Julius
> With his triumphe, laureat ful hye.

Upon this point of Chaucer's attributing an account of a triumph of Julius Cæsar to Lucan, Skeat says: "See Lucan's *Pharsalia*, iii, 79: 'Perdidit o qualem vincendo plura triumphum.' But Chaucer's reference, evidently made at random, is unlucky. Lucan laments that he had no triumph to record." [1] Lounsbury explains Chaucer's mistake about the triumph as due to careless reading of Lucan: [2]

> Pro, si remeasset in urbem,
> Gallorum tantum populis arctoque subacta,
> Quam seriem rerum longa praemittere pompa.
> Quas potuit belli facies! ut vincula Rheno
> Oceanoque daret, celsos ut Gallia currus

---

[1] *Oxford Chaucer*, V, 153.
[2] *Studies in Chaucer*, II, 254.

Nobilis et flavis sequeretur mixta Britannis!
Perdidit o qualem vincendo plura triumphum.
                              (*Pharsalia*, iii, 73–79.)

But two other passages in the *Pharsalia*, to which
attention has not been called, much more directly
suggest that Cæsar expected to enjoy a triumph
after his defeat of Pompey, and from these Chaucer
may have inferred that the triumph was actually
celebrated. The first passage is:

> Campis prostrata iacere
> Agmina nostra putes; nec enim felicibus armis
> Misceri damnata decet, partemque triumphi
> Captos ferre tui; turba haec sua fata peregit,
> Hoc petimus, victos ne tecum vincere cogas.
>   (*Pharsalia*, iv, 358–362.)

Here the soldiers who have deserted Pompey's side
and fled to Cæsar are begging not to be made a
part of Cæsar's triumphal procession, assuming
apparently that a triumph will certainly be enjoyed
by him. The second passage is a boast of Cæsar
himself in an address to his mutinous soldiers:

> Anne fugam Magni tanta cum classe secuntur
> Hesperiae gentes, nobis victoria turbam
> Non dabit, inpulsi tantum quae praemia belli
> Auferat et vestri rapta mercede laboris
> Lauriferos nullo comitetur volnere currus?
> Vos despecta, senes, exhaustaque sanguine turba
> Cernetis nostros iam plebs Romana triumphos.
>   (*Pharsalia*, v, 328–334.)

The first three stanzas "de Julio Caesare" in the
Monk's Tale are a rapid summing up of the main
facts of the *Pharsalia*. Lines B 3863–3864,

> Up roos he, Julius the conquerour,
> That wan al th' occident by lond and see,

appear to be Chaucer's condensation of Lucan's
rather long roll call of the various Gallic and Germanic tribes that were subject to Cæsar.[1] Lucan
begins by saying (ll. 393–396),

> Caesar, ut acceptum tam prono milite bellum
> Fataque ferre videt, ne quo lanquore moretur
> Fortunam, sparsos per Gallica rura cohortes
> Evocat et Romam motis petit undique signis.

After enumerating the tribes, Lucan tells of
Cæsar's advance into Italy and the terror that his
coming created; he was to be greatly feared because,

> Hunc inter Rhenum populos Alpemque jacentes
> Finibus arctois patriaque a sede revolsos,
> Pone sequi jussamque feris a gentibus urbem
> Romano spectanti rapi.
>   (i, 481–484.)

In lines B 3871–3872 about Pompey,

> That of th' orient hadde al the chivalrye
> As fer as that the day beginneth dawe,

Chaucer apparently is thinking of Lucan's exalta-
tion of Pompey. In the *Pharsalia*, Lucan represents
Pompey, his hero, as the leader of all the nations of
the East which have flocked to his standard because he is so great and famous a general. In trying
to arouse his soldiers to battle, Pompey boasts of

[1] See *Pharsalia*, i, 393–465.

the nations that he has conquered (*Pharsalia*, ii,
583 ff.). A little later Lucan says that Pompey,
when all hope in Italy is gone, looks toward the
East and sends his eldest son to arouse the nations
of the Orient. (*Pharsalia*, ii, 628–644. See also vii,
360–364.)

Though Pompey is his hero, Lucan of necessity
gives Julius Cæsar much prominence. Pompey and
Cæsar are the two opposing forces struggling for
control of the known world. Chaucer dramatically
presents one as the conqueror of the Occident and
the other as the leader of all the forces of the Orient.
Chaucer mentions the country where the contest
between Cæsar and Pompey took place in line
B 3869,

> O mighty Cesar, that in Thessalye.

The fact that Lucan makes so much of Thessaly
(*Pharsalia*, vi, 333–412), giving an account of its
inhabitants, boundaries, mountains, and rivers,
served no doubt to impress the name upon Chaucer's mind.

Chaucer interrupts his account of Cæsar to be-
wail the fate of Pompey, with which Lucan is so
much concerned (ll. 3877–3884):

> But now a litel whyl I wol biwaille
> This Pompeius, this noble governour
> Of Rome, which that fleigh at this bataille;
> I seye, oon of his men, a fals traitour
> His heed of smoot, to winnen him favour

> Of Julius, and him the heed he broghte.
> Allas Pompey, of th' orient conquerour
> That fortune unto swich a fyn thee broghte.

Of the three authors, Lucan, Suetonius, and Valerius, to whom Chaucer refers the reader in the closing stanza of the story of Julius Cæsar, it is easy to see from which one he derived the very concrete statement that one of Pompey's own men cut off his head. Suetonius [1] merely says that Pompey was killed before Cæsar's arrival. Valerius Maximus,[2] though mentioning the fact that Pompey's head was cut off, attributes it to Egyptian treachery. But Lucan gives in full the details which Chaucer evidently had in mind (*Pharsalia*, viii, 592–673).

It would seem clear enough that Chaucer names his authorities correctly when he says (ll. 3909–3911):

> Lucan, to thee this storie I recommende
> And to Sweton, and to Valerie also
> That of this storie wryten word and ende.

One of Chaucer's feats was condensing in brief form some of the Latin epics. He gives a summary of the entire *Æneid* in the first book of the *House of Fame*, and of the *Thebaid* toward the end of *Troilus and Criseyde*. In the *Monk's Tale* he has summarized in three stanzas practically all the important points in the *Pharsalia*. The rest of the

[1] *C. Julius Caesar*, xxxv.
[2] *De factis et dictis Memorabilibus*, v, i, 10.

story of Julius Cæsar, which Lucan does not tell,
— how Brutus Cassius, as Chaucer calls him, at-
tacked Cæsar, and how Cæsar drew his mantle
about him while dying, — Chaucer obtained from
Suetonius [1] and Valerius Maximus.[2]

If Lucan was a popular poet in the Middle Ages [3]
and Chaucer was acquainted with his poem, the
question naturally arises, why did Chaucer make
so little use of it in his works? The answer is not
far to seek. Lucan's subject-matter and style were
not such as to make an appeal to our English story-
teller poet. Lucan's long speeches, eloquent as
they are, smack of the rhetorician's art and seem to
be introduced to display the poet's power of dec-
lamation, as do also the long descriptions of
peoples and places in which he indulges. Consider,
for instance, his ethnological and geographical
account of Thessaly. To Lucan, Pompey was the
representative of freedom, which was hopelessly
crushed by Julius Cæsar's superior force. Chaucer,
however, had no concern with the political or historical events of antiquity, for

> They are gone: ay, ages long ago.

The element of human interest for which he had so
keen an appreciation was not to be found in the
Pharsalia.

[1] *C. Julius Caesar,* lxxxii.

[2] Valerius Maximus, *De factis et dictis Memorabilibus,* iv, v, 6.

[3] Sandys, *History of Classical Scholarship,* I, 641.

VALERIUS FLACCUS

THOUGH Valerius Flaccus seems to have been held in high regard by the men of his own time, — for he was praised by Quintilian and imitated by Statius,[1] — yet after his death he was apparently read by only a few, and in later times no writer or grammarian mentions him or quotes from his work.[2] This accounts for the paucity of manuscripts of his epic, the *Argonauticon*, in the Middle Ages. The traditional statement is that it was practically unknown, because the only two extant manuscripts of the Middle Ages are the one in the Vatican (Codex Vaticanus 3277 of the ninth century) and the Codex Sangallensis, ascribed by scholars to the tenth century. But the Codex Sangallensis was not known until discovered by Poggio at St. Gallen in 1416.[3]

Yet in the face of the silence among ancient writers and grammarians and the ignorance of the

[1] See Teuffel, *Geschichte der Römischen Literatur*, sechste Auflage (Leipzig, 1910), sec. 317, 4.

[2] See O. Kramer, *C. Valeri Flacci Argonauticon* (Lipsiae, 1913), Praef., p. v.

[3] W. Shepherd, *Life of Poggio Bracciolini* (Liverpool, 1837), pp. 97–98. See also B. A. Wise, *Influence of Statius upon Chaucer*, p. 39; Lounsbury, *Studies in Chaucer*, II, 258–260.

Middle Ages concerning Valerius Flaccus, it appears that he must have been known to some extent to Chaucer. There are indications of this knowledge in several places in Chaucer's poetry.

The first of these, in the *House of Fame*, is his locating the abode of Æolus, God of the Winds, in Thrace:

> In Trace ther ye shul him finde.
>
> (l. 1572.)

> In a contree that highte Trace,
> This Eolus, with harde grace,
> Held the windes in distresse.
>
> (ll. 1585–1587.)

This location of the home of Æolus has never before been attributed to Valerius Flaccus, but no satisfactory authority has been found for it in any of the other classical writers.[1] According to Virgil, who has been the source of this myth for succeeding times, Æolus held sway over the winds in Sicily. Skeat[2] says the connection between Æolus and Thrace is not obvious, but suggests that it may be based upon Ovid's phrase, "Threicio Borea," in *Ars Amatoria*, ii, 431. But Æolus is more directly connected with Thrace in an account of an attack by the winds upon the Argonauts given by Valerius Flaccus in *Argonauticon*, i, 596–613. Boreas, whose

---

[1] C. G. Child (*M. L. N.*, XI, 487) suggests Boethius, Book iv, and *Met.*, iii; but though these refer to Boreas, Æolus is not mentioned.

[2] *Oxford Chaucer*, III, 279, note to line 1571.

home was on Pangaeus, a mountain in Thrace, sees the ship of the Greeks, and desirous of overwhelming it, appeals at once to Æolus for permission. When this is granted and Æolus releases all the winds from their prison, they are called, as they rush forth, the *Thracian horses:*

Nuntius hunc solio Boreas proturbat ab alto:
Pangaea quod ab arce nefas, ait, Aeole vidi!
Graia novam ferro molem commenta juventus
Pergit, et ingenti gaudens domat aequora velo:
Nec mihi libertas imis freta tollere harenis.
Qualis eram, nondum vinclis et carcere clausus!
Huic animi structaeque viris fiducia puppis,
Quod Boream sub rege vident. Da mergere Graios,
Insanamque ratem; mil me mea pignora tangunt,
Tantum hominum compresce minas, dum litora juxta
Thessala, nec dum aliae viderunt carbasa terrae.
Dixerat; at cuncti fremere intus et aequora venti
Poscere. Tum valido contortam turbine portam
Inpulit Hippotades: fundunt se carcere laeti
Thraces equi: Zephyrusque, et nocti concolor alas
Nimborum cum prole Notus; crinemque procellis
Hispidus, et multa flavus caput Eurus arena,
Induxere hiemem.

In calling the winds Thracian horses, Valerius Flaccus is following Apollonius Rhodius,[1] who seems to place Æolus in Thrace. Earlier in the account quoted from, Valerius mentions Æolia as the home of Æolus, apparently following Virgil.[2] In this same connection, Valerius uses the adjec-

---

[1] Apollonius Rhodius, i, 954; iv, 765.
[2] *Æn.*, i, 52.

tives Tyrrhenian [1] and Trinacrian;[2] but without a pretty thorough knowledge of classical geography, which we have little reason to suppose Chaucer had, he might still have had a very hazy idea of the location of Æolia. Especially is this likely when we consider that there were also apparently an Æolia in Greece and one in Asia Minor. The reference to Thrace was plain, and Æolia, a name derived from the god's own, might well have been supposed to indicate the immediate location of his abode in Thrace.

What may be another trace of knowledge of Valerius Flaccus occurs in *Troilus*, v, 8,

> The golden-tressed Phebus heighe on lofte.

Skeat [3] says, "For *golden tressed* the MS. Harl. 3493 has *Auricomus tressed* (!). Cf. Sol auricomus, cingentibus Horis, Val. Fl. Argonauticon iv, 92." Though *auricomus* would seem a most appropriate epithet for Sol or Phoebus, no ancient poet other than Valerius Flaccus has used it with regard to him. Martianus Capella, a satirist of the fifth century, whom Mr. Wise [4] cites as the source of this

---

[1] Continuo Aeolium Tyrrhenaque tendit ad antra
   Concitus.
       (ll. 576–577.)

[2] Aequore Trinacrio, refugique a parte Pelori
   Stat rupes horrenda fretis.
           (ll. 579–580.)

[3] *Oxford Chaucer*, II, 495.

[4] *Influence of Statius upon Chaucer*, p. 20.

epithet, pedantically explains why the sun is called *auricomus*. Martianus was known to Chaucer, so that we can feel no certainty as to whether he owed his epithet to the poet, or the satirist, or both.

A third reference to Valerius Flaccus, this time by name, appears in line A 280 of the Prologue to the *Legend of Good Women:*

What seith Valerie, Titus, or Claudian?

Skeat seems rather inconsistent with regard to this line. He refers Titus to Livy and mentions his story of Lucretia; he takes the reference to Claudian to be to the *De Raptu Proserpinae;* and he attributes the "Valerie" in the line to *Valerius ad Rufinum de non ducenda uxore.* He then classes all three as writers against women, thus making it Chaucer's argument that even those who wrote against women had to admit that some were good. But neither Livy nor Claudian can be said to write against women. The context where "Valerie" occurs in the *Wife of Bath's Prologue*, which Skeat cites in corroboration, shows certainly that Chaucer is referring there to *Valerius ad Rufinum.* But it by no means follows that the "Valerie" in the Prologue to the *Legend of Good Women* is the same.[1] Lounsbury[2] takes "Valerie" in the Prologue to be Valerius Maximus. But his *Facta et Dicta Memora-*

---

[1] *Oxford Chaucer*, III, 302.
[2] *Studies in Chaucer*, II, 276.

bilia treats of women only incidentally and of almost none who is famous in history or literature. Such accounts as he gives are told in the barest outline, with the purpose of illustrating the abstract virtues which his epitome aims to set forth. Lounsbury cites Claudian's *Laus Serenae*, which it is most reasonable to suppose Chaucer had in mind here instead of the *De Raptu Proserpinae;* for I believe that Chaucer means to refer to those who have praised women, particularly for steadfastness in love. If this is true, then "Valerie" must refer to Valerius Flaccus, who in the *Argonauticon* treats of two women faithful in love, to both of whom Chaucer has given places in the *Legend of Good Women*. The story of Hypsipyle and Jason is found in Book ii, and that of Medea and Jason in Book vii of the *Argonauticon.*

In Chaucer's own version of the first of these stories, the *Legend of Hypsipyle*, he refers to Valerius Flaccus' poem by its correct title, intimating that he knows something of its contents, and shows in two other passages some resemblance to it.

In the early part of this *Legend*, Chaucer cites Guido delle Colonna as his authority and summarizes Guido's account from line 1396 to line 1461. But near the close of this passage he refers the reader who wishes to know who went with Jason to the *Argonauticon*, where he will find a long enough tale:

> Anoon Argus his shippes gan devyse;
> With Jasoun wente the stronge Ercules,
> And many an-other that he with him chees.
> But whoso axeth who is with him gon,
> Lat him go reden Argonauticon
> For he wol telle a tale longe y-now.
>
> (*L. G. W.*, ll. 1453–1458.)

Guido gives no list of the Argonauts. That given by Statius in *Thebaid*, v, 335–444, is only incidental to the attempt of the Argonauts to land at Lemnos, and is not long enough to warrant Chaucer's reference to its length. Valerius Flaccus, on the other hand, gives a long list of the names and identities of the heroes who joined Jason while he was preparing for the journey, and it is just at that point that Chaucer introduces the reference to it in his account. Bech [1] has pointed out in Dares a passage similar to Chaucer's, but Chaucer could hardly have derived the correct title of Valerius' poem from Dares' "Argonautas." [2] Besides, Dares says nothing about the list being a long and dreary one, as it is.

Immediately following this reference to the *Argonauticon* Chaucer has ten lines in which he tells how, when the wind was good, Jason sailed out of Thessaly and at length arrived at the isle of Lemnos, — circumstances he says, which though not rehearsed by Guido, are told by Ovid in his Epistle,

---

[1] *Anglia*, V, 325–326.
[2] See Wise, *Influence of Statius upon Chaucer*, p. 39.

— and how the queen of this isle was the fair young Hypsipyle, the daughter of the former King Thoas. After these ten lines Chaucer gives an account of the landing of Jason and his companions at Lemnos, of the reception accorded them, and of the wooing and winning of Hypsipyle, which is quite independent of Ovid, or any other known version of the story. Ovid gives none of this at all.

Valerius Flaccus, however, gives an account of the visit of the Argonauts to Lemnos, very different in most respects, to be sure, from Chaucer's, but similar to it in two features.

After the Lemnians decide to receive the Argonauts in a friendly manner, Hypsipyle sends a messenger to invite the Greeks to come ashore. By Valerius Flaccus this messenger is named Iphinoe, a woman:

> portatque preces ad litora Graiis
> Iphinoe.
> > (*Argonauticon*, ii, 326–327.)

Chaucer has made this messenger a man, a change which may be due to Virgil.[1]

> This messagere adoun him gan to hye.[2]
> > (*L. G. W.*, l. 1479.)

---

[1] For a discussion of the influence of Virgil upon Valerius Flaccus in this story, see p. 211.

[2] Statius gives an account of a battle that raged between the Argonauts and the Lemnian women before a landing was effected. But his narrative seems to have nothing in common with Chaucer's. See Wise, *Influence of Statius upon Chaucer*, p. 38.

In the account of Hypsipyle's entertainment of the Argonauts, Chaucer again shows resemblance to Valerius Flaccus:

> And to the castel with her ledeth she
> Thise straunge folk, and doth hem greet honour,
> And axeth hem of travail and labour
> That they han suffred in the salte see.
>
> (*L. G. W.*, ll. 1507–1510.)

After describing the banquet which Hypsipyle gave to the Argonauts, Valerius Flaccus says that she inquired about the fortunes of the leader, what fates were drawing him on, and what was the goal of the journey.

> Praecipueque ducis casus mirata requirit
> Hypsipyle, quae fata trahunt, quae regis agat vis.
>
> (*Argonauticon*, ii, 351–352.)

The facts that confront us then with regard to Chaucer's use of Valerius Flaccus are: (1) that he got the suggestion of Thrace as the abode of Æolus in the *House of Fame* from the *Argonauticon;* (2) that he may have adopted Valerius Flaccus' epithet "auricomus" for the Sun; (3) that he refers to Valerius Flaccus as a writer upon faithful women in the Prologue to the *Legend of Good Women;* (4) that he knew the correct title of Valerius' epic and refers to his long list of Argonautic heroes in the *Legend of Hypsipyle;* and (5) that he twice used suggestions from the *Argonauticon* further on in the same legend.

In view of Chaucer's apparent acquaintance with
the *Argonauticon*, we must reconsider the question
of the MSS. Does Poggio's discovery of the Codex
Sangallensis in 1416, though it marks the revival of
a knowledge of Valerius Flaccus in Italy, preclude
the possibility of his being known previously in the
Middle Ages and consequently to Chaucer? It
would seem not.

The history and parentage of the Codex Vaticanus indicate pretty clearly that in Britain, at
least, some interest in Valerius Flaccus was kept
alive during the Middle Ages. And this, of course,
bears directly upon Chaucer's connection with the
question.

Otto Kramer, one of the latest students of Valerius Flaccus, has made a thorough investigation
of the history of the MSS and gives the result of his
studies in the preface to his edition of the *Argonauticon*. The following is a translation of that part of
his Latin preface which relates to the history of the
Codex Vaticanus:

> Besides, from other indications it is possible to recog-
> nize much more certainly the native land of Codex
> Vaticanus, or rather its archetype. For it is not dis-
> proved by these arguments that the Codex Vaticanus
> was brought out of remote Germany, as indeed Pius
> affirmed formerly in his preface. We find on page 140
> *recto* the word *uulfered*, which F. Holthausen kindly
> confirmed for me, when I was somewhat doubtful, as

being an Anglo-Saxon name. Nor is there any doubt but that either the scribe himself placed his own name upon the Codex, or — what not seldom happened, from the archetype the name of the scribe or critic was transcribed upon the apograph. Moreover in the Codex Vaticanus itself the letter (g) preserves the insular form (z) in two places. In fine, many changes of letters are scarcely intelligible except from insular writing. . . . Not only the archetype of the Codex Vaticanus seems to have been written in the insular handwriting, but the source of the archetype, and it seems that the errors and corrections of the archetype ought to be attributed to a scribe who was not sufficiently acquainted with insular letters. Moreover, other obvious changes in the Codex Vaticanus are more easily intelligible from the accustomed minuscular handwriting. . . . Therefore it seems to me that the archetype of Codex Vaticanus was written in minuscular characters from some codex written in insular handwriting either in Britain or in some monastery in Germany. Then indeed from that exemplar of minuscular writing the Codex Vaticanus sprang in Germany. In what year it was brought into Italy we do not know. But that this was done a little after Poggio found the Codex Sangallensis is evident from the fact that comparatively few apographs of the St. Gallen MS. are to be met with. To be sure, the learned men preferred the fuller MS. to the mutilated one.[1]

There are two manuscripts of excerpts from numerous classical and late Latin writers which contain some fragments of Valerius Flaccus — the Codex Parisinus 7647 and the Codex del Escurial Q 1, 14. Scholars generally agree that the Parisinus

---

[1] O. Kramer, *C. Valeri Flacci Argonauticon*, Praef., pp. xiv–xv.

is derived from the Codex Vaticanus or from the same archetype, and that the Escurial was copied from the Parisinus, or that both came independently from a common source. Hence these fragments seem to trace back to the same source as the Vaticanus.

There is also the history of another MS., now lost, to be considered, called the Codex Carrionis, after the name of Ludavicus Carrio, who claimed to have used it. Carrio published an edition of Valerius Flaccus in 1565 at Antwerp, in the preface of which he says that he has corrected his text in six hundred or more places by the authority of a very ancient MS., written six hundred years before, that is, in the tenth century. This statement of Carrio's went unchallenged for a long time. But Thilo in his edition of Valerius Flaccus (1863), questions the good faith of Carrio, or his critical judgment, concerning the date of the MS. he employed. Thilo contends that the Codex Carrionis must have been transcribed from the Codex Vaticanus and so was a fifteenth-century MS. He suggests that the scribe may have gone to the trouble of imitating the handwriting of the tenth century, and in this way Carrio was deceived. Some scholars say that the Carrio MS. derived from the Vaticanus, but was corrected by another of better source: others say that the Carrio was from the same archetype as the Vaticanus, or rather from some twin of its archetype.[1] But Carrio's text was acknowledged by succeeding commentators to be a very superior one, showing marked improvements over those taken from the Vaticanus solely. When all is said on the question of Carrio's MS., it is by no means certain that he did not have, what he in good faith claimed to have, a tenth-century MS. of Valerius Flaccus, which he found in Belgium.

Besides the two MSS of excerpts still extant and the lost Carrio, there is a record of the existence of a MS. of Valerius Flaccus preserved in a catalogue of MSS in the monastery of Bobbio, where it is listed among those of the tenth century.[2] As it was catalogued merely as *Valerii Flacci Liber I*, we cannot now tell whether it was the entire poem, or only a part of the poem of Valerius Flaccus. Kramer, who cites Becker, says that we have no knowledge of whether it was the whole poem, or part, or sentences only, or by what chain of necessity it was connected with the other MSS, or whence it came.[3]

But I think we can tell probably whence this MS. came and what was the chain of circumstances

[1] For a good summary of divergent opinions, see Kramer, Praef., p. xlvii.

[2] See G. Becker, *Catalogi Bibliothecarum Antiqui*. See also Leon Maître, *Ecoles*, p. 298, who records the same MS.

[3] Kramer, Praef., p. v.

connecting it with the other Valerius Flaccus MSS, by considering the history of the monastery of Bobbio and its founder.

The monastery of Bobbio was founded by an Irish monk, Columbanus, who went from Ireland to Gaul with twelve other monks and settled in Burgundy, where he founded several monasteries — as many as three. Later he was banished from Burgundy, and, after several years of wandering, he brought up in Italy, where he founded the monastery of Bobbio about 613.[1] This monastery became a house of learning and many MSS were contributed to its library. Columbanus himself was a man finely educated in the Classics, and among the requirements of his "Rule" was one imposing the necessity of copying MSS. The indications are pretty clear, therefore, that a Valerius Flaccus MS. came from Britain with this company of Irish monks, or with others who came later travelling to the Continent and found a copyist in the monastery of Bobbio. If this perfectly natural and logical thing happened, we can readily see how the MS. at Bobbio, as well as the Vaticanus, goes back to a British original. Likewise, the MS. which Carrio

---

[1] See *Life of St. Columban*, translated and edited by D. C. Monro, Dept. of History, Univ. of Pa., 1895; also Manitius, *Geschichte der Lat. Lit. des Mittelalter*, München, 1911 ("Columbanus," pp. 181 ff.). On the relation of the Irish monks to Britain, see Zimmer, *The Celtic Church in Britain and Ireland*, translated by Meyer, London, 1902.

found in Belgium may have been copied from one left there by these or other British monks.

But our chain of circumstances has one more interesting link. When Columbanus left Switzerland for Italy where he was to found the monastery of Bobbio, St. Gallus, an Irish monk who had accompanied him from Britain, remained on the Lake of Constance and with several other Irish monks founded the now famous monastery of St. Gallen.[1] This too became a treasure house of Latin as well as Irish literature.[2] It was here, that Poggio made his notable discovery of the MS. of Valerius Flaccus known as the Codex Sangallensis.

With this connection between St. Gallen and Britain in mind, let us consider the evidence that modern scholarship has to give on the relation of the Codex Sangallensis to the Codex Vaticanus. Kramer says that scholars have disagreed as to the exact relationship between these two MSS. Some have contended that Codex Sangallensis came from the Vaticanus, while others have argued that they were twin MSS.[3] After giving the reasons for his belief, Kramer states his own conclusion, which is that the Sangallensis was transcribed from the Vaticanus.[4]

[1] A. Potthast, "Das Leben des heiligen Gallus," *Die Geschichtschreiber der deut. Vorzeit* (Berlin, 1857), IV, 3 ff.

[2] J. E. Sandys, *History of Classical Scholarship*, I, 455.

[3] Kramer, Praef., p. xxxviii.   [4] Praef., p. xlii.

It would seem evident from the history of the monasteries where the MSS of Valerius Flaccus have been discovered and from the internal evidence of the MSS themselves that the knowledge of Valerius Flaccus during the Middle Ages traces directly back to the British Isles, while at the same time a profound ignorance of him prevailed generally upon the Continent.

We can now understand how Chaucer, the lover of books, was able to know the *Argonauticon* and to refer to it by its proper title while his predecessors and contemporaries on the Continent maintained a universal silence with regard to it. Where he got his MS. of Valerius Flaccus we can no more tell than where he got his MS. of Ovid, or Virgil, or any other ancient, but it seems clear enough that it was possible for him to have seen one.

CLAUDIAN

THOUGH Chaucer's use of Claudian [1] is not extensive, his knowledge of this Roman poet is unmistakable, for he refers to him by name or quotes from him in at least four different poems.

Lines 99–105 of the *Parliament of Fowls*, which relate how dreams are often the result of the mind's activity during the day, are a free translation of the opening lines of the Preface to Claudian's panegyric on the sixth consulship of the Emperor Honorius.[2]

Lines 176–182 of the *Parliament of Fowls*, which give the "tree-list" with the various epithets for each, are, to be sure, more or less conventional, and probably no very definite conclusion can be drawn from them. Professor Lounsbury [3] thought the correspondences between Chaucer and Claudian were nearer than those between Chaucer and the other writers [4] who have given similar lists. Professor Root,[5] however, has produced evidence by a detailed comparison of Chaucer's list with that of each of the earlier authors to show that Chaucer

[1] On Claudian in the Middle Ages, see Manitius, *Rhein. Mus.*, XLVII, 103–105.

[2] See Lounsbury, *Studies in Chaucer*, II, 257.

[3] Ibid., p. 256.   [4] See *Oxford Chaucer*, I, 511.

[5] *Mod. Phil.*, XV, 18–22.

agrees with Joseph of Exeter more completely than with any of the others.

In line 449 of the *House of Fame* Chaucer advises reading for the torments of hell

> On Virgile or on Claudian.

Here the reference is evidently to the *De Raptu Proserpinae*.

In lines 1507–1512 of the *House of Fame* is found Chaucer's description of Claudian:

> And next him on a piler stood
> Of soulfre, lyk as he were wood,
> Dan Claudian, the soth to telle,
> That bare up al the fame of helle,
> Of Pluto, and of Proserpyne,
> That quene is of the derke pyne.

Professor Lounsbury says, "'Like as he were wood' is an expression, which, common as it is in Chaucer, may be thought to show here his appreciation of the fervor and fire, and rhetorical diction which modern critics have regarded as special characteristics of Claudian's style. On the other hand, it is possible that he may have had in mind the fierce invectives against Eutropius and Rufinius." [1] I think it is much more likely that Claudian's own words near the beginning of the *De Raptu Proserpinae* (i, 4–6) furnished the suggestion for the epithet. There the poet says the *divine madness,*

[1] *Studies in Chaucer,* II, 255.

which is upon him, has removed from his breast all human sensibilities:

> gressus removete profani
> Jam furor humanos nostro de pectore sensus
> Expulit et totum spirant praecordia Phoebum.

In the Prologue to the *Legend of Good Women*, line A 280, Claudian is mentioned by name —

> What seith Valerie, Titus, or Claudian?

The reference is probably to the *Laus Serenae*, where several famous women of antiquity are named as noble examples of womanhood — Alcestis, Penelope, Laodamia, Lucretia, Atalanta, Deianira.[1]

In the *Merchant's Tale*, lines E 2227–2233, Chaucer refers to Proserpina gathering flowers in the mead and being carried off by Pluto in his fiery chariot, and adds,

> In Claudian ye may the story rede.

This passage shows a knowledge of the *De Raptu Proserpinae*, though Claudian does not, of course, represent Pluto and his queen as fairies as Chaucer does.

[1] See Lounsbury, II, 257–258. See also the discussion of this line under Valerius Flaccus, p. 344.

HORACE

HORACE was a popular poet in the Middle Ages, as the number of manuscripts of his works testifies.[1] It is, therefore, quite possible that Chaucer may have become acquainted with his poems, but we find no evidence that he did.

All the passages in Chaucer that seem to have Horace as their ultimate source have been collected and published by Miss Harriet Seibert in *Modern Language Notes*, XXXI, 304–307.[2] She enumerates eight, for five of which some convenient second-hand source has already been found. Though she failed to note the juxtaposition of Orpheus and Amphion as musicians both by Chaucer in the *Merchant's Tale*, lines E 1715–1717, and by Horace in the *Ars Poetica*, lines 394 ff., this is not sufficient evidence of a first-hand knowledge. Besides, as has already been shown, Chaucer knew of Amphion as a musician from *Metamorphoses*, vi, 177–179. See page 319.

The three remaining passages, for which no second-hand sources have been suggested, and

---

[1] See A. Graf, *Roma nella memoria e nelle imaginazione del medio evo*, pp. 593–595; J. E. Sandys, *History of Classical Scholarship*, I, 635–638; Teuffel-Schwabe, *History of Roman Literature*, trans. by G. C. W. Warr, I, 453–477; Manitius, *Rhein. Mus.*, XLVII, 28–31.

[2] See also C. L. Wrenn, *Mod. Lang. Rev.*, XVIII, 286–292.

which seem to indicate some knowledge of Horace by Chaucer, have been considered by Miss Seibert. Her suggestion of John of Salisbury's *Metalogicus* as the source for *Troilus*, ii, 22 ff., must give place to the explanation by Professor Lowes that these lines were suggested by Dante's *Convivio*.[1] The second passage, *Troilus*, ii, 1028–1036, with regard to a harper who continually plays upon one string, she rightly says, was too much of a commonplace for us to draw any conclusion from it. Her third citation, *Troilus*, ii, 1041–1043, she suggests as due to John of Salisbury's *Policraticus*, ii, 18, and this is probably correct.

Chaucer nowhere mentions Horace by name. When we consider the readily accessible second-hand sources from which he could acquire some ideas from Horace, we are forced to the conclusion that he was not familiar at first hand with the works of this one of the Roman poets.

[1] *Mod. Phil.*, XIV, 134.

JUVENAL

AS JUVENAL was well known during the Middle Ages,[1] there is no ground for denying a knowledge of his works to Chaucer. Yet the material upon which to base a judgment is very meagre. It is in fact confined to two references to the poet by name and a correct quotation from his work in each case.

The first of these is in the *Wife of Bath's Tale*, lines D 1192–1194:

> Juvenal seith of povert merily:
> "The povre man, whan he goth by the weye,
> Bifore the theves he may singe and pleye."

As has been noted by Skeat and others, these lines are a very happy rendering of Juvenal's

> Cantabit vacuus coram latrone viator.
> *(Sat.,* x, 21.)

The second is in *Troilus*, iv, 197–201:

> O Juvenal, lord! trewe is thy sentence,
> That litel witen folk what is to yerne
> That they ne finde in hir desyr offence:
> For cloud of errour lat hem nat descerne
> What best is.

---

[1] See J. E. Sandys, *History of Classical Scholarship*, pp. 644–645; Teuffel-Schwabe, *History of Roman Literature*, trans. by G. C. W. Warr, II, 147–153; Manitius, *Rhein. Mus.*, XLVII, 66–68.

This is a pretty close translation of Juvenal's

> pauci dinoscere possunt
> Vera bona atque illis multum diversa, remota
> Erroris nebula.
> (*Sat.*, x, 2–4.)

Chaucer's use of the proper name Arviragus [1] in the *Franklin's Tale* has no significance in connection with Juvenal, though Juvenal does use it as the name of a Celtic king in Britain. The names of the other characters in the *Franklin's Tale* are decidedly Celtic, and the setting of the story is Celtic. So it seems more reasonable to attribute Chaucer's use of Arviragus to the Breton *lai*, from which he must have derived his tale, than to Juvenal's *Satire*, iv, 127.

As no easily accessible second-hand sources are available to which to attribute Chaucer's knowledge of Juvenal, and as the quotations from him are such evident translations, the conclusion seems inescapable that Chaucer must have known his work at first hand. That more borrowing from it does not appear in Chaucer's poems is not strange. The didactic quality of the Roman's invectives against particular vices was not such as to appeal to the humanity-loving nature of the English teller of stories.

[1] See Lounsbury, *Studies in Chaucer*, II, 260.

PERSIUS

UNWILLING as we are to be too dogmatic about Chaucer's knowledge of Juvenal on the basis of two quotations, we are more so with regard to his acquaintance with Persius.[1] For in this case we have only one quotation, correct to be sure, in the Prologue to the *Franklin's Tale* (l. F 721):

> I sleep never on the mount of Pernaso.

This line, as noted by Skeat, is very close to the idea contained in the first three lines of the *Prologus* of the *Satires* of Persius:

> Nec fonte labra prolui caballino,
> Neque in bicipiti somniasse Parnasso
> Memini, ut repente sic poeta prodirem.

Whether this means an actual reading of Persius by Chaucer or a culling from some convenient florilegium, no living mortal can tell.

---

[1] On Persius in the Middle Ages, see Teuffel-Schwabe, *History of Roman Literature*, trans. by G. C. W. Warr, II, 75–78; J. E. Sandys, *History of Classical Scholarship*, I, 645; Manitius, *Rhein. Mus.*, XLVII, 52–54.

CATULLUS

THOUGH traces of Catullus in English poetry from the time of the Renaissance have long been observed, no suggestion has ever been made, so far as I am aware, that evidence of his influence is to be found in Chaucer. Yet there are three passages in Chaucer's poetry which point significantly to Catullus as their source.

The first of these is in the *House of Fame* (lines 269–285), where Chaucer halts in the midst of the story of Dido and Æneas to make some general observations upon the deceitful nature of men with regard to love:

> Lo, how a woman doth amis,
> To love him that unknowen is!
> For, by Crist, lo! thus hit fareth;
> Hit is not al gold, that glareth.
> For, also brouke I wel myn heed,
> Ther may be under goodliheed
> Kevered many a shrewed vyce;
> Therfor be no wight so nyce,
> To take a love only for chere,
> For speche, or for frendly manere;
> For this shal every woman finde
> That som man, of his pure kinde,
> Wol shewen outward the faireste,
> Til he have caught that what him leste;
> And thanne wol he causes finde,
> And swere how that she is unkinde,
> Or fals, or prevy, or double was.[1]

[1] That the theme was a favorite one with Chaucer is apparent from his repetition of it in the *Anelida and Arcite*, ll. 97–98, 148–151,

With Dido particularly in mind (as well as all the others whom Ovid treats in the *Heroides*, so many of whom are included by name in the *House of Fame*), it might have been easy enough for Chaucer to make application of Æneas' conduct to men in general. Possibly, too, his own observation of life might have brought him to this conclusion. But it is noteworthy that in the *Heroides*, which exerted so great an influence upon the *Anelida and Arcite*, the *House of Fame*, and the *Legend of Good Women*, Ovid makes the heroines, with one apparent exception, emphasize merely the unfaithfulness of the heroes to them individually.[1]

Catullus, however, in the story of Ariadne, which he tells in No. LXIV of his poems, has a passage upon the faithlessness of men similar to Chaucer's. According to this account, Ariadne, after reciting the fair promises Theseus had made to her of a happy marriage and eagerly wished-for espousal, says the winds of heaven now blow them abroad in vain:

311–314; in *Troilus and Criseyde*, ii, 786–788; and in the *Legend of Good Women*, ll. 1885, 2387–2391, 2559.

[1] The only exception to this is to be found in the words of Helen to Paris:

> Sed quia credulitas damno solet esse puellis,
> Verbaque dicuntur vestra carere fide.
>
> (*Her.*, xvi, 39–40.)

But here Helen is merely voicing a fear and the idea is not expanded, as in the *House of Fame* and in Catullus.

> At non haec quondam blanda promissa dedisti
> Voce mihi; non haec miseram sperare jubebas,
> Sed conubia laeta, sed optatos hymenaeos:
> Quae cuncta aerii discerpunt irrita venti.
>
> (lxiv, 139–142.)

Then she draws the conclusion for all women suggested by her own fate: henceforth let no woman trust in the oaths of a man; let her not hope that he will be faithful to his promises. When their eager mind desires to obtain something, men do not fear to swear, and do not hesitate to promise, but as soon as the lust of their passionate mind is satisfied, they respect their words no longer and care nothing for their false oaths.

> Jam, jam nulla viro juranti femina credat,
> Nulla viri speret sermones esse fideles;
> Quis dum aliquid cupiens animus praegestit apisci,
> Nil metuunt jurare, nihil promittere parcunt:
> Sed simul accupidae mentis satiata libidost,
> Dicta nihil metuere, nihil perjuria curant.
>
> (lxiv, 143–148.)

The lyric intensity with which Catullus makes Ariadne generalize her own particular misfortune must have expressed for Chaucer his own reaction to his reading of the *Heroides*.

A less conclusive but possible bit of evidence for Chaucer's acquaintance with Catullus is to be found in the *Legend of Ariadne*, where Theseus is represented as a youth of twenty-three:

> And yong, but of a twenty yeer and three.
>
> (*L. G.W.*, l. 2075.)

Boccaccio, to be sure, writes in the *De Genealogia Deorum* of "seven noble youths" (*VII nobiles juvenes*) being sent each year to Crete. This hint from Boccaccio as to Theseus' age might have been sufficient to suggest Chaucer's description of Theseus as twenty-three years old. But in Catullus we find Theseus twice specifically called *juvenis*, that is, one who is in the flower of his youth, older than *adolescens* and younger than *senior:*

Immemor at juvenis fugiens pellit vada remis.
(lxiv, 58.)

Talia complexum juveni mandata dedisse.
(lxiv, 214.)

The occurrence of this word here assumes significance when we consider that both of Chaucer's other analogies with Catullus are from this same story of Theseus and Ariadne. And the evidence of the third is more convincing than either of those already mentioned.

In the introductory lines of the *Legend of Ariadne* is found the statement that the gods were angry with Theseus for his treatment of Ariadne and took vengeance upon him for it:

But for to clepe agein unto memorie
Of Theseus the grete untrouthe of love;
For which the goddes of the heven above
Ben wrothe, and wreche han take for thy sinne.
(*L. G. W.*, ll. 1889–1892.)

No comment has ever been made upon these lines, nor any indication given that they differ from the usual version of the story of Ariadne. But though the death of Theseus' father is recounted by Boccaccio,[1] he gives no hint that this grief was sent upon Theseus by the gods as a retribution for his desertion of Ariadne. In fact, Chaucer is here at variance with all the other accounts of this episode except that of Catullus. The idea that the gods took cognizance of Theseus' abandonment of Ariadne is consonant with the very theme of Catullus' poem, No. LXIV. He introduces the Ariadne story, which he tells mainly in agreement with other accounts, apparently for the purpose of the dramatic contrast that it offers between the favor of the gods toward the nuptials of Peleus and Thetis and their vengeance upon Theseus for his broken vows. In developing this new slant, which, by the way, is an interesting bit of creative adaptation, Catullus represents Ariadne as appealing to the Eumenides, the Goddesses of Vengeance, to bring retribution upon Theseus for his conduct:

Vos nolite pati nostrum vanescere luctum;
Sed quali solam Theseus me mente reliquit,
Tali mente, deae, funestet seque suosque.

(lxiv, 199–201.)[2]

[1] *De Genealogia Deorum*, lib. x, cap. xlviii.
[2] Cf. the whole passage, ll. 192–201.

This prayer to the avenging Fates Jupiter hears, and grants his assent with a nod that makes the earth and seas tremble and the heavens shake (lxiv, 202–206). The fulfilment of Jupiter's vengeance, Catullus says, came when Theseus on his arrival home found that his father had drowned himself because he saw Theseus' ship returning with the black sails, which the son had neglected to change to white in accordance with their agreement if he returned alive. In the loss of his father by his forgetfulness of mind Theseus received such grief as he had caused to the daughter of Minos:

> Sic funestra domus ingressus tecta paterna
> Morte ferox Theseus qualem Minoidi luctum
> Obtulerat mente immemori talem ipse recepit.
> (lxiv, 246–248.)

We can readily see how the poetic justice that Catullus develops would appeal to Chaucer. And, as the idea is common to these two only among the various narrators of the story of Theseus and Ariadne, the conclusion seems inevitable that Chaucer must have taken it from Catullus.

Number LXIV of Catullus' poems is the only one of the series that contains a story which Chaucer has retold from the Classics, or indeed any story which we should expect him to be interested in. Hence it was that his borrowing was restricted to the episode of Theseus and Ariadne.

That Chaucer could have known Catullus is
quite possible. The history of the manuscripts of
his poems [1] is very simple. With the exception of
one fragment, Codex Thuaneus, they trace back
to the Codex Veronensis, which is known to have
been in Verona early in the fourteenth century.
Of this MS. two transcripts exist, Codex Sanger-
manensis or Parisiensis (1375) and Codex Oxonien-
sis (*ca.* 1400).

[1] See J. E. Sandys, *A History of Classical Scholarship*, p. 633.

CONCLUSION

THE one dominant idea that emerges from the consideration of Chaucer's relation to the Roman poets is his intimate knowledge of even the details of Ovid's poetry. Ovid was so familiar to him that he doubtless knew many lines and passages of his poetry from memory. This is illustrated by his inserting phrases from Ovid's description of the cave of the God of Sleep in the account of Fame's dwelling in the *House of Fame*. Sometimes he followed Ovid so closely as to indicate the reading of his MS., where the MSS offer variations in the text.[1] In using material from Ovid he translated, adapted, modified, shortened, expanded, referred or alluded to it. It is interesting to observe that the other great genius of English literature, Shakspere, loved Ovid and referred more frequently to him than to any other ancient writer.[2]

The points of similarity in taste and poetic gifts between Chaucer and Ovid are so many that we cannot wonder at the extent of the Roman's influence upon the Englishman. One of the most easily discernible characteristics of Ovid as a poet is the facility and grace of his verse. Chaucer was

---

[1] See pp. 6, 279.
[2] See J. Q. Adams, *A Life of William Shakespeare*, p. 57.

similarly gifted; he carries the reader along with
the smoothness of his diction. Both were not only
masters but creators of verse forms. Ovid extended
the use of the elegiac metre into practically a new
medium for his love-poetry, as Chaucer invented
the Rhyme Royal for the *Troilus and Criseyde*.
The verse of the two poets is indicative of their
characters: Ovid's shows the softness of his nature,
while Chaucer's evinces simplicity and manly
vigor.

These poets exhibit a resemblance of manner in
introducing into their poems literary references
and allusions. To Ovid naturally these came from
Greek and Roman mythology. To Chaucer the
classical myths likewise appealed, though he
adapted them to the conditions of his own day.
In order to produce local color he filled the *Troilus*
with such references. Yet he almost invariably
stripped the stories he retold from the Classics of
their pagan significance, especially such supernatural occurrences as were unnecessary to the
plot. This is characteristic of his use of material
from the first book of the *Æneid* in the *Legend of
Dido*, and of his discarding the metamorphosis
regularly in stories taken from Ovid. To him the
characters in the *Metamorphoses*, the *Heroides*,
and the *Æneid* appealed as real men and women,
unrelated to mythological symbolism.

In insight into woman's nature Ovid particularly excels. Possibly the lack of heroic qualities in himself made him more sensitive to feminine charms and more sympathetic with woman. Rarely has a keener psychological analysis been written than his account of the struggle that Biblis undergoes between her love and her reason.[1] She vacillates and comes to a decision, only immediately to reopen the question, until the reader is eager to know what the final conclusion is to be. The same characteristics mark the debate in Medea's mind about her duty to her father and her native land when it lies in conflict with her consuming love.[2] Much of Chaucer's poetry, too, concerns itself with women in love. The outstanding characters of his creation are Criseyde and the Wife of Bath, and the catholicity of his understanding of feminine emotions is illustrated in these two types of woman. Criseyde is young and beautiful, living in an atmosphere of the Court of Love, yet breaking its conventions in following her own impulse to love. The Wife of Bath is frankly animal in her nature, mature, experienced and supremely realistic, with no romantic illusions. Like Mona Lisa's smile, these two women, after all the centuries, still defy complete analysis.

[1] *Met.*, ix, 425 ff.
[2] *Ibid.*, vii, 1–94.

The world in which Ovid moved was the luxurious and decadent society of the later days of Augustus, and in some of his poems he gives a true and realistic picture of the times. In this realism lay the seeds of inspiration to Chaucer which were slowly and gradually to grow into the great idea of portraying the English people in the days of Richard II. Rich and full as is the picture in the *Canterbury Tales*, it shows much the same lightness and vivacity that belong to Ovid. The reason that Chaucer tells us so little of the ravages of the plague, the wars with France, or the peasant rebellion is that these themes did not appeal to him as material for his genius any more than the heroic appealed to Ovid. He was interested in the essentially human qualities of men and women, which he treats with a sureness of touch and restraint of style that stamp him as the genius of England in his day. John Gower pursued his pedantic way to the grave without suspecting that in life interpreted realistically rather than allegorically lay the pathway to literary fame.

The peculiar excellence of Ovid's narrative verse lies in its dramatic quality. He knew how to secure a highly emotional effect without sacrificing continuity in the story. Chaucer's mastery of vivid narrative must have attained much of its perfection from long familiarity with Ovid's poems. We have found him leaving practically untouched such masterpieces as Ovid's accounts of Thisbe and Lucretia, and retaining the graphic features of a story like Ariadne's. Few poets of any age or time have excelled or equalled Ovid in vividness. He possessed unusual powers of seeing and making others see the objects of his portrayal, whether he was dealing with outdoor nature or with human nature.

The congeniality of spirit and temperament between the two poets is apparent in the assimilation that Chaucer made of Ovid's works. The creative fancy running through all of Ovid's poetry appears at its best in the *Heroides* and the *Metamorphoses*. These two poems stand out in Chaucer's relation to Ovid, the *Metamorphoses* as the great treasure house of story and incident, and the *Heroides* as the source of imaginative inspiration.

It is easy to see why to Chaucer the appeal of Ovid was greater than that of any other single writer who contributed to his literary development. The subjects as well as the poetic forms of the other Roman writers held no such attraction for him as the stories of Ovid. As a consequence he used the work of the other poets chiefly for illustrative episodes or enrichment of ideas. Yet there is something about all the Classics which seems to temper one's disposition to tolerance and restraint.[1] The very definite conception of a poem like the *Æneid*, the *Thebaid*, the *Metamorphoses*, or the *Heroides*, carried to its conclusion by adherence to the single idea running through it all, was bound to have a moulding influence upon the mind of a man like Chaucer. By this I do not mean to imply that he was not at the same time mediaeval. He must absorb what the classical poets could teach him and make it his own in the midst of his mediaeval surroundings. Otherwise he would have become a mere sounding brass and tinkling cymbal of antiquity — a thing of which he surely cannot be accused. Much as he owed to the Classics, he never failed to be himself. And the fullest revelation of himself he has made, of course, in the *Canterbury Tales*. Nor should I wish to seem guilty of maintaining that all of Chaucer's tolerance, temperance, restraint, and polish in thought and style were the result of his classical studies only. That he was naturally endowed with such qualities made him the more responsive to these characteristics in the Roman poets.

Had Chaucer continued to follow his early French models he would never have attained the position he occupies in English literature. His preëminence is due in great measure to the influence upon him of the Italian Renaissance. This

[1] See Henry Osborn Taylor, *The Mediaeval Mind*, II, 164.

great intellectual rebirth was well under way when he made his first visit to Italy in 1372. His second journey in 1378 doubtless served to deepen the impressions gained from his earlier contacts. The essence of the Renaissance, lay in its directing the minds of men to the ideals of antiquity. So different were these ideals with their emphasis upon the interests of men in the present-day world [1] as contrasted with those of the Middle Ages, which looked for the attainment of human happiness in the far-away future, that a perception of them amounted really to the discovery of a new intellectual realm. The Renaissance in Italy in its inception was largely a Latin influence because of the lack of a knowledge of Greek. Petrarch, we know, wept over a MS. of Homer which he was unable to read, and Boccaccio made rather ineffectual efforts to master the Greek language. But the opening of the way to an understanding of the spirit of classical Latin literature — a service which Petrarch and Boccaccio rendered to Chaucer, at least through their writings, possibly also through personal contact — was destined to work wonders in his intellectual development. The burden of Petrarch's teaching and Boccaccio's practice was to direct men to the artistic purpose of the writers of antiquity, who portrayed life directly and

[1] See H. O. Taylor, *The Mediaeval Mind*, II, 135.

realistically. All this literature of the past was quite different from the mysticism and allegory that shadowed the Middle Ages, and it was entirely at variance with the incubus of feudalism and the Church, which had so long dominated the minds of men. Though Chaucer laid under tribute rather extensively Boccaccio's Italian works, the great benefit he derived from Italy was the direction to the Classics as the source of inspiration. When we speak of the Italian period in Chaucer's literary career, we mean quite as much the classical period, for the Italy of his day was responding to the spirit of individual freedom and realism which animated Roman literature.

Like many another man, Chaucer found that a vision beyond that of his contemporaries brought embarrassment to him in his art. So long as he followed Old French models no problem was raised by the creations of his imagination. But once he had caught the spark of inspiration from the leaders of the Renaissance in Italy, misconception by his contemporaries in England was inevitable. He was no longer primarily a mediaeval but a Renaissance poet. In the ardor of the new-found source of ideas he wrote the *House of Fame* and the *Troilus and Criseyde*, in the latter of which he first attained full imaginative freedom. He must have recognized the artistic superiority of the *Troilus*

over the usual Court of Love poem popular among
the royal coterie, yet he was uncertain of its reception. The unfavorable judgment of the court circle
would not be aimed at the art of the *Troilus*, for
that it would never see. It could not, being mediaeval. Its censure would be that it was different.
Criseyde, in acting as a human being in her love
affairs, had violated the rules of the Court of Love.
To make amends he responded with the *Legend of
Good Women*. Though the inability of his friends
and patrons at court to appreciate his poetry fully
must have been disappointing, Chaucer's wisdom
and sense of humor did not desert him. Nothing
could be more graceful and happy than the Prologue to the *Legend of Good Women* for meeting the
situation that confronted him.

But there was the possibility that the *Troilus
and Criseyde* might offend another part of his public, that is, the Church. It was likely to prove more
inimical than the circle of the Court. The latter
might interfere with his joys and prospects here on
earth, but the former could damn his soul.

> Of cursing oghte ech guilty man him drede —
> For curs wol slee, right as assoiling saveth —
> And also war him of a *significavit*.
>
> (Prologue, ll. 660–662.)

The condemnation of the Church, like that of the
Court, would not be against the art of the *Troilus*,

but against its frank realism. The whole machinery of the Church was set strongly against the most common of the Seven Deadly Sins, lechery. The poet, no less than the painter, had to be on his guard against offending. It was probably fear of the Church that Chaucer had in mind in the *Knight's Tale*, when he expresses the limitations upon his freedom of speech. In describing the rites of Emily in the temple of Diana he says (ll. A 2284–2288):

> But how she dide hir ryte I dar not telle,
> But it be any thing in general;
> And yet it were a game to heren al;
> To him that meneth wel, it were no charge:
> But it is good a man ben at his large.

He would like to be frank and outspoken, but he dares not. A poet intent upon revealing human nature as it is would surely be classed as one "that meneth wel." For him and apparently for all men it is a good thing, in Chaucer's view, to be at liberty to speak. But he could not enjoy indulging his tendency toward realistic portrayal without some misgivings churchward. It may be for this reason that he gives the religious turn to the closing stanzas of the *Troilus*.

The story is well known how Boccaccio was affected by the appearance of a priest before him to tell him of his certain damnation if he did not repent. Another striking example of the hold the

Church had upon the minds of men in the Middle
Ages is the case of Pierpaolo Boscoli, who lived
more than a hundred years after Chaucer.[1] Boscoli
had spent his life following the ancient ideals of
liberty and of paganism in general. But when he
was put in prison for political reasons and condemned to die, he turned to the Church for consola-
tion, and passed his last days in making such preparations for death as the Church prescribed.
Michael Angelo was criticized as being unchristian
for daring to use the nude in his paintings and
sculptures. The attitude of the Church on this
subject was due to its conception of the body as the
source of corruption of man's soul. This belief
made it strive to keep the body in subjection and
refuse to allow its beauty and perfection to be depicted realistically as had been done by the Greeks
and Romans.

> Quite from the mark of painting, bless us all!
> Faces, arms, legs, and bodies like the true
> As much as pea and pea! it's devil's game![2]

It was not that the Church wished to prohibit art
so much as to restrict it to purely religious aims.
This perhaps accounts for the ecclesiastical subject-matter of so much of the mediaeval and early
Renaissance art.

[1] See J. Burckhardt, *The Civilization of the Renaissance in Italy*,
pp. 542–543.
[2] Browning's *Fra Lippo Lippi*, ll. 176–178.

The pathway of one who would be a realist anywhere during the Middle Ages was a thorny one. But Chaucer's position in England was, it may be surmised, more difficult than Boccaccio's, because the entire atmosphere in Italy was more sympathetic with art. To John Gower and the author of *Piers Plowman* freedom of imagination was not an acute problem, for neither basked in court favor, nor did they venture upon the perilous paths of undisguised realism. But to Chaucer the question was a "living option." That Chaucer was far in advance of the England of his day is clear from the failure of any of his contemporaries or successors to catch the spirit of his work. One hundred and fifty years later England was ready for what Chaucer had discovered for himself. Sir Philip Sidney's tribute is well known: "Chaucer, undoubtedly, did excellently well in his *Troilus and Criseyde:* of whom, truly, I know not whether to marvel more, either that he in that misty time could see so clearly, or that we in this clear age go so stumblingly after him" (*Apology of Poetry*).

Though we may read with pangs of regret the "retraction" at the end of the *Canterbury Tales*, it serves to suggest the anxieties that Chaucer may have experienced while engaged in writing his greatest poems. We can rejoice, however, that his creative impulse was strong enough to rise superior to all misgivings and produce those masterpieces which display an imagination enlightened and emancipated by the Classics — the *House of Fame*, *Troilus and Criseyde*, the *Legend of Good Women*, and the *Canterbury Tales*.

APPENDIX

APPENDIX

REFERENCES TO ALLUSIONS AND BORROWINGS IN CHAUCER'S WORK WHICH HAVE NOT HITHERTO BEEN CITED

SPECIFIC passages which have not been cited before, though the general sources have been noted by previous commentators, are marked by asterisks.

Passages in Chaucer	Reference to Source	Page
Duch., 163–164	*Met.*, xi, 591	6
Duch., 72	*Met.*, xi, 514–515	7
Duch., 152	*Met.*, xi, 586	8
Duch., 170–171	*Met.*, xi, 594–596	8
P. F., 10–13	*Am.*, i, i, 21–26	13
	Am., ii, 1	13
	Am., iii, 1	13
	Ars Am., i, 9	14
	Rem. Am., 1–40	14
P. F., 288	*Fasti*, iii, 9–45	15
Anelida, 21	*Am.*	21
	Her.	36
Anelida, 201–202	*Am.*, ii, xix, 3.	42
	Am., iii, iv, 17	42
	Am., iii, iv, 25–26	42
Anelida, 207	*Her.*, x, 137–138	38
Anelida, 208–209	*Her.*, x, 140	38
Anelida, 214	*Her.*, x, 139	38
Anelida, 229–234	*Her.*, xii, 175–178	39
Anelida, 247–255	*Her.*, ii, 49	39
Anelida, 273–277	*Her.*, ii, 63–66	40
	Her., iii, 144	40
Anelida, 284–289	*Her.*, iii, 139–141	41
Anelida, 328–334	*Her.*, xv, 123 ff.	41
Anelida, 342–348	*Her.*, vii, 3–6	42
Former Age, 12	*Met.*, i, 101–102	45
	Met., i, 109	45

Passages in Chaucer	Reference to Source	Page
Troil., i, 58–60	*Her.*, xiii, 97	121
Troil., i, 712–714	*ex Ponto*, ii, vii, 41–42	124
	ex Ponto, iv, xvi, 51–52	124
Troil., ii, 409–427	*Her.*, xvi, 111–114	162
Troil., ii, 480	*Her.*, xvi, 17–18	162
Troil., ii, 659 ff.	*Her.*, xvi	167
Troil., ii, 727–728	*Her.*, xvi, 17–18	162
Troil., ii, 758–759	*Her.*, xvi, 136–137	163
Troil., ii, 786–788	*Her.*, xvi, 39–40	163
Troil., ii, 793	*Her.*, xvi, 39–40	163
Troil., ii, 1213–1214	*Her.*, xvi, 143–144	165
Troil., iii, 155–161	*Her.*, xvi, 261–263	161
Troil., iii, 731	*Ars Am.*, i, 261–262	132
Troil., iii, 1390–1391	*De Casibus*, vi, 7	133
Troil., iii, 1450–1460	**Am.*, i, xiii, 9	135
	*Am., i, xiii, 33, 39–40	135
	*Am., i, xiii, 41–42	135
	*Am., i, xiii, 45–46	136
	De Gen., xiii, 1	136
	Met., iv, 171–172	137
Troil., iii, 1807–1809	*Ars Am.*, iii, 3	139
	Ars Am., iii, 769–770	139
	Am., i, xiv, 33–34	139
	Ars Am., ii, 593–594	139
Troil., iv, 120–126	*Met.*, xi, 194–210	141
	Her., xv, 181–182	142
Troil., iv, 789–791	*Met.*, x, 45–48	144
Troil., iv, 1543–1545	*Met.*, i, 192–193	147
Troil., iv, 1548–1553	*Her.*, xiii, 53–54	148
	Her., i, 33–34	148
	Ars. Am., ii, 133–134	148
	Her., vii, 145	149
Troil., v, 319–320	*Met.*, vi, 432	151
	Met., x, 453	151
	Met., xv, 791	151
Troil., v, 601–602	*Met.*, iii, 131–315	151
	Met., iv, 416–542	151
Troil., v, 644	*Met.*, xiv, 75	152
	Æn., iii, 420	152
Troil., v, 904–910	*Her.*, xv, 17–18; 41–42	166
Troil., v, 916–917	*Her.*, xv, 17–18; 41–42	166

INDEX

INDEX

Achates, 214

Achilleis, 329

Achilles, 62

Adams, J. Q., 371 n. 2

Adonis, 132

Ægeus, 244, 245, 254

Æneas, in *House of Fame*, 55–66; in *Legend of Dido*, 196–208

Æneid, xx, 15, 48, 55, 57, 59, 75, 83, 92, 93, 97, 104, 106, 110, 121, 138, 140, 145, 152, 158, 196, 197, 198, 199, 200, 201, 202, 203, 204, 206, 212, 213, 214 n. 1, 228, 285, 304, 319, 332. *See also* under Virgil.

Æolus, 91; as trumpeter, 92, 95; in Thrace, 341

Albricus Philosophus, 93

Alcyone, 3 ff.

Amores, xv, 13, 22, 23, 24, 25, 27, 42, 44, 90, 122, 134, 135, 136, 137, 139, 144 n. 2, 147, 158, 331

Amorosa Visione, 72, 75

Amorum, 22, 23, 24, 27

Androgeus, 244

Anelida and Arcite, 15 ff.

Anna, sister of Dido, 201, 202

Anthon, 95

Apollo and Daphne, 131

Apollonius Rhodius, 342

Appendix, references to allusions and borrowings in Chaucer's works not hitherto cited, 387–391

Argonauticon, 97, 150, 211, 212, 213, 214, 341, 343, 345, 346, 348, 349, 355

Ariadne, 62; in *House of Fame*, 66–74; *Legend of*, 228–258

Ars Amatoria, influence upon mediaeval literature, xiv ff., 13, 14, 27, 89, 128, 139, 148, 153, 305, 315, 318, 323

Arviragus, 362

Ascalaphus, 151

Augustine, 221

Bartsch, xiv n. 2, 23 n. 1

Bech, M., 181, 202, 211 n. 3, 216 n. 1, 285 n. 3, 346 n. 1

Becker, G., 23 n. 2, 352 n. 2

Benoit de Ste. More, 11

Blomfield, H. G., 211 n. 3

Bobbio, monastery of, 352, 353

Boccaccio, 96, 103, 120, 129, 137, 138, 143, 145, 146, 150, 151, 152, 153, 156, 159, 160, 181, 182, 183, 185, 186, 187, 188, 189, 190, 229, 231, 232, 234, 236, 237, 238, 239, 240, 241, 245, 246, 247, 249, 250, 251, 254, 284, 286, 292, 302, 304, 305, 367, 377, 378

Boethius, 45, 313, 314

Book of the Duchess, xvi, 3–12, 53, 114, 117, 330

Briseis, 62

Brown, C., 189 n. 1

Browning, Robert, 381 n. 2

Burckhardt, J. C., 381 n. 1

Burmann, 25, 310

Busiris, 312 ff.

Calipsa, 90

Calliope, 130